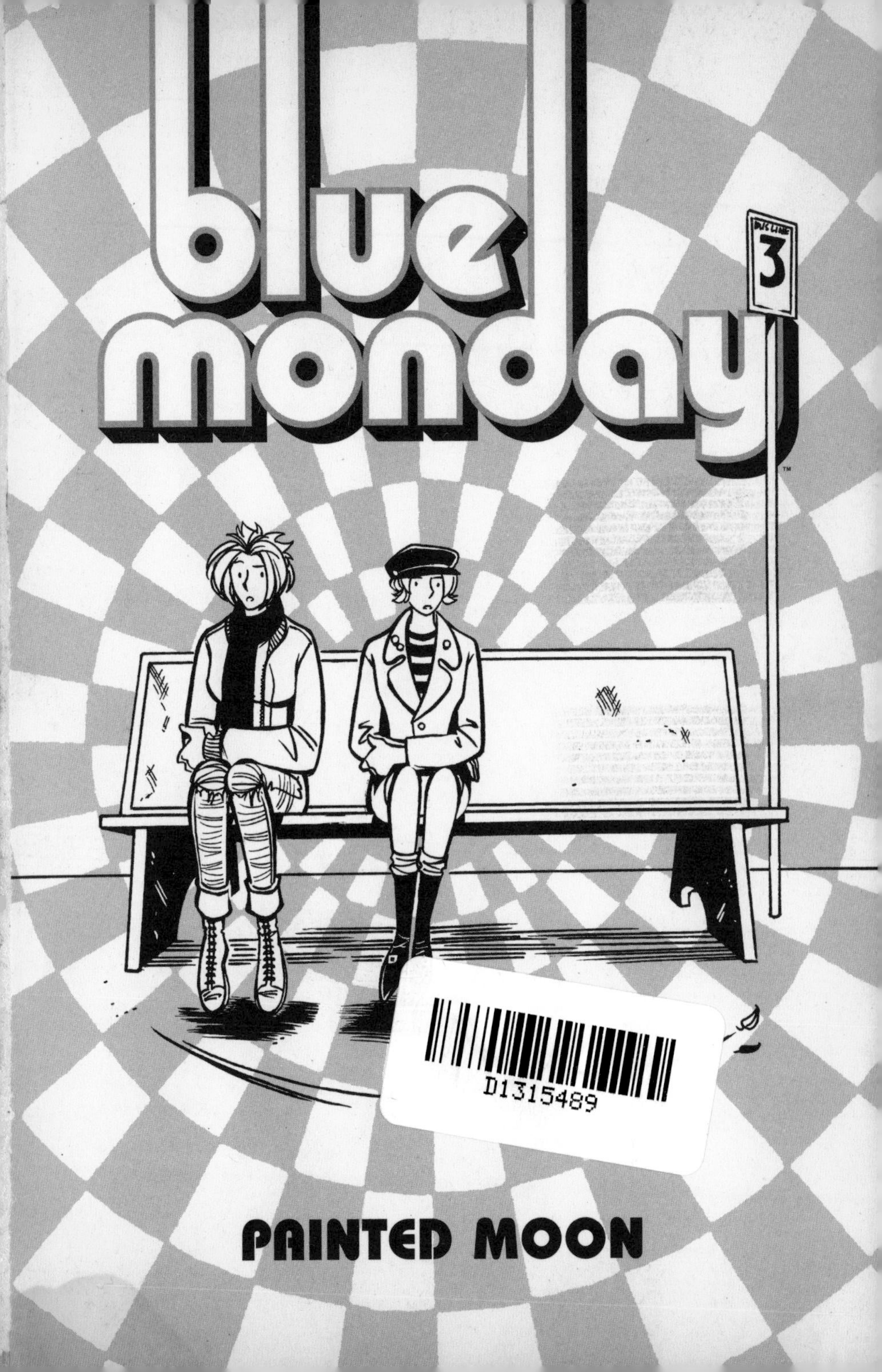
blue monday™
BUS LINE
3
PAINTED MOON

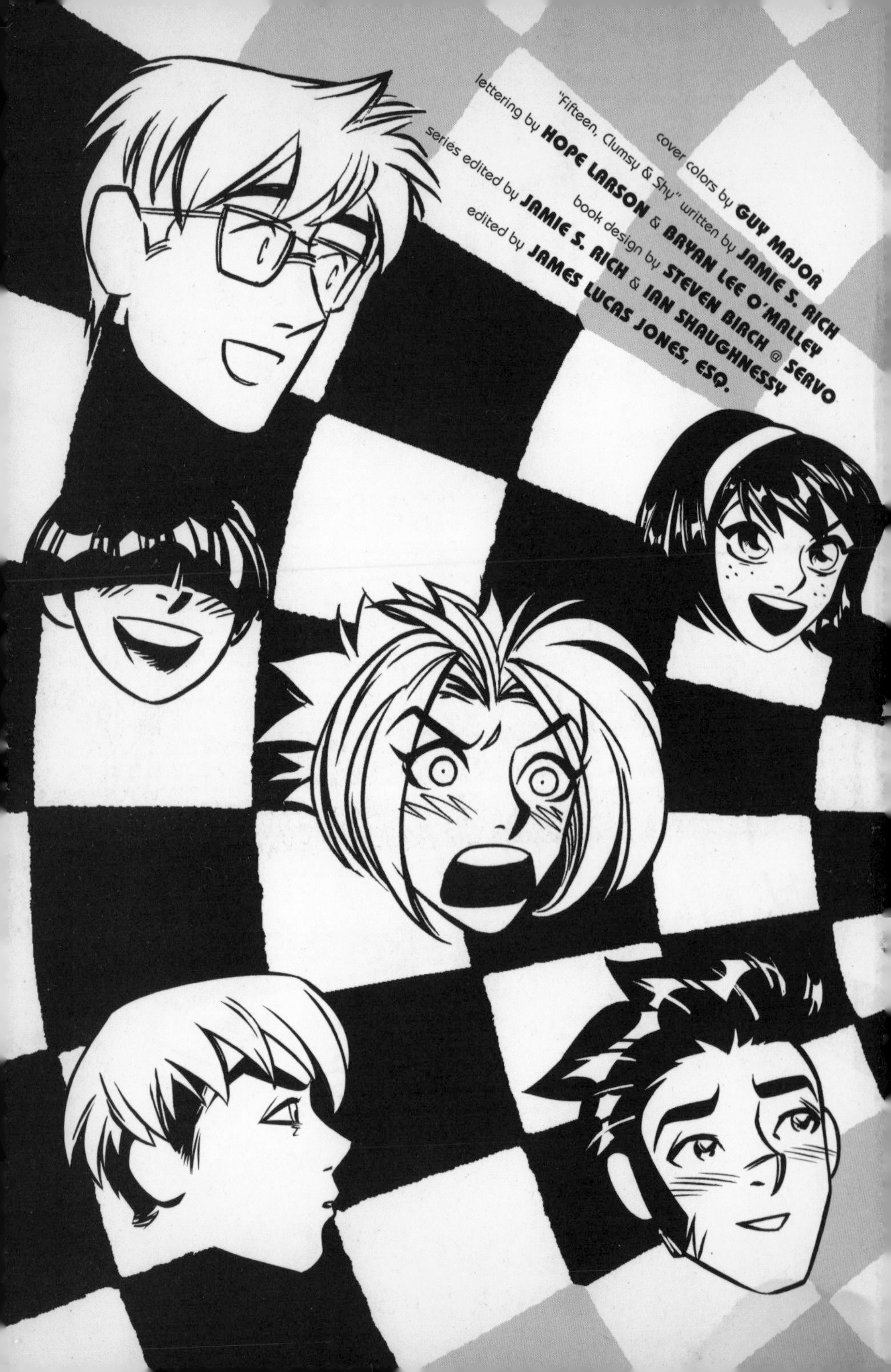
cover colors by GUY MAJOR
"Fifteen, Clumsy & Shy" written by JAMIE S. RICH
lettering by HOPE LARSON & BRYAN LEE O'MALLEY
book design by STEVEN BIRCH @ SERVO
series edited by JAMIE S. RICH & IAN SHAUGHNESSY
edited by JAMES LUCAS JONES, ESQ.

blue monday

PAINTED MOON

written and illustrated by
CHYNNA CLUGSTON

Published by Oni Press, Inc.
JOE NOZEMACK publisher
JAMES LUCAS JONES editor in chief
RANDAL C. JARRELL managing editor
MARYANNE SNELL marketing & sales director
DANIEL RAY editorial intern

This collects issues 1-4 of the Oni Press comics series *Blue Monday: Painted Moon*™

J

ONI PRESS, INC.
1305 SE Martin Luthe King Jr. Blvd.
Suite A
Portland, OR 97214
USA

www.onipress.com

Second edition: April 2005
ISBN 1-932664-11-4

1 3 5 7 9 10 8 6 4 2
PRINTED IN CANADA

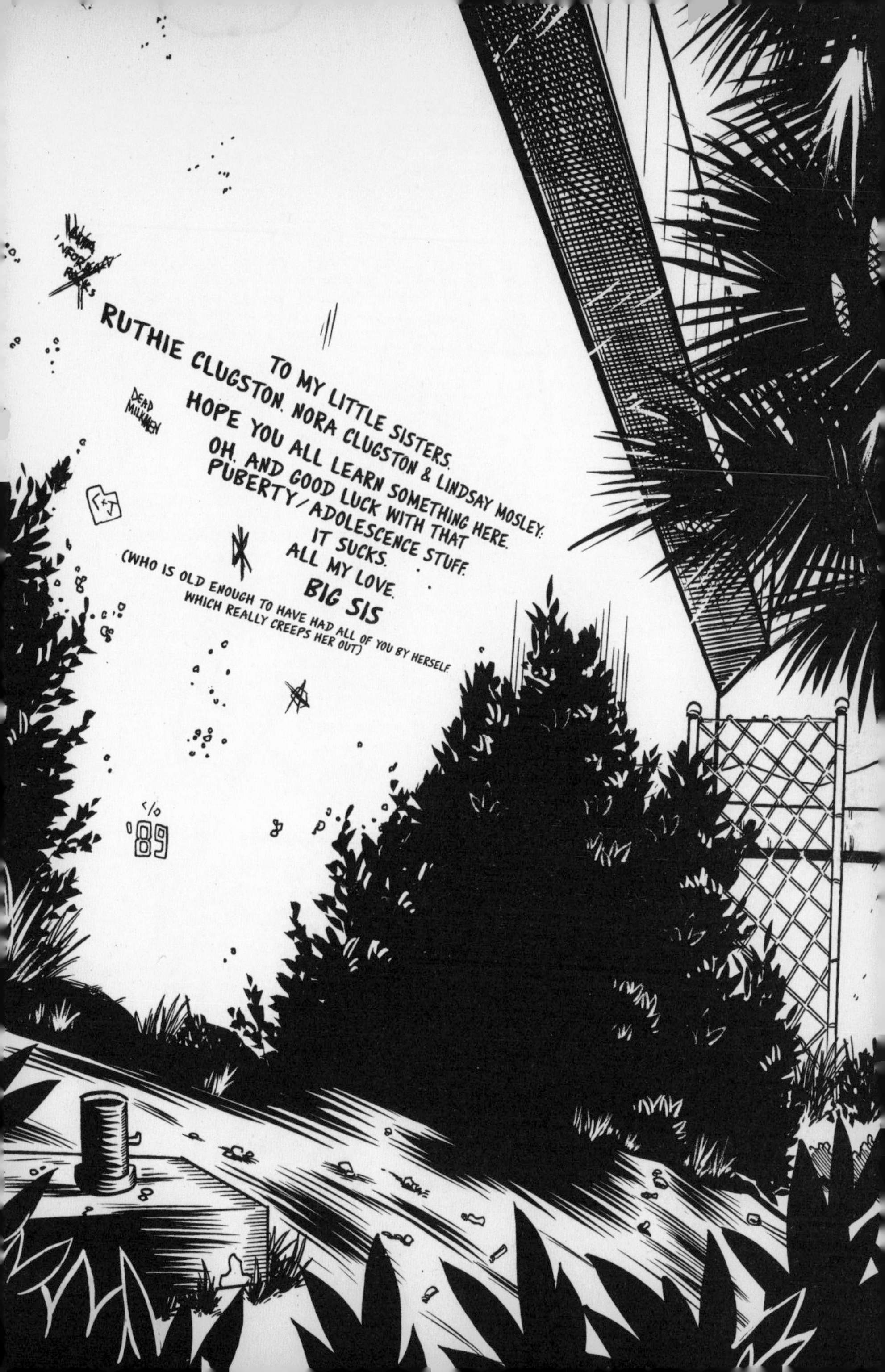
DEAD MILKMEN
'89

TO MY LITTLE SISTERS,
RUTHIE CLUGSTON, NORA CLUGSTON & LINDSAY MOSLEY:
HOPE YOU ALL LEARN SOMETHING HERE.
OH, AND GOOD LUCK WITH THAT
PUBERTY/ADOLESCENCE STUFF.
IT SUCKS.
ALL MY LOVE,
BIG SIS
(WHO IS OLD ENOUGH TO HAVE HAD ALL OF YOU BY HERSELF,
WHICH REALLY CREEPS HER OUT)

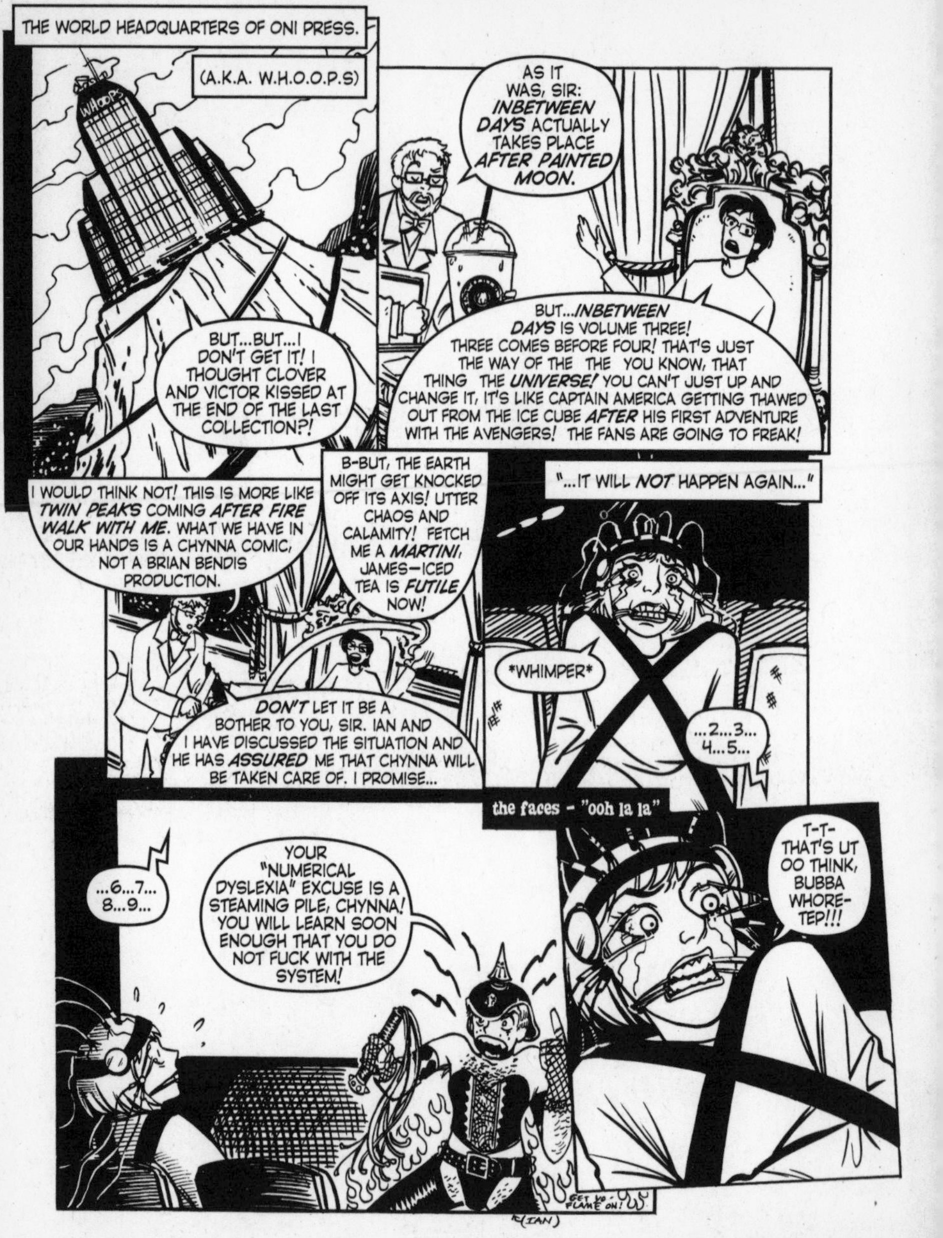
THE WORLD HEADQUARTERS OF ONI PRESS.
(A.K.A. W.H.O.O.P.S)
WHOOPS
BUT...BUT...I DON'T GET IT! I THOUGHT CLOVER AND VICTOR KISSED AT THE END OF THE LAST COLLECTION?!
AS IT WAS, SIR: INBETWEEN DAYS ACTUALLY TAKES PLACE AFTER PAINTED MOON.
BUT...INBETWEEN DAYS IS VOLUME THREE! THREE COMES BEFORE FOUR! THAT'S JUST THE WAY OF THE THE YOU KNOW, THAT THING THE UNIVERSE! YOU CAN'T JUST UP AND CHANGE IT, IT'S LIKE CAPTAIN AMERICA GETTING THAWED OUT FROM THE ICE CUBE AFTER HIS FIRST ADVENTURE WITH THE AVENGERS! THE FANS ARE GOING TO FREAK!
I WOULD THINK NOT! THIS IS MORE LIKE TWIN PEAKS COMING AFTER FIRE WALK WITH ME. WHAT WE HAVE IN OUR HANDS IS A CHYNNA COMIC, NOT A BRIAN BENDIS PRODUCTION.
B-BUT, THE EARTH MIGHT GET KNOCKED OFF ITS AXIS! UTTER CHAOS AND CALAMITY! FETCH ME A MARTINI, JAMES—ICED TEA IS FUTILE NOW!
DON'T LET IT BE A BOTHER TO YOU, SIR. IAN AND I HAVE DISCUSSED THE SITUATION AND HE HAS ASSURED ME THAT CHYNNA WILL BE TAKEN CARE OF. I PROMISE...
"...IT WILL NOT HAPPEN AGAIN..."
WHIMPER
...2...3...
4...5...
the faces - "ooh la la"
...6...7...
8...9...
YOUR "NUMERICAL DYSLEXIA" EXCUSE IS A STEAMING PILE, CHYNNA! YOU WILL LEARN SOON ENOUGH THAT YOU DO NOT FUCK WITH THE SYSTEM!
T-T-THAT'S UT OO THINK, BUBBA WHORE-TEP!!!
GET YO- FLAME ON!
K(IAN)

chapter one:
"HOW SOON IS NOW?"

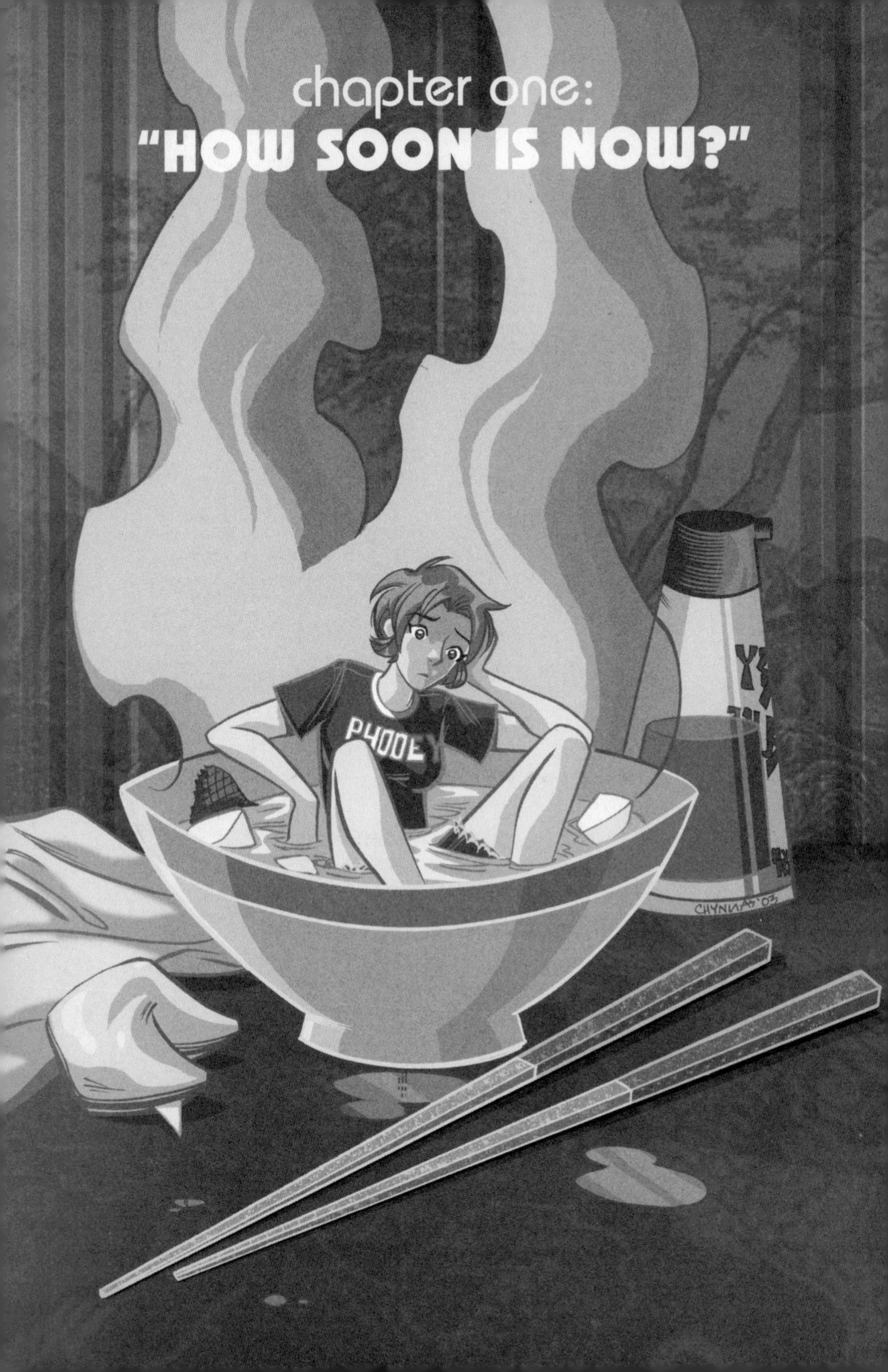

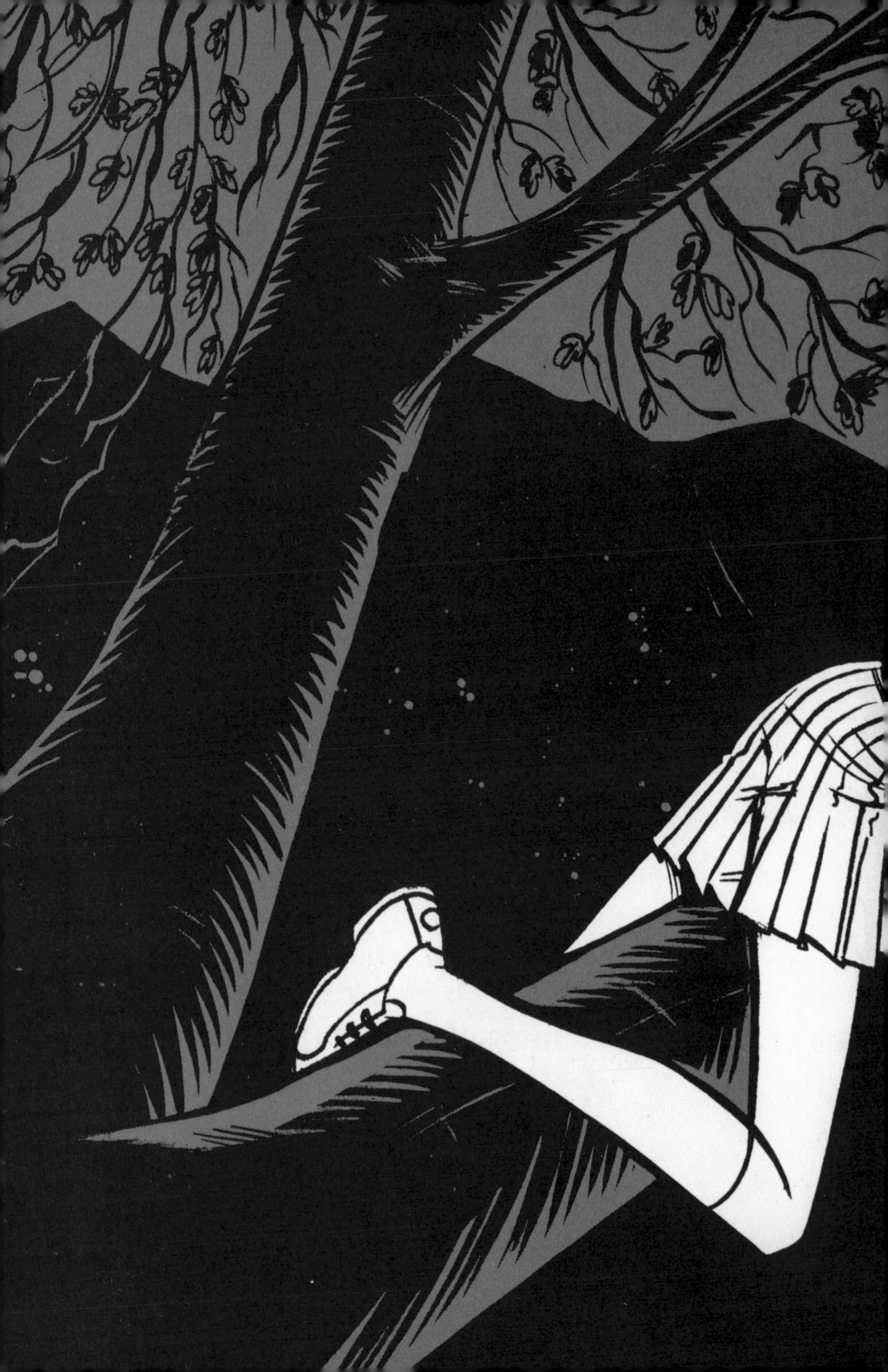

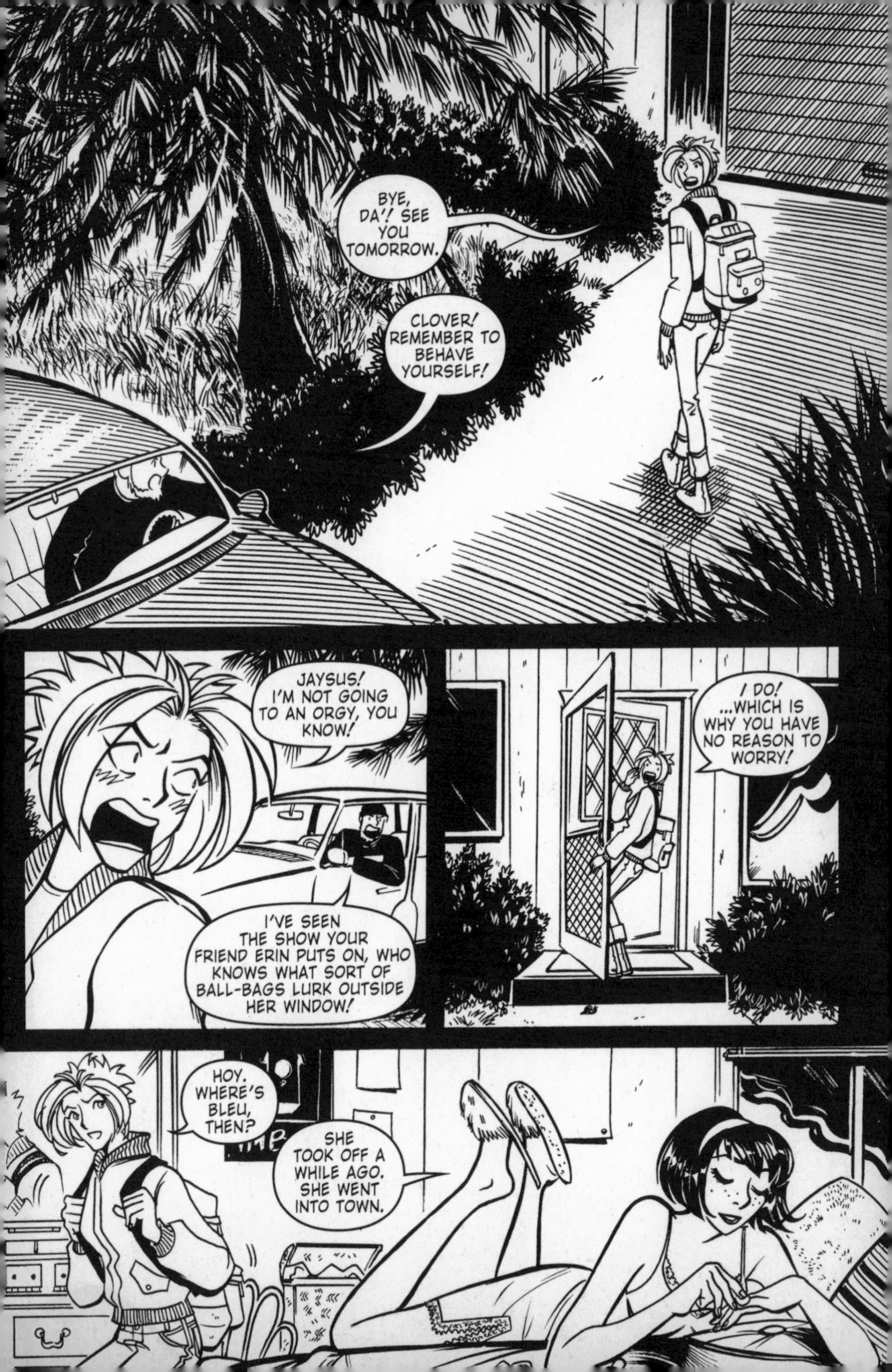
BYE, DA'! SEE YOU TOMORROW.
CLOVER! REMEMBER TO BEHAVE YOURSELF!
JAYSUS! I'M NOT GOING TO AN ORGY, YOU KNOW!
I'VE SEEN THE SHOW YOUR FRIEND ERIN PUTS ON, WHO KNOWS WHAT SORT OF BALL-BAGS LURK OUTSIDE HER WINDOW!
I DO! ...WHICH IS WHY YOU HAVE NO REASON TO WORRY!
HOY. WHERE'S BLEU, THEN?
SHE TOOK OFF A WHILE AGO. SHE WENT INTO TOWN.

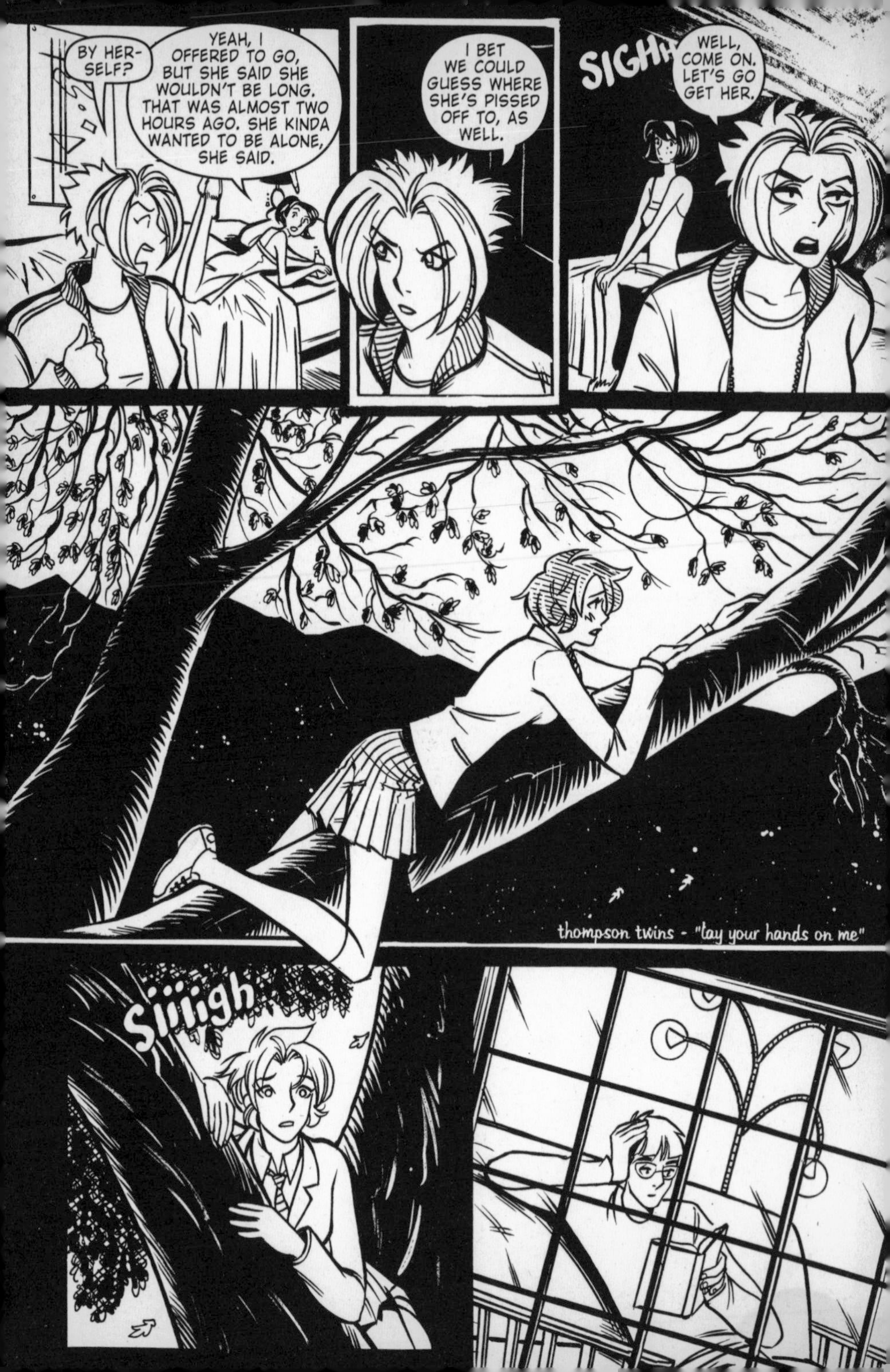
BY HER-SELF?
YEAH, I OFFERED TO GO, BUT SHE SAID SHE WOULDN'T BE LONG. THAT WAS ALMOST TWO HOURS AGO. SHE KINDA WANTED TO BE ALONE, SHE SAID.
I BET WE COULD GUESS WHERE SHE'S PISSED OFF TO, AS WELL.
SIGH
WELL, COME ON. LET'S GO GET HER.
thompson twins - "lay your hands on me"
Siiiigh

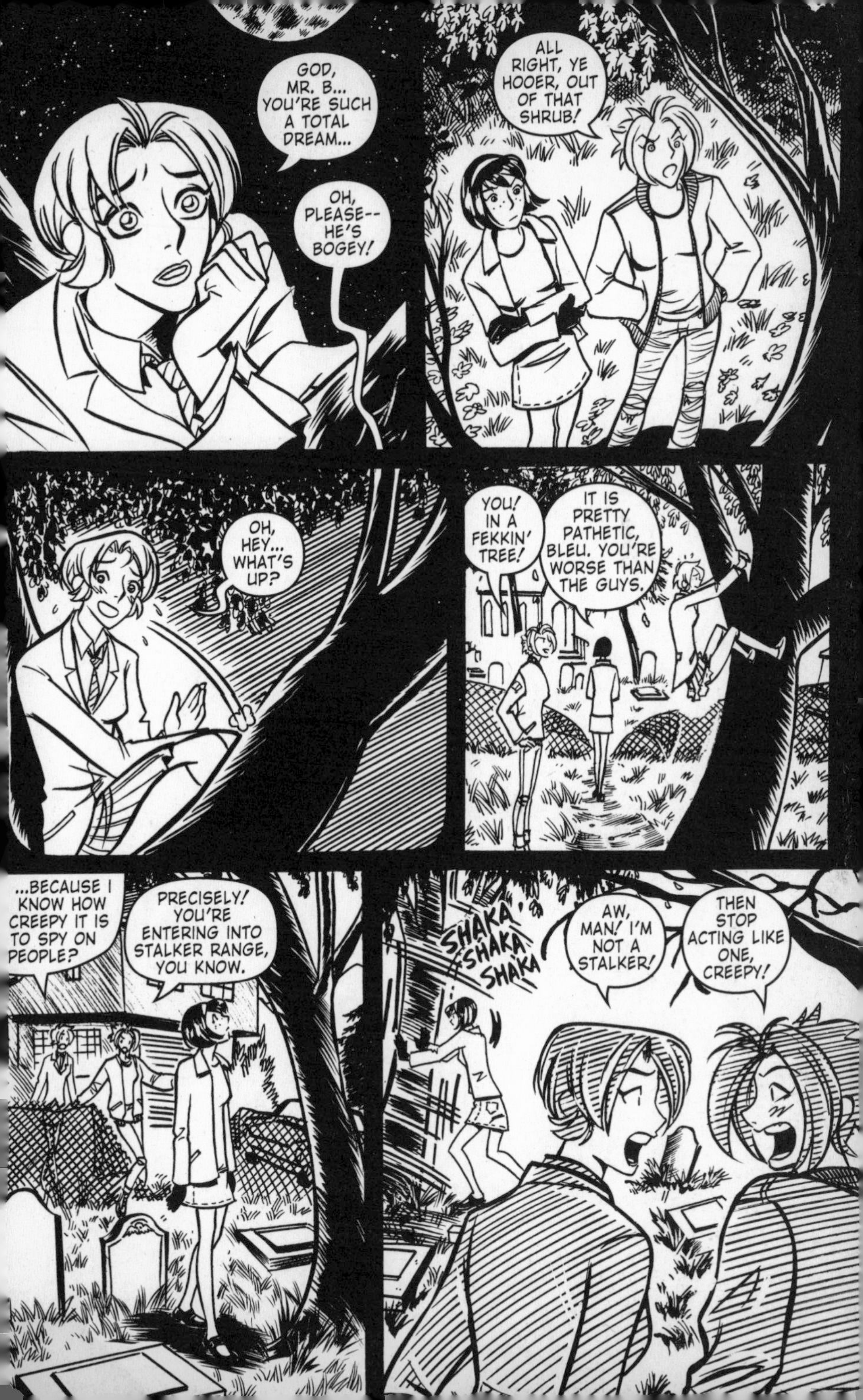
GOD, MR. B... YOU'RE SUCH A TOTAL DREAM...
OH, PLEASE-- HE'S BOGEY!
ALL RIGHT, YE HOOER, OUT OF THAT SHRUB!
OH, HEY... WHAT'S UP?
YOU! IN A FEKKIN' TREE!
IT IS PRETTY PATHETIC, BLEU. YOU'RE WORSE THAN THE GUYS.
...BECAUSE I KNOW HOW CREEPY IT IS TO SPY ON PEOPLE?
PRECISELY! YOU'RE ENTERING INTO STALKER RANGE, YOU KNOW.
SHAKA SHAKA SHAKA
AW, MAN! I'M NOT A STALKER!
THEN STOP ACTING LIKE ONE, CREEPY!

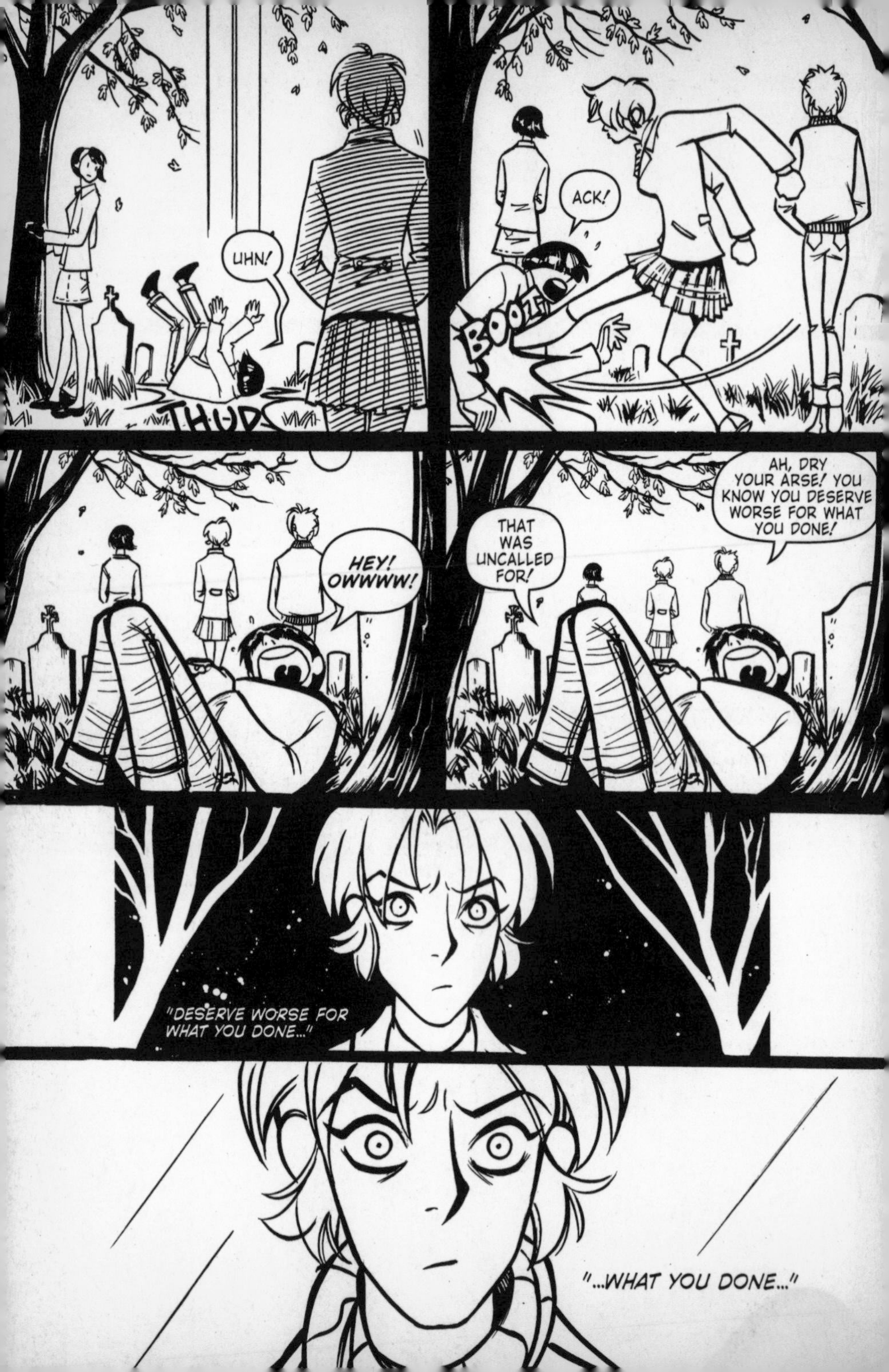
UHN!
THUD
ACK!
BOOT
HEY! OWWWW!
THAT WAS UNCALLED FOR!
AH, DRY YOUR ARSE! YOU KNOW YOU DESERVE WORSE FOR WHAT YOU DONE!
"DESERVE WORSE FOR WHAT YOU DONE..."
"...WHAT YOU DONE..."

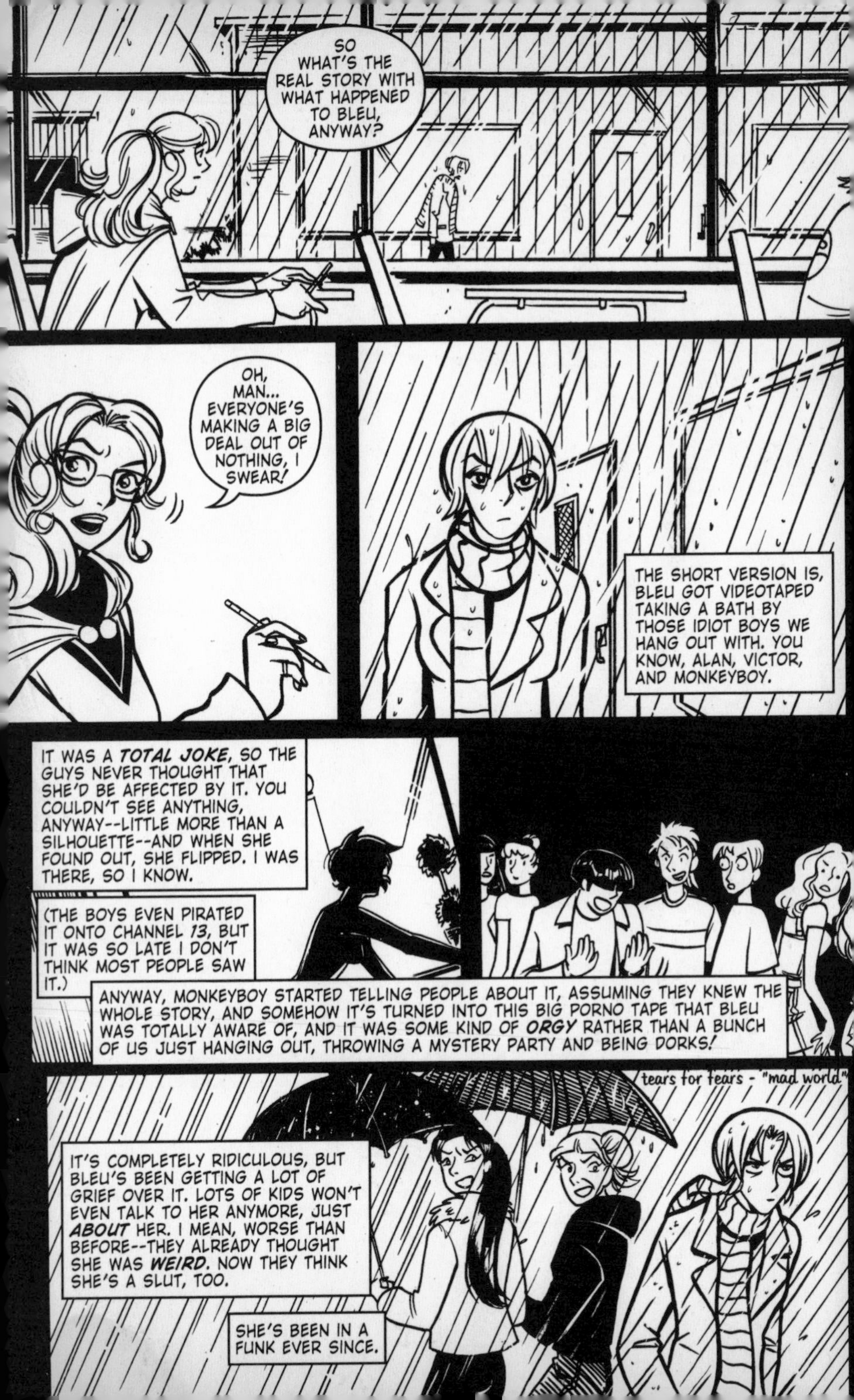
SO WHAT'S THE REAL STORY WITH WHAT HAPPENED TO BLEU, ANYWAY?
OH, MAN... EVERYONE'S MAKING A BIG DEAL OUT OF NOTHING, I SWEAR!
THE SHORT VERSION IS, BLEU GOT VIDEOTAPED TAKING A BATH BY THOSE IDIOT BOYS WE HANG OUT WITH. YOU KNOW, ALAN, VICTOR, AND MONKEYBOY.
IT WAS A TOTAL JOKE, SO THE GUYS NEVER THOUGHT THAT SHE'D BE AFFECTED BY IT. YOU COULDN'T SEE ANYTHING, ANYWAY--LITTLE MORE THAN A SILHOUETTE--AND WHEN SHE FOUND OUT, SHE FLIPPED. I WAS THERE, SO I KNOW.
(THE BOYS EVEN PIRATED IT ONTO CHANNEL 13, BUT IT WAS SO LATE I DON'T THINK MOST PEOPLE SAW IT.)
ANYWAY, MONKEYBOY STARTED TELLING PEOPLE ABOUT IT, ASSUMING THEY KNEW THE WHOLE STORY, AND SOMEHOW IT'S TURNED INTO THIS BIG PORNO TAPE THAT BLEU WAS TOTALLY AWARE OF, AND IT WAS SOME KIND OF ORGY RATHER THAN A BUNCH OF US JUST HANGING OUT, THROWING A MYSTERY PARTY AND BEING DORKS!
tears for fears - "mad world"
IT'S COMPLETELY RIDICULOUS, BUT BLEU'S BEEN GETTING A LOT OF GRIEF OVER IT. LOTS OF KIDS WON'T EVEN TALK TO HER ANYMORE, JUST ABOUT HER. I MEAN, WORSE THAN BEFORE--THEY ALREADY THOUGHT SHE WAS WEIRD. NOW THEY THINK SHE'S A SLUT, TOO.
SHE'S BEEN IN A FUNK EVER SINCE.

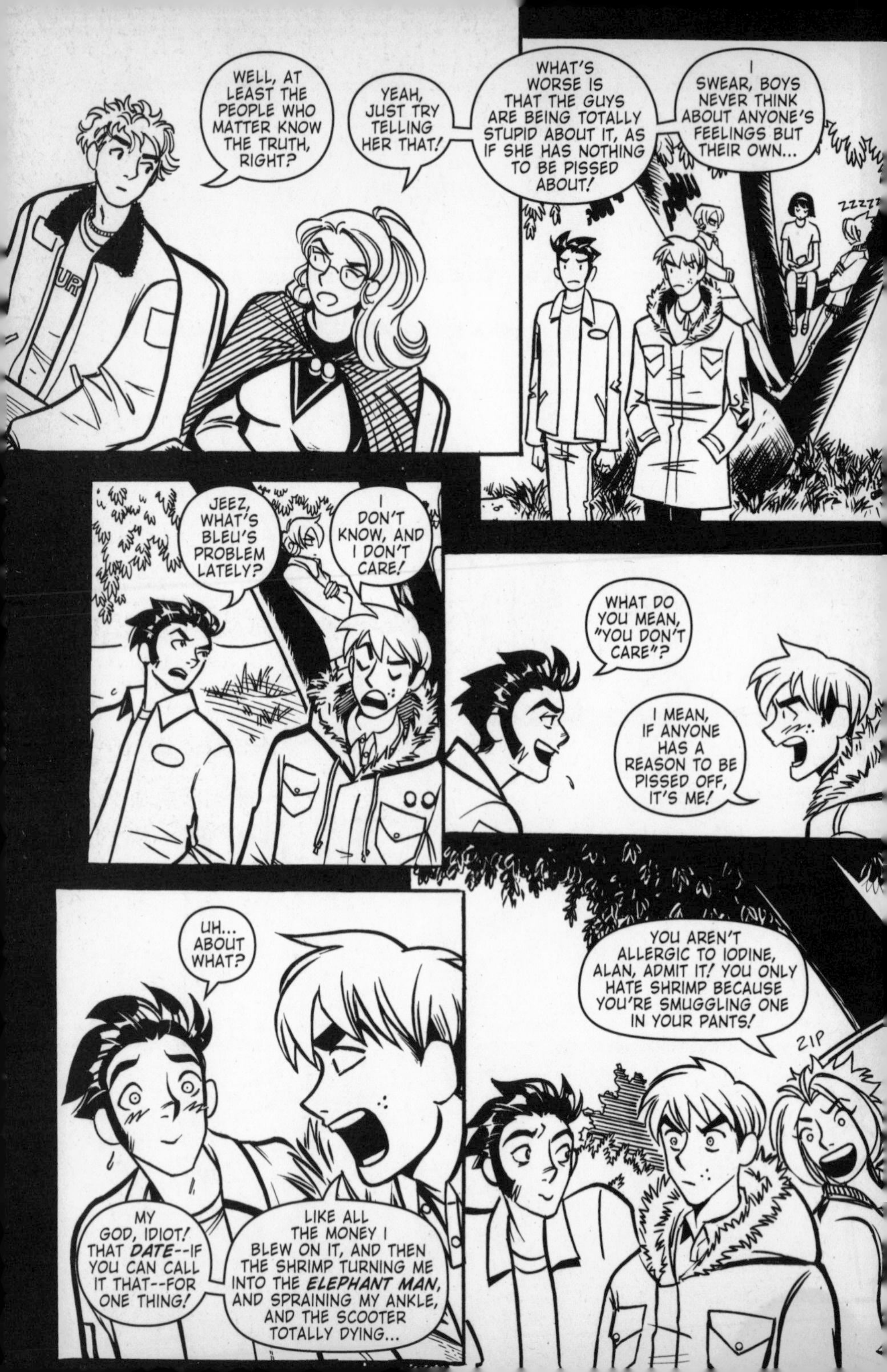
WELL, AT LEAST THE PEOPLE WHO MATTER KNOW THE TRUTH, RIGHT?
YEAH, JUST TRY TELLING HER THAT!
WHAT'S WORSE IS THAT THE GUYS ARE BEING TOTALLY STUPID ABOUT IT, AS IF SHE HAS NOTHING TO BE PISSED ABOUT!
I SWEAR, BOYS NEVER THINK ABOUT ANYONE'S FEELINGS BUT THEIR OWN...
ZZZZZ
JEEZ, WHAT'S BLEU'S PROBLEM LATELY?
I DON'T KNOW, AND I DON'T CARE!
WHAT DO YOU MEAN, "YOU DON'T CARE"?
I MEAN, IF ANYONE HAS A REASON TO BE PISSED OFF, IT'S ME!
UH... ABOUT WHAT?
MY GOD, IDIOT! THAT DATE--IF YOU CAN CALL IT THAT--FOR ONE THING!
LIKE ALL THE MONEY I BLEW ON IT, AND THEN THE SHRIMP TURNING ME INTO THE ELEPHANT MAN, AND SPRAINING MY ANKLE, AND THE SCOOTER TOTALLY DYING...
YOU AREN'T ALLERGIC TO IODINE, ALAN, ADMIT IT! YOU ONLY HATE SHRIMP BECAUSE YOU'RE SMUGGLING ONE IN YOUR PANTS!
ZIP

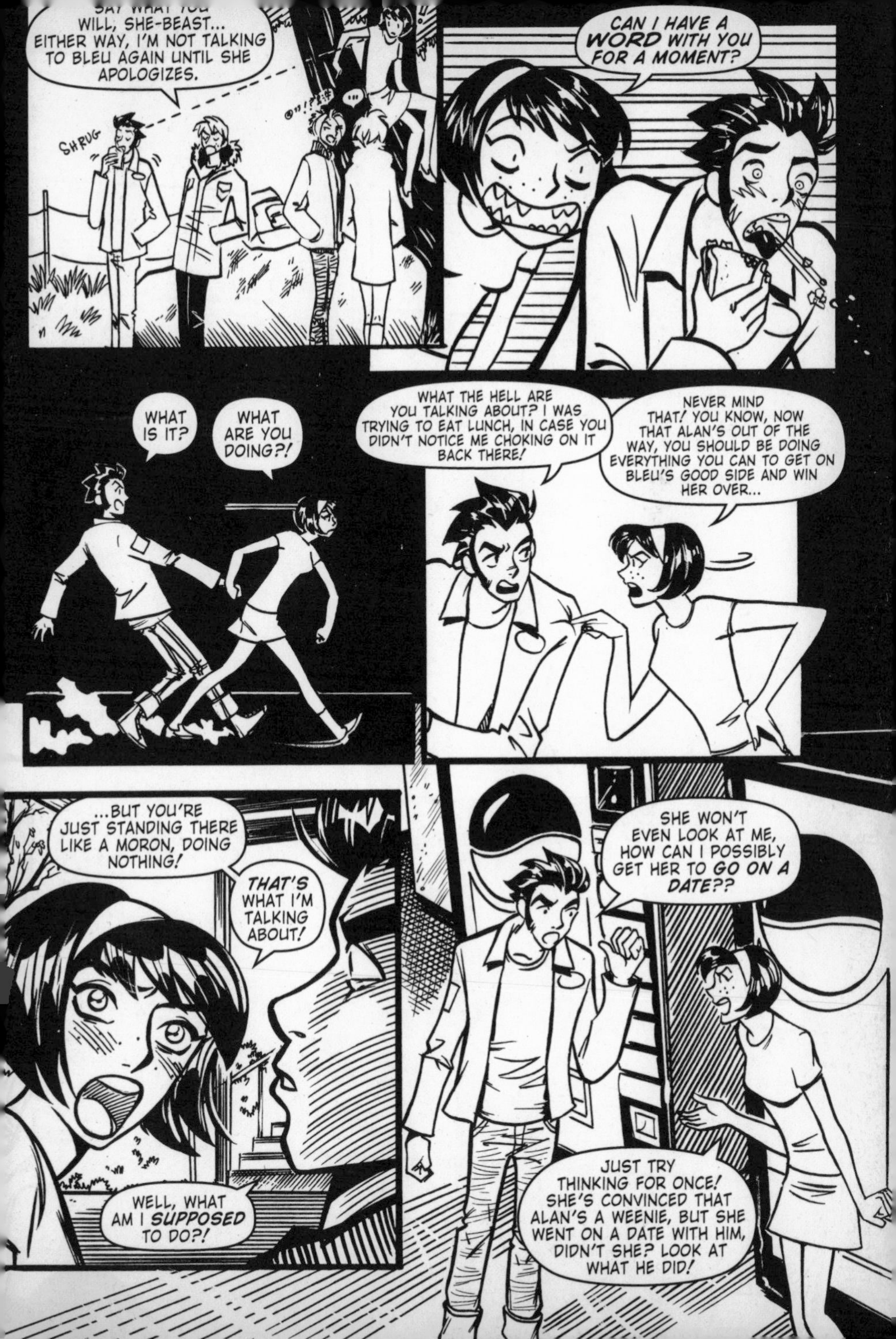
SAY WHAT YOU WILL, SHE-BEAST... EITHER WAY, I'M NOT TALKING TO BLEU AGAIN UNTIL SHE APOLOGIZES.
SHRUG
...
CAN I HAVE A **WORD** WITH YOU FOR A MOMENT?
WHAT IS IT?
WHAT ARE YOU DOING?!
WHAT THE HELL ARE YOU TALKING ABOUT? I WAS TRYING TO EAT LUNCH, IN CASE YOU DIDN'T NOTICE ME CHOKING ON IT BACK THERE!
NEVER MIND THAT! YOU KNOW, NOW THAT ALAN'S OUT OF THE WAY, YOU SHOULD BE DOING EVERYTHING YOU CAN TO GET ON BLEU'S GOOD SIDE AND WIN HER OVER...
...BUT YOU'RE JUST STANDING THERE LIKE A MORON, DOING NOTHING!
THAT'S WHAT I'M TALKING ABOUT!
WELL, WHAT AM I ***SUPPOSED*** TO DO?!
SHE WON'T EVEN LOOK AT ME, HOW CAN I POSSIBLY GET HER TO ***GO ON A DATE***??
JUST TRY THINKING FOR ONCE! SHE'S CONVINCED THAT ALAN'S A WEENIE, BUT SHE WENT ON A DATE WITH HIM, DIDN'T SHE? LOOK AT WHAT HE DID!

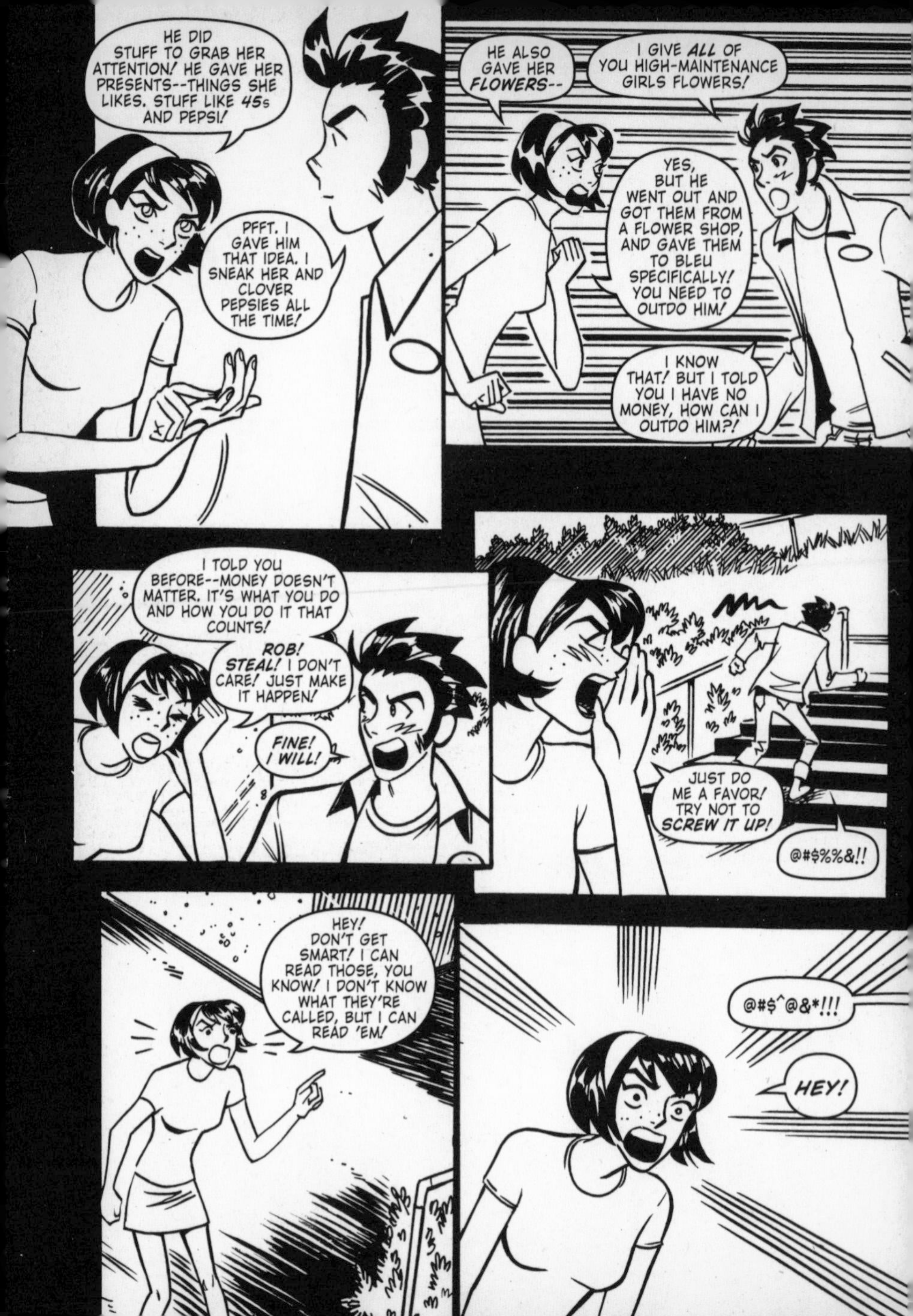
HE DID STUFF TO GRAB HER ATTENTION! HE GAVE HER PRESENTS--THINGS SHE LIKES. STUFF LIKE 45s AND PEPSI!
PFFT. I GAVE HIM THAT IDEA. I SNEAK HER AND CLOVER PEPSIES ALL THE TIME!
HE ALSO GAVE HER FLOWERS--
I GIVE ALL OF YOU HIGH-MAINTENANCE GIRLS FLOWERS!
YES, BUT HE WENT OUT AND GOT THEM FROM A FLOWER SHOP, AND GAVE THEM TO BLEU SPECIFICALLY! YOU NEED TO OUTDO HIM!
I KNOW THAT! BUT I TOLD YOU I HAVE NO MONEY, HOW CAN I OUTDO HIM?!
I TOLD YOU BEFORE--MONEY DOESN'T MATTER. IT'S WHAT YOU DO AND HOW YOU DO IT THAT COUNTS!
ROB! STEAL! I DON'T CARE! JUST MAKE IT HAPPEN!
FINE! I WILL!
JUST DO ME A FAVOR! TRY NOT TO SCREW IT UP!
@#$%%&!!
HEY! DON'T GET SMART! I CAN READ THOSE, YOU KNOW! I DON'T KNOW WHAT THEY'RE CALLED, BUT I CAN READ 'EM!
@#$^@&*!!!
HEY!

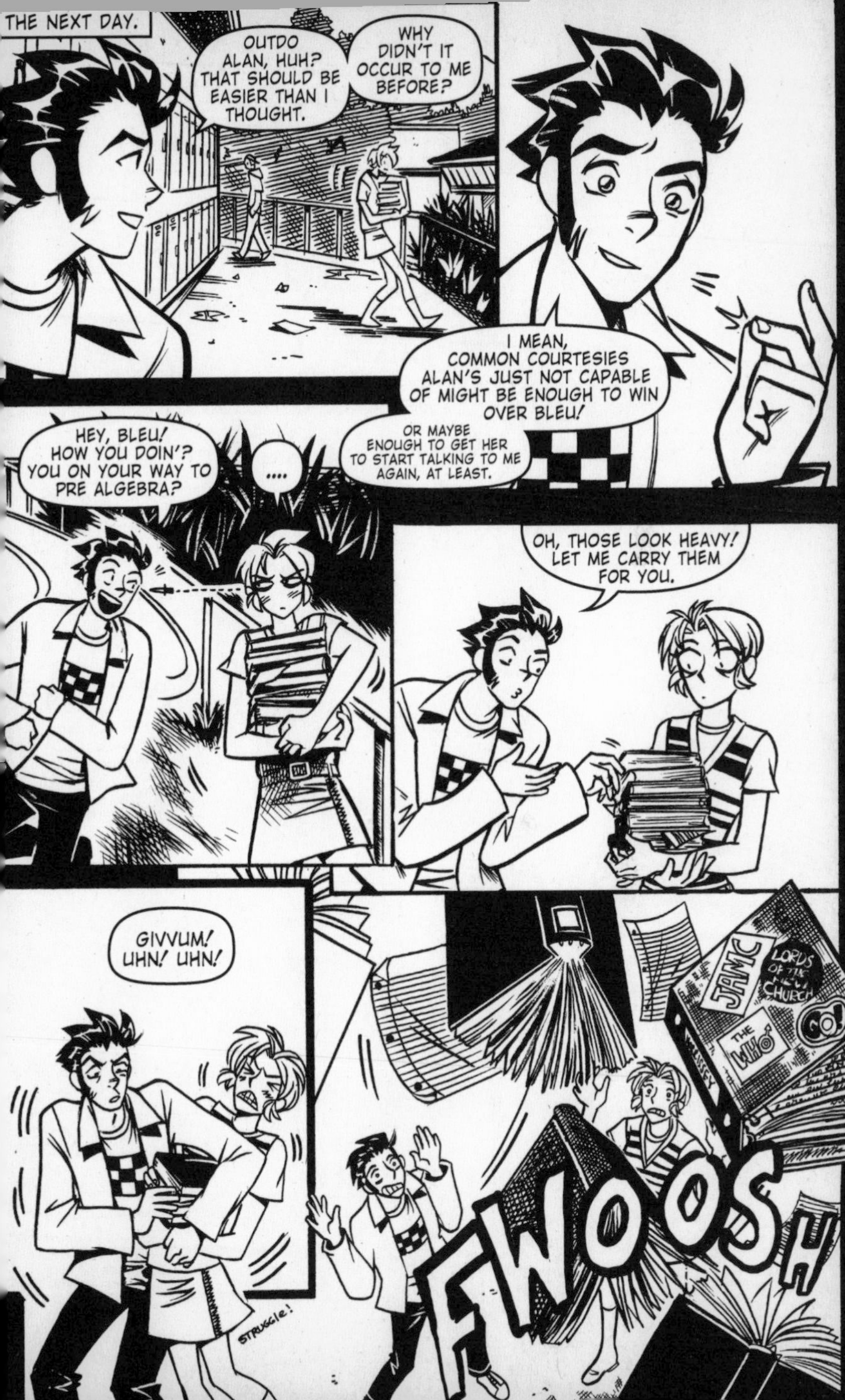
THE NEXT DAY.
OUTDO ALAN, HUH? THAT SHOULD BE EASIER THAN I THOUGHT.
WHY DIDN'T IT OCCUR TO ME BEFORE?
I MEAN, COMMON COURTESIES ALAN'S JUST NOT CAPABLE OF MIGHT BE ENOUGH TO WIN OVER BLEU!
OR MAYBE ENOUGH TO GET HER TO START TALKING TO ME AGAIN, AT LEAST.
HEY, BLEU! HOW YOU DOIN'? YOU ON YOUR WAY TO PRE ALGEBRA?
....
OH, THOSE LOOK HEAVY! LET ME CARRY THEM FOR YOU.
GIVVUM! UHN! UHN!
STRUGGLE!
JAMC
LORDS OF THE NEW CHURCH
THE WHO
GO!
FWOOSH

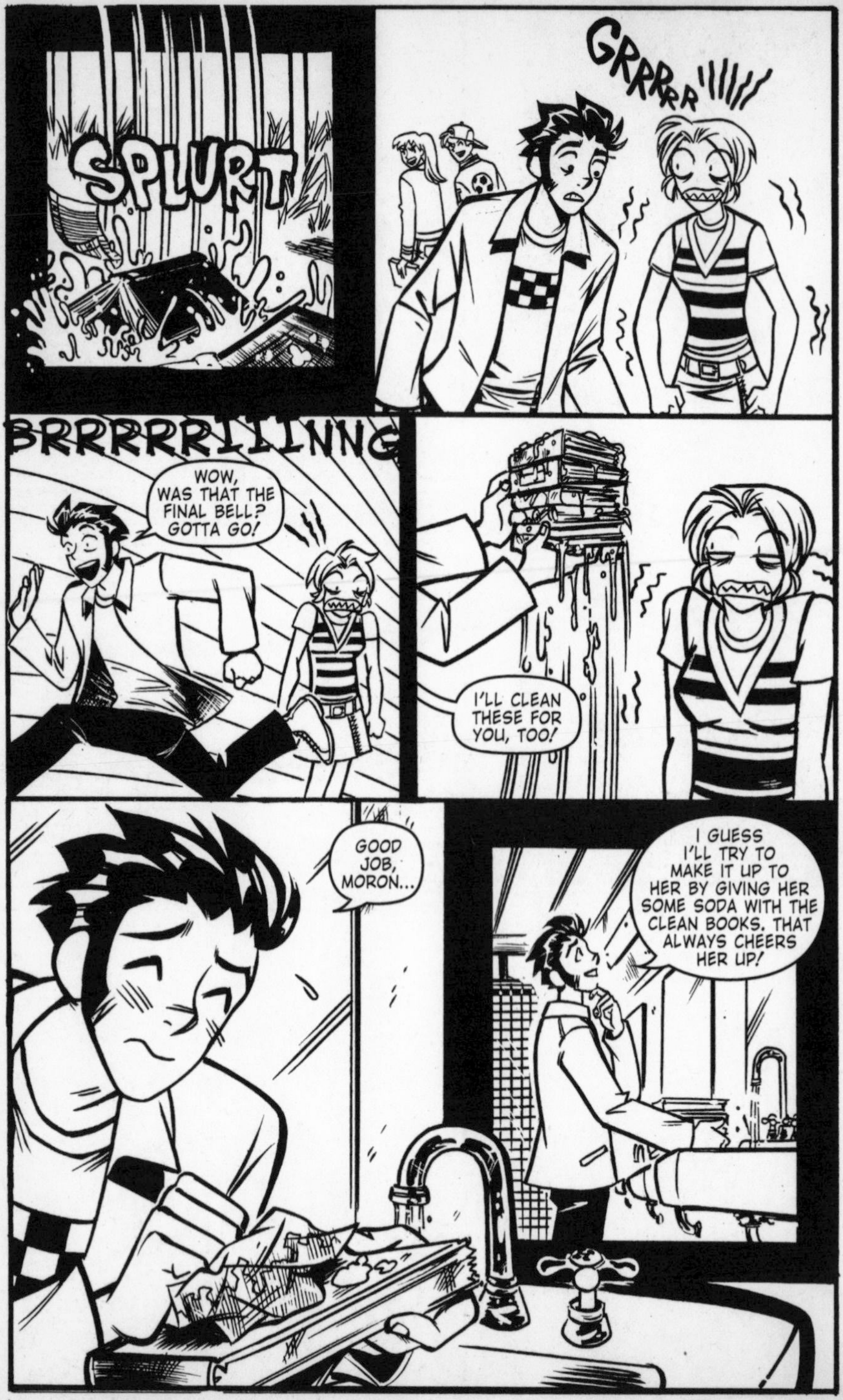

SPLURT
GRRRRR
BRRRRRRIIINNG
WOW, WAS THAT THE FINAL BELL? GOTTA GO!
I'LL CLEAN THESE FOR YOU, TOO!
GOOD JOB, MORON...
I GUESS I'LL TRY TO MAKE IT UP TO HER BY GIVING HER SOME SODA WITH THE CLEAN BOOKS. THAT ALWAYS CHEERS HER UP!

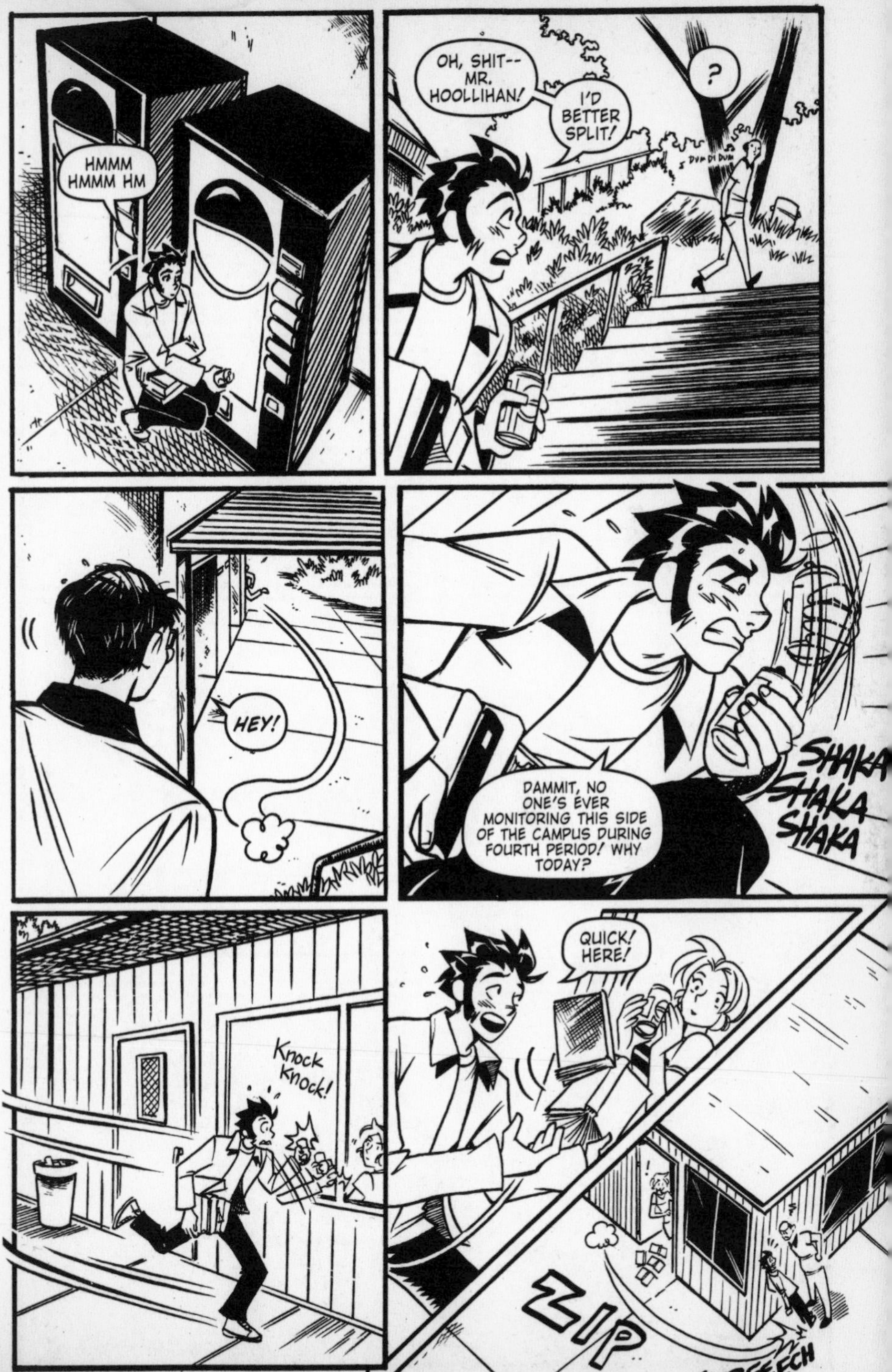
HMMM HMMM HM
OH, SHIT-- MR. HOOLLIHAN!
I'D BETTER SPLIT!
?
DUM DI DUM
HEY!
DAMMIT, NO ONE'S EVER MONITORING THIS SIDE OF THE CAMPUS DURING FOURTH PERIOD! WHY TODAY?
SHAKA SHAKA SHAKA
Knock knock!
QUICK! HERE!
ZIP
SKREEECH

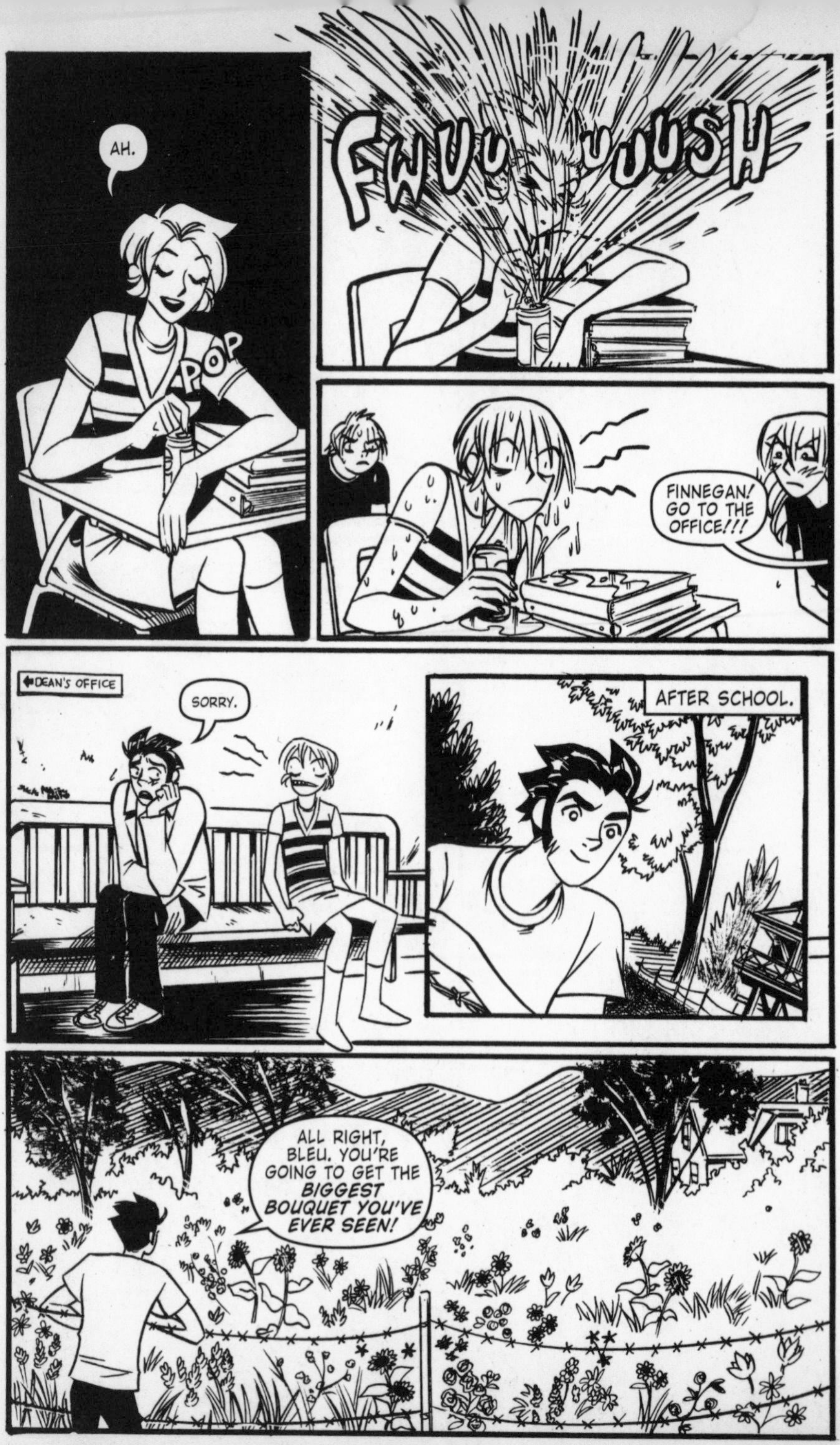
AH.
POP
FWUU UUUSH
FINNEGAN! GO TO THE OFFICE!!!
DEAN'S OFFICE
SORRY.
AFTER SCHOOL.
ALL RIGHT, BLEU. YOU'RE GOING TO GET THE BIGGEST BOUQUET YOU'VE EVER SEEN!

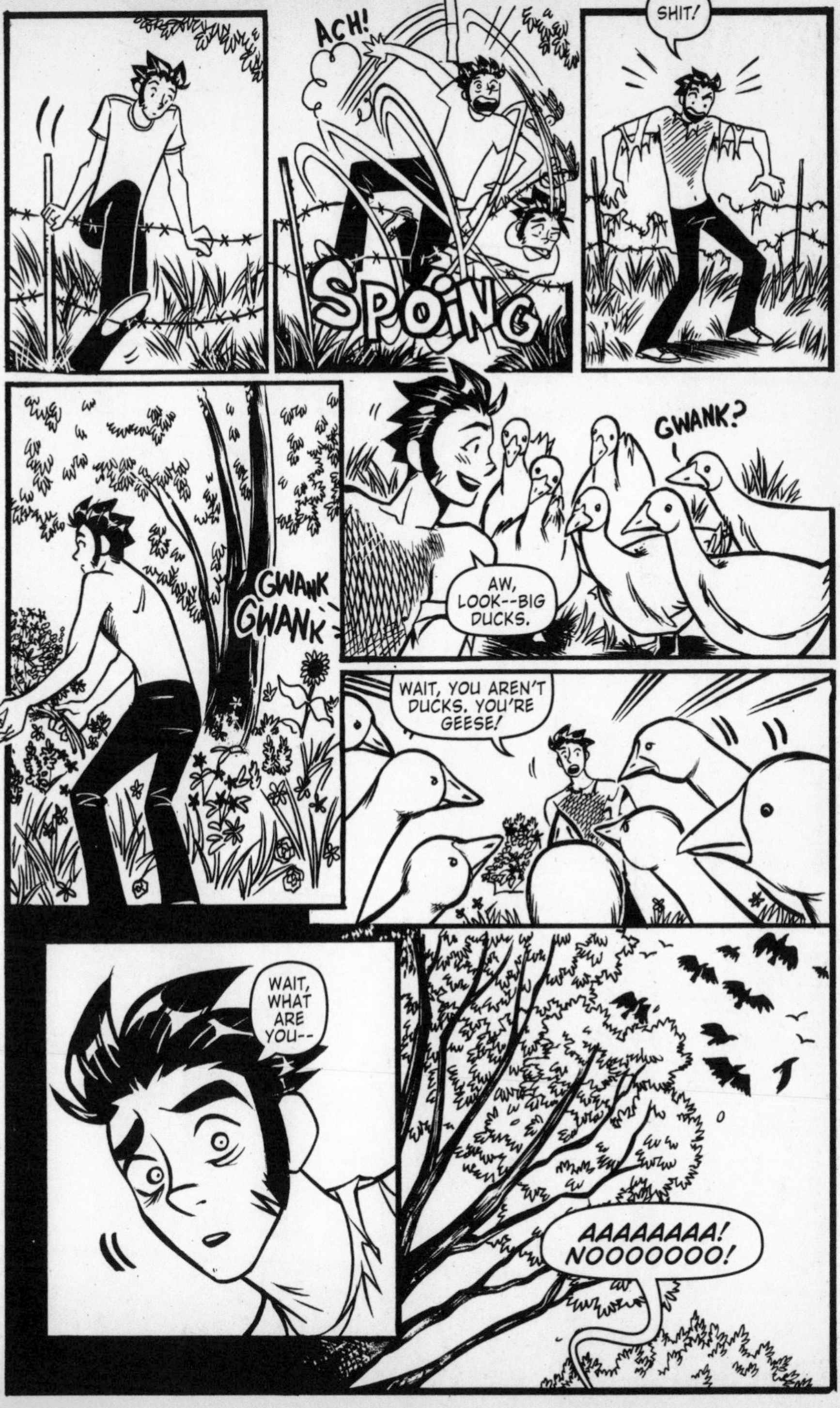
ACH!
SPOING
SHIT!
GWANK
GWANK
AW, LOOK--BIG DUCKS.
GWANK?
WAIT, YOU AREN'T DUCKS. YOU'RE GEESE!
WAIT, WHAT ARE YOU--
AAAAAAAA! NOOOOOOO!

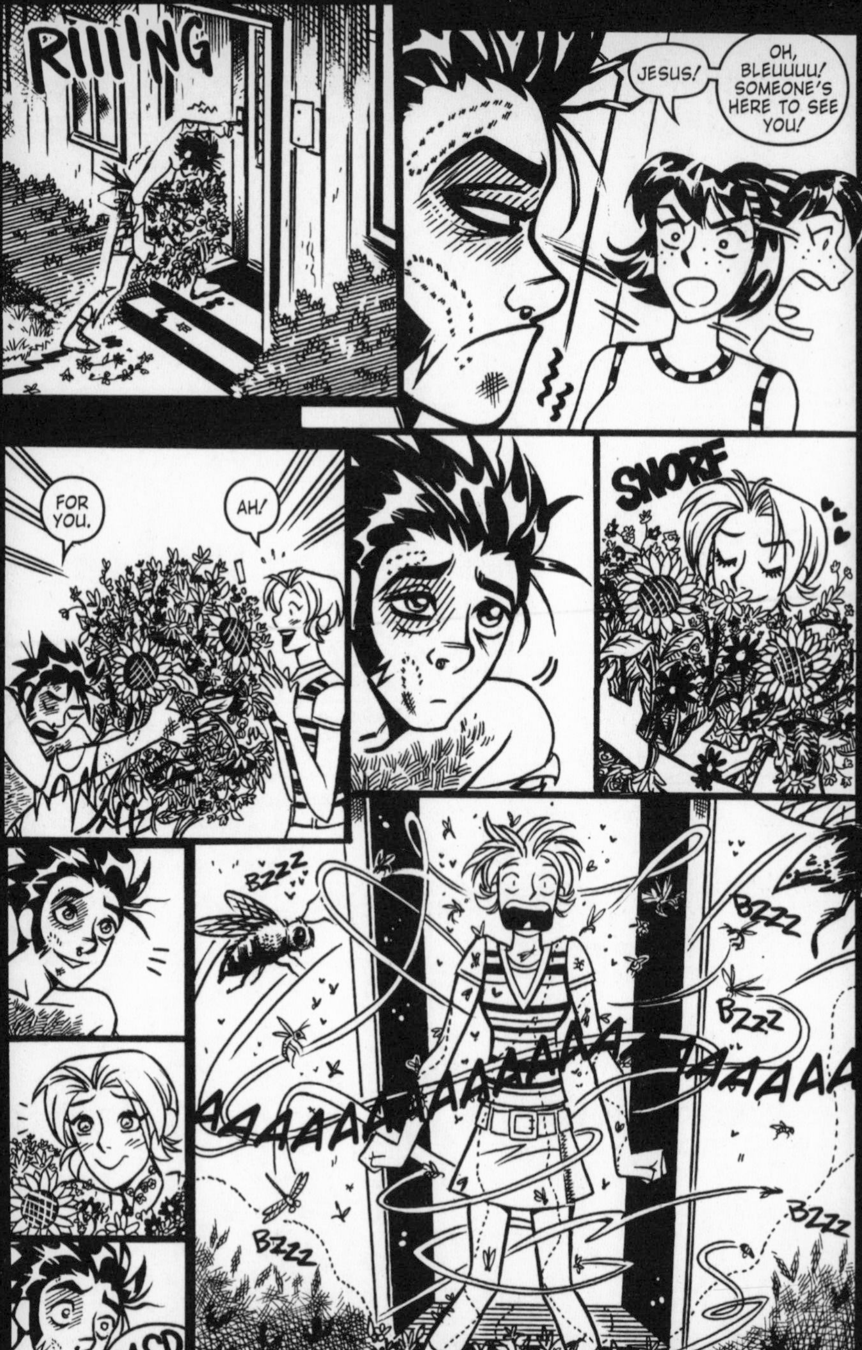
RIIIING
JESUS!
OH, BLEUUUU! SOMEONE'S HERE TO SEE YOU!
FOR YOU.
AH!
SNORF
BZZZ
BZZZ
BZZZ
AAAAAAAAAAAAAAAAAAAAAAAAAA
BZZZ
BZZZ
GASP

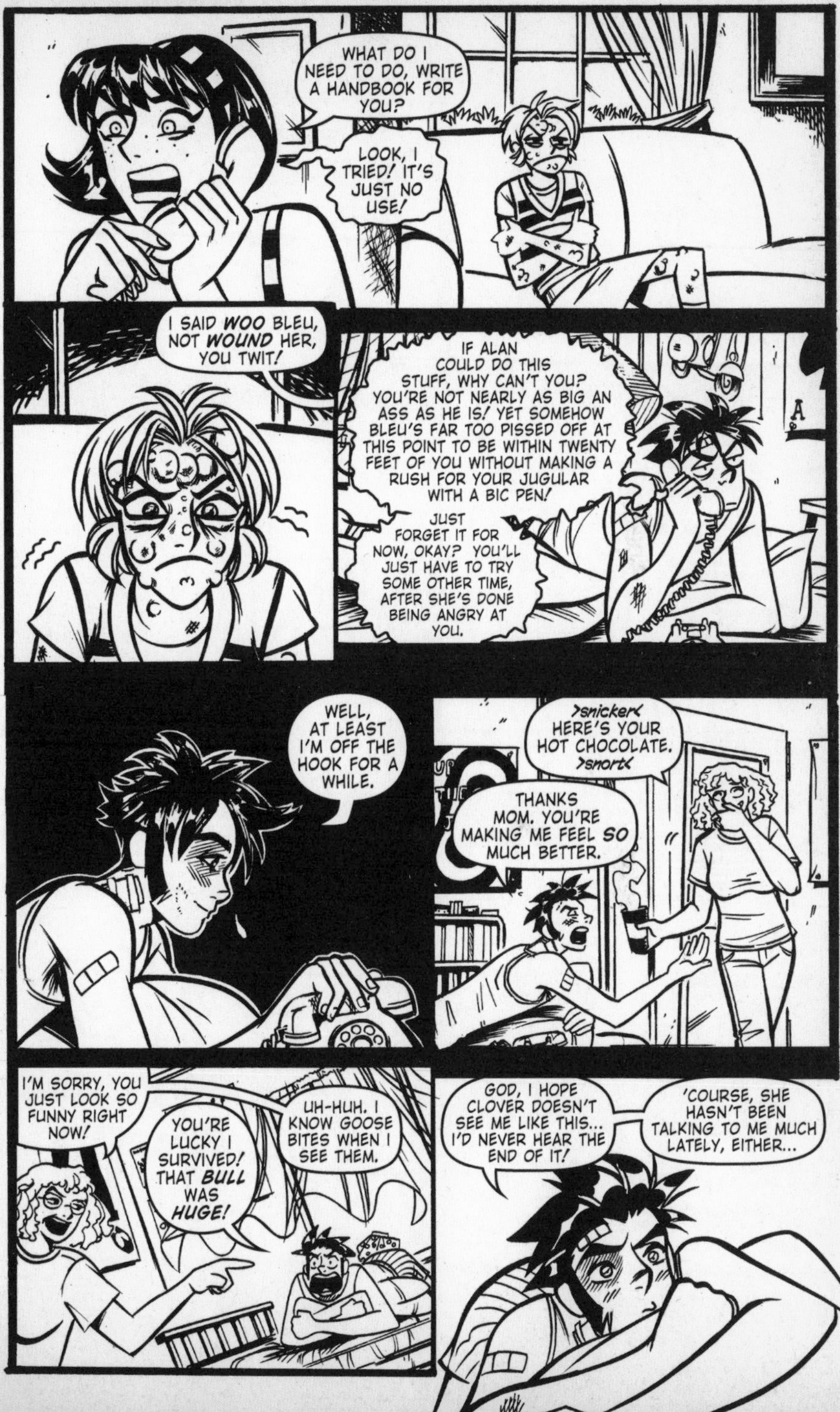
WHAT DO I NEED TO DO, WRITE A HANDBOOK FOR YOU?
LOOK, I TRIED! IT'S JUST NO USE!
I SAID **WOO** BLEU, NOT **WOUND** HER, YOU TWIT!
IF ALAN COULD DO THIS STUFF, WHY CAN'T YOU? YOU'RE NOT NEARLY AS BIG AN ASS AS HE IS! YET SOMEHOW BLEU'S FAR TOO PISSED OFF AT THIS POINT TO BE WITHIN TWENTY FEET OF YOU WITHOUT MAKING A RUSH FOR YOUR JUGULAR WITH A BIC PEN!
JUST FORGET IT FOR NOW, OKAY? YOU'LL JUST HAVE TO TRY SOME OTHER TIME, AFTER SHE'S DONE BEING ANGRY AT YOU.
WELL, AT LEAST I'M OFF THE HOOK FOR A WHILE.
>snicker< HERE'S YOUR HOT CHOCOLATE. *>snort<*
THANKS MOM. YOU'RE MAKING ME FEEL **SO** MUCH BETTER.
I'M SORRY, YOU JUST LOOK SO FUNNY RIGHT NOW!
YOU'RE LUCKY I SURVIVED! THAT **BULL** WAS **HUGE!**
UH-HUH. I KNOW GOOSE BITES WHEN I SEE THEM.
GOD, I HOPE CLOVER DOESN'T SEE ME LIKE THIS... I'D NEVER HEAR THE END OF IT!
'COURSE, SHE HASN'T BEEN TALKING TO ME MUCH LATELY, EITHER...

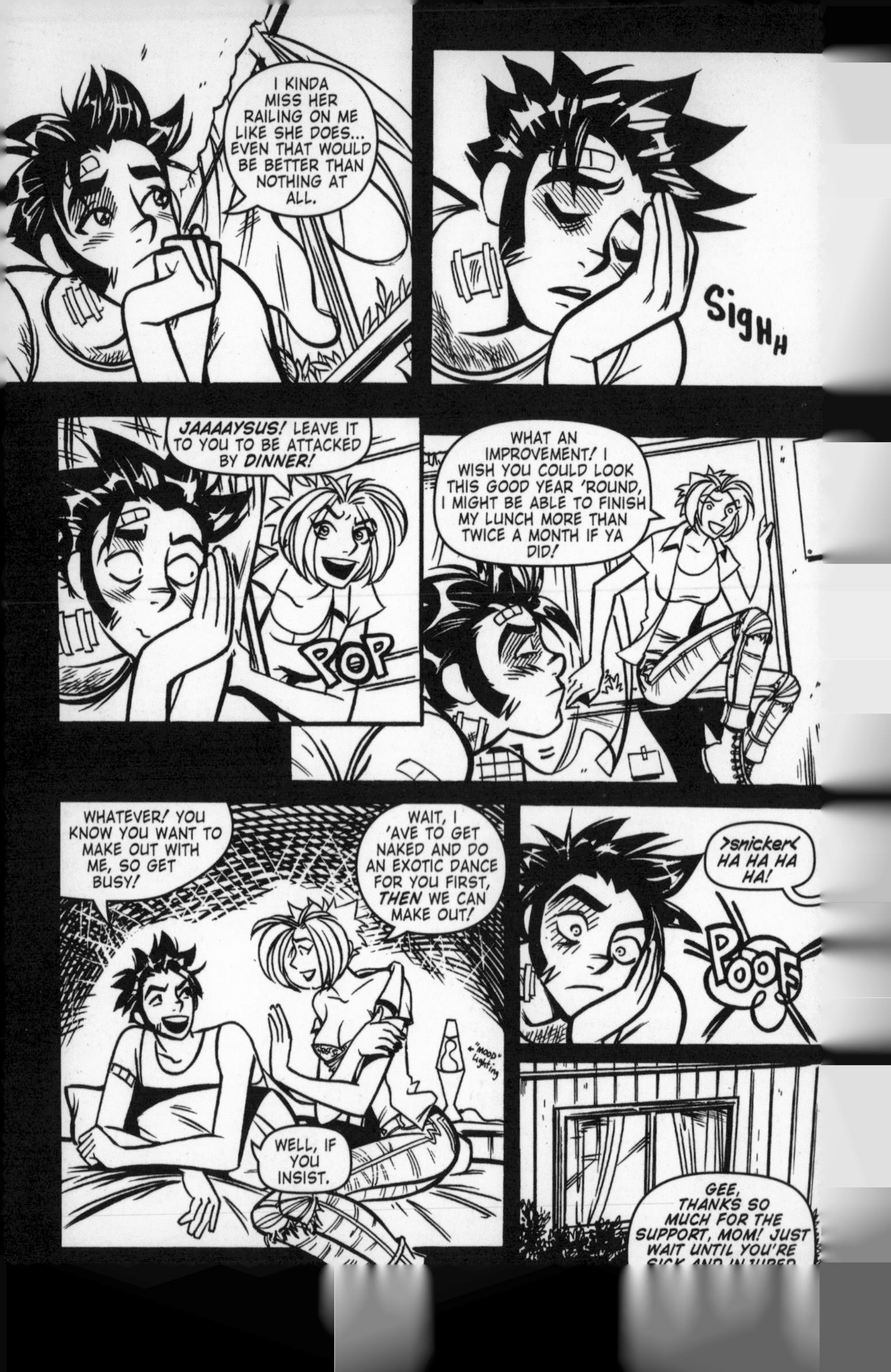
I KINDA MISS HER RAILING ON ME LIKE SHE DOES... EVEN THAT WOULD BE BETTER THAN NOTHING AT ALL.
SIGHHH
JAAAAYSUS! LEAVE IT TO YOU TO BE ATTACKED BY DINNER!
POP
WHAT AN IMPROVEMENT! I WISH YOU COULD LOOK THIS GOOD YEAR 'ROUND, I MIGHT BE ABLE TO FINISH MY LUNCH MORE THAN TWICE A MONTH IF YA DID!
WHATEVER! YOU KNOW YOU WANT TO MAKE OUT WITH ME, SO GET BUSY!
WAIT, I 'AVE TO GET NAKED AND DO AN EXOTIC DANCE FOR YOU FIRST, THEN WE CAN MAKE OUT!
WELL, IF YOU INSIST.
"MOOD" lighting
>snicker< HA HA HA HA!
POOF
GEE, THANKS SO MUCH FOR THE SUPPORT, MOM! JUST WAIT UNTIL YOU'RE

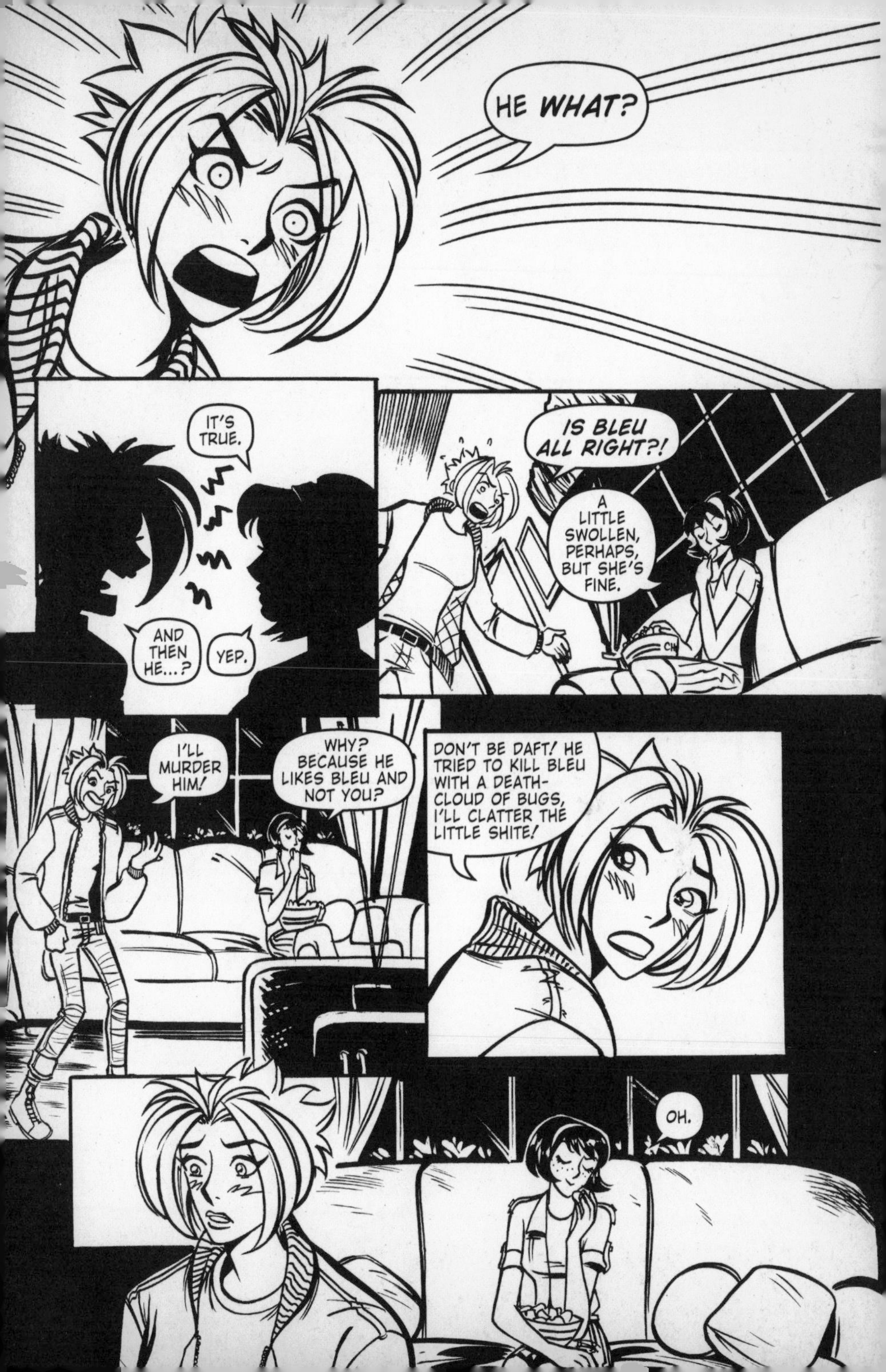

HE WHAT?
IT'S TRUE.
AND THEN HE...?
YEP.
IS BLEU ALL RIGHT?!
A LITTLE SWOLLEN, PERHAPS, BUT SHE'S FINE.
I'LL MURDER HIM!
WHY? BECAUSE HE LIKES BLEU AND NOT YOU?
DON'T BE DAFT! HE TRIED TO KILL BLEU WITH A DEATH-CLOUD OF BUGS, I'LL CLATTER THE LITTLE SHITE!
OH.

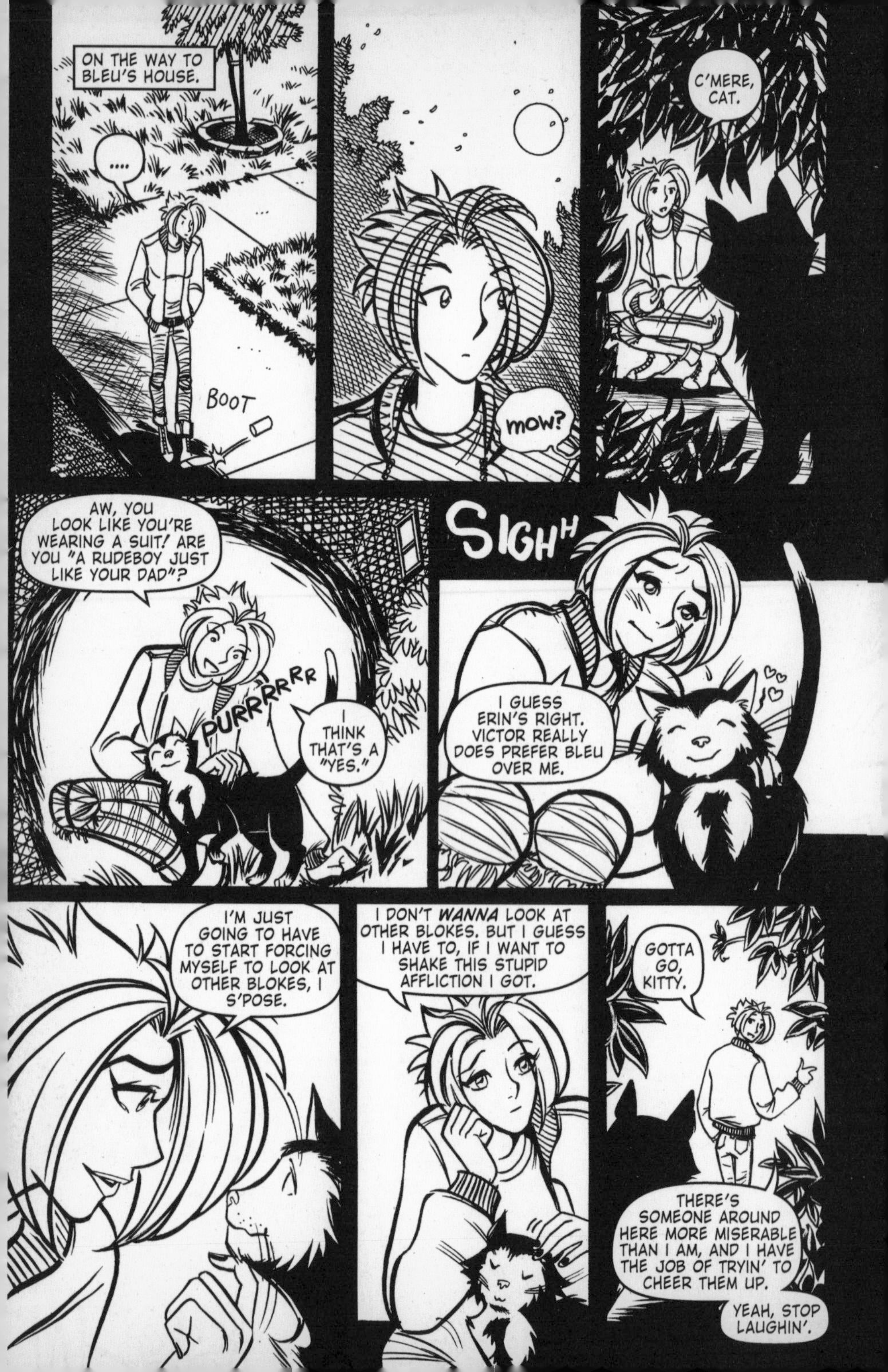

ON THE WAY TO BLEU'S HOUSE.
....
...
BOOT
mow?
C'MERE, CAT.
AW, YOU LOOK LIKE YOU'RE WEARING A SUIT! ARE YOU "A RUDEBOY JUST LIKE YOUR DAD"?
PURRRRRR
I THINK THAT'S A "YES."
SIGHH
I GUESS ERIN'S RIGHT. VICTOR REALLY DOES PREFER BLEU OVER ME.
I'M JUST GOING TO HAVE TO START FORCING MYSELF TO LOOK AT OTHER BLOKES, I S'POSE.
I DON'T *WANNA* LOOK AT OTHER BLOKES. BUT I GUESS I HAVE TO, IF I WANT TO SHAKE THIS STUPID AFFLICTION I GOT.
GOTTA GO, KITTY.
THERE'S SOMEONE AROUND HERE MORE MISERABLE THAN I AM, AND I HAVE THE JOB OF TRYIN' TO CHEER THEM UP.
YEAH, STOP LAUGHIN'.

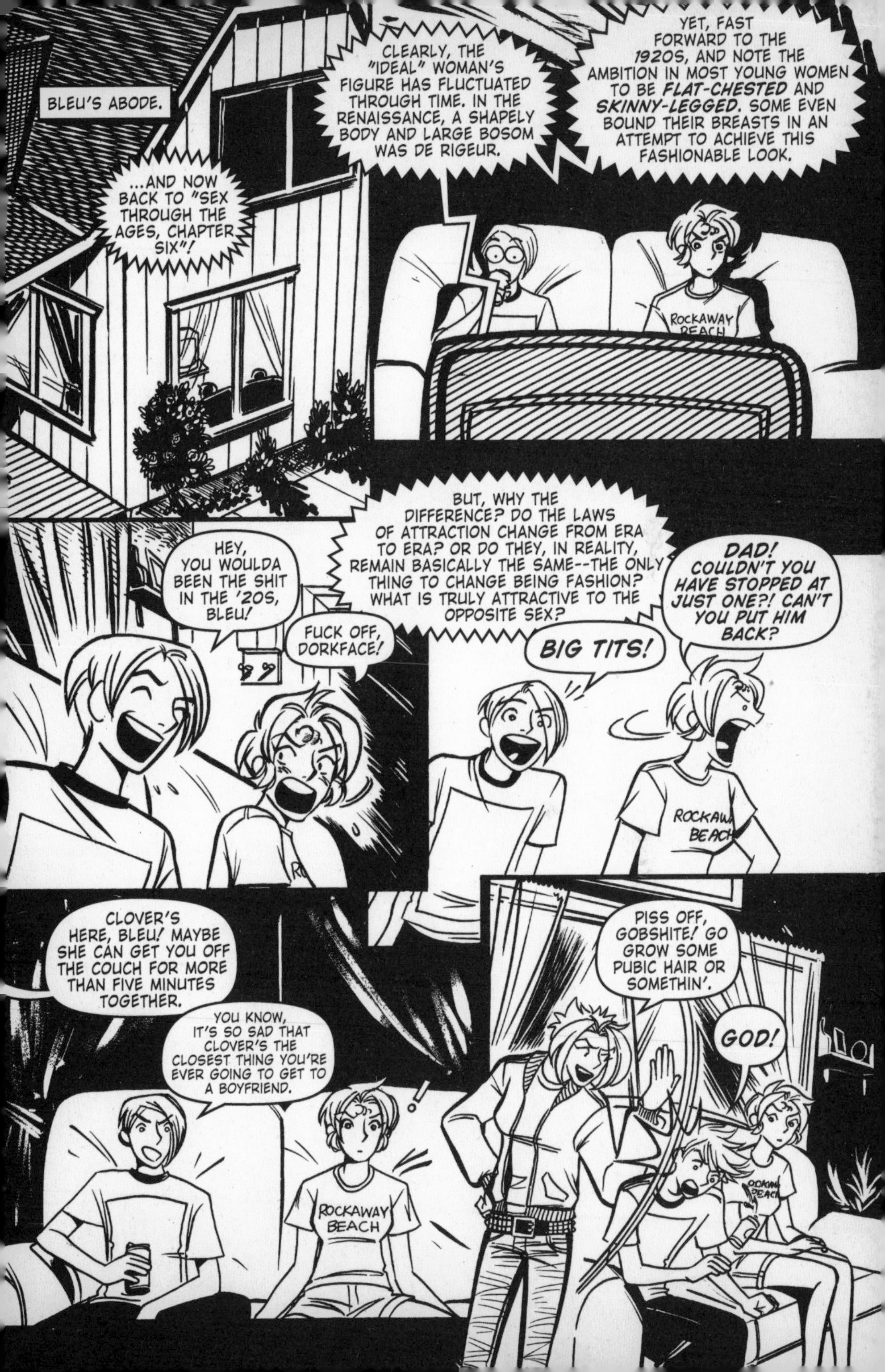
BLEU'S ABODE.
...AND NOW BACK TO "SEX THROUGH THE AGES, CHAPTER SIX"!
CLEARLY, THE "IDEAL" WOMAN'S FIGURE HAS FLUCTUATED THROUGH TIME. IN THE RENAISSANCE, A SHAPELY BODY AND LARGE BOSOM WAS DE RIGEUR.
YET, FAST FORWARD TO THE 1920S, AND NOTE THE AMBITION IN MOST YOUNG WOMEN TO BE FLAT-CHESTED AND SKINNY-LEGGED. SOME EVEN BOUND THEIR BREASTS IN AN ATTEMPT TO ACHIEVE THIS FASHIONABLE LOOK.
ROCKAWAY BEACH
HEY, YOU WOULDA BEEN THE SHIT IN THE '20S, BLEU!
FUCK OFF, DORKFACE!
BUT, WHY THE DIFFERENCE? DO THE LAWS OF ATTRACTION CHANGE FROM ERA TO ERA? OR DO THEY, IN REALITY, REMAIN BASICALLY THE SAME--THE ONLY THING TO CHANGE BEING FASHION? WHAT IS TRULY ATTRACTIVE TO THE OPPOSITE SEX?
BIG TITS!
DAD! COULDN'T YOU HAVE STOPPED AT JUST ONE?! CAN'T YOU PUT HIM BACK?
CLOVER'S HERE, BLEU! MAYBE SHE CAN GET YOU OFF THE COUCH FOR MORE THAN FIVE MINUTES TOGETHER.
YOU KNOW, IT'S SO SAD THAT CLOVER'S THE CLOSEST THING YOU'RE EVER GOING TO GET TO A BOYFRIEND.
ROCKAWAY BEACH
PISS OFF, GOBSHITE! GO GROW SOME PUBIC HAIR OR SOMETHIN'.
GOD!

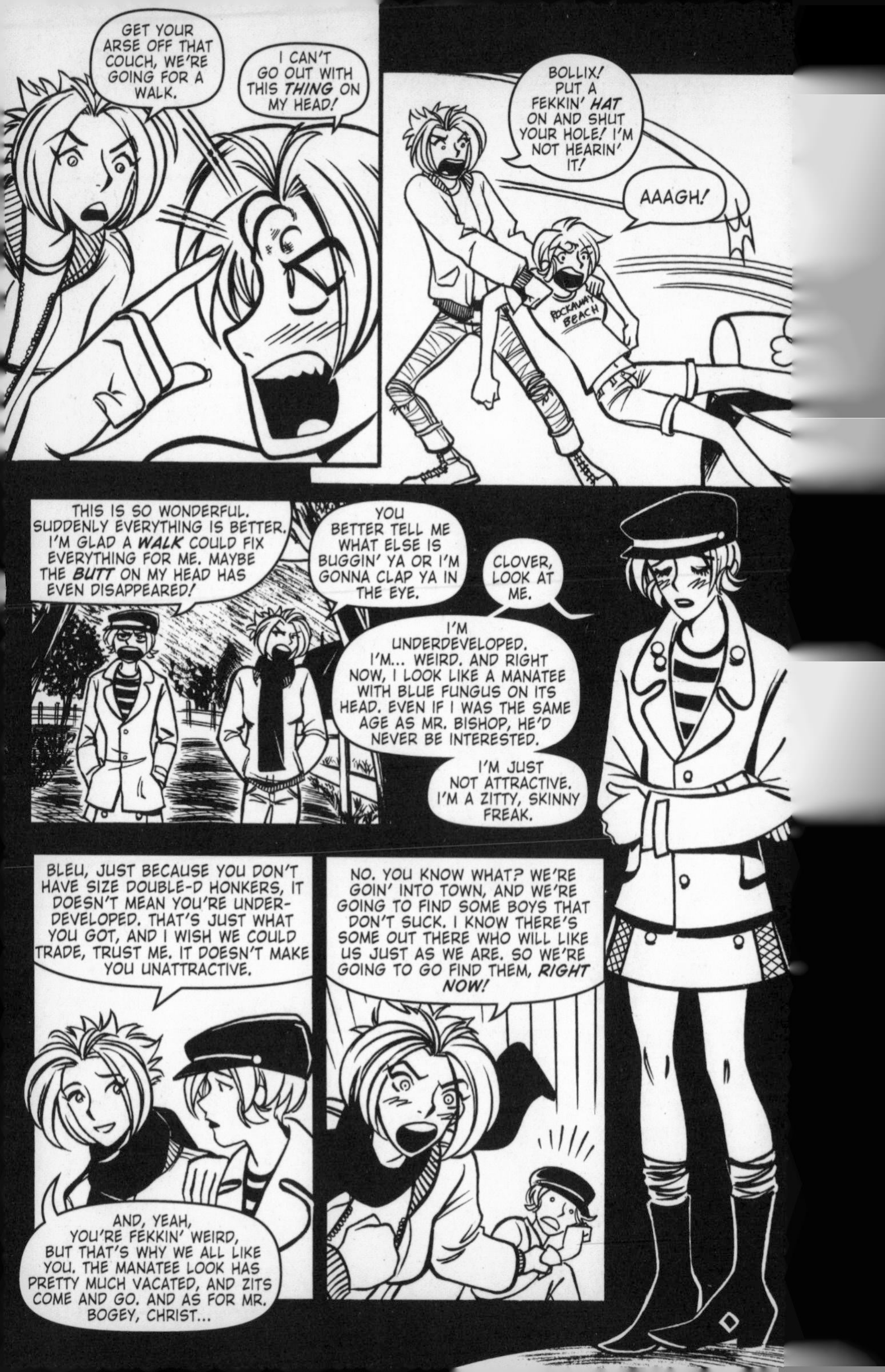
GET YOUR ARSE OFF THAT COUCH, WE'RE GOING FOR A WALK.
I CAN'T GO OUT WITH THIS *THING* ON MY HEAD!
BOLLIX! PUT A FEKKIN' *HAT* ON AND SHUT YOUR HOLE! I'M NOT HEARIN' IT!
AAAGH!
ROCKAWAY BEACH
THIS IS SO WONDERFUL. SUDDENLY EVERYTHING IS BETTER. I'M GLAD A *WALK* COULD FIX EVERYTHING FOR ME. MAYBE THE *BUTT* ON MY HEAD HAS EVEN DISAPPEARED!
YOU BETTER TELL ME WHAT ELSE IS BUGGIN' YA OR I'M GONNA CLAP YA IN THE EYE.
CLOVER, LOOK AT ME.
I'M UNDERDEVELOPED. I'M... WEIRD. AND RIGHT NOW, I LOOK LIKE A MANATEE WITH BLUE FUNGUS ON ITS HEAD. EVEN IF I WAS THE SAME AGE AS MR. BISHOP, HE'D NEVER BE INTERESTED.
I'M JUST NOT ATTRACTIVE. I'M A ZITTY, SKINNY FREAK.
BLEU, JUST BECAUSE YOU DON'T HAVE SIZE DOUBLE-D HONKERS, IT DOESN'T MEAN YOU'RE UNDER-DEVELOPED. THAT'S JUST WHAT YOU GOT, AND I WISH WE COULD TRADE, TRUST ME. IT DOESN'T MAKE YOU UNATTRACTIVE.
AND, YEAH, YOU'RE FEKKIN' WEIRD, BUT THAT'S WHY WE ALL LIKE YOU. THE MANATEE LOOK HAS PRETTY MUCH VACATED, AND ZITS COME AND GO. AND AS FOR MR. BOGEY, CHRIST...
NO. YOU KNOW WHAT? WE'RE GOIN' INTO TOWN, AND WE'RE GOING TO FIND SOME BOYS THAT DON'T SUCK. I KNOW THERE'S SOME OUT THERE WHO WILL LIKE US JUST AS WE ARE. SO WE'RE GOING TO GO FIND THEM, *RIGHT NOW!*

the smiths - "stop me if you think you've heard this one before"

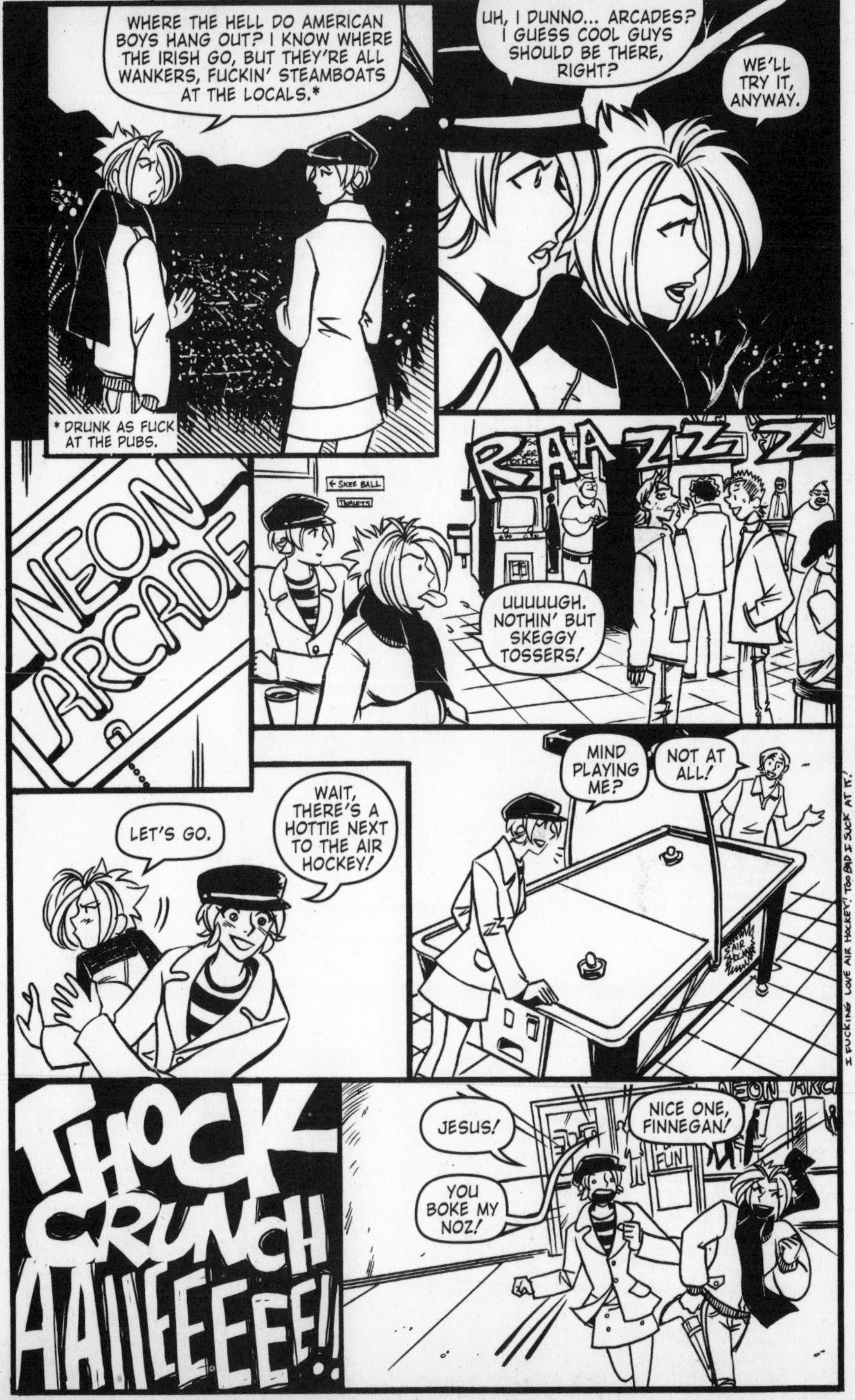
WHERE THE HELL DO AMERICAN BOYS HANG OUT? I KNOW WHERE THE IRISH GO, BUT THEY'RE ALL WANKERS, FUCKIN' STEAMBOATS AT THE LOCALS.*
* DRUNK AS FUCK AT THE PUBS.
UH, I DUNNO... ARCADES? I GUESS COOL GUYS SHOULD BE THERE, RIGHT?
WE'LL TRY IT, ANYWAY.
NEON ARCADE
← SKEE BALL
RAAZZZ
UUUUUGH. NOTHIN' BUT SKEGGY TOSSERS!
LET'S GO.
WAIT, THERE'S A HOTTIE NEXT TO THE AIR HOCKEY!
MIND PLAYING ME?
NOT AT ALL!
THOCK CRUNCH AAIIEEEEEE!!
JESUS!
NICE ONE, FINNEGAN!
YOU BOKE MY NOZ!

I FUCKING LOVE AIR HOCKEY! TOO BAD I SUCK AT IT.

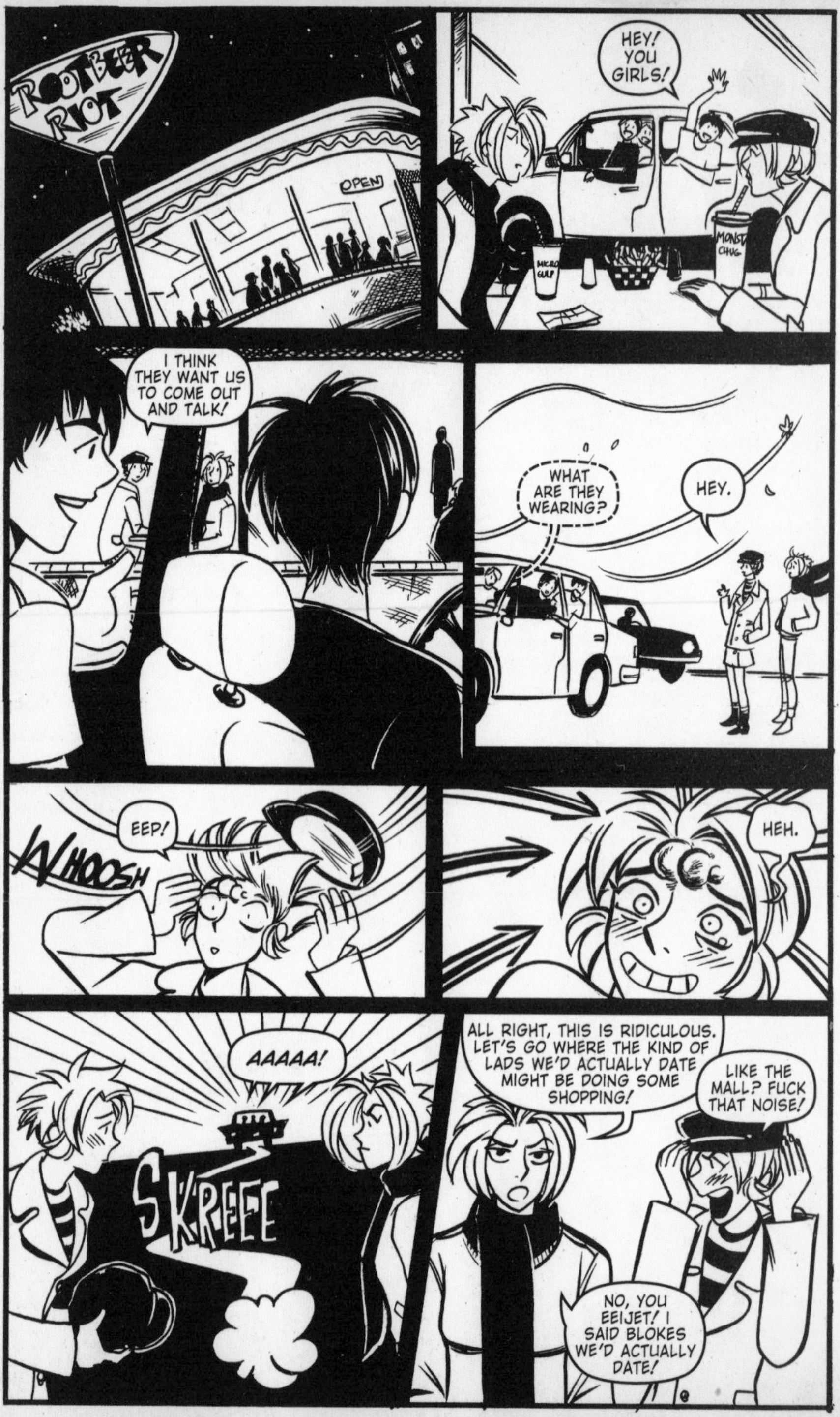
ROOTBEER RIOT
OPEN
HEY! YOU GIRLS!
MICRO GULP
MONST CHUG
I THINK THEY WANT US TO COME OUT AND TALK!
WHAT ARE THEY WEARING?
HEY.
EEP!
WHOOSH
HEH.
AAAAA!
SKREEE
ALL RIGHT, THIS IS RIDICULOUS. LET'S GO WHERE THE KIND OF LADS WE'D ACTUALLY DATE MIGHT BE DOING SOME SHOPPING!
LIKE THE MALL? FUCK THAT NOISE!
NO, YOU EEIJET! I SAID BLOKES WE'D ACTUALLY DATE!

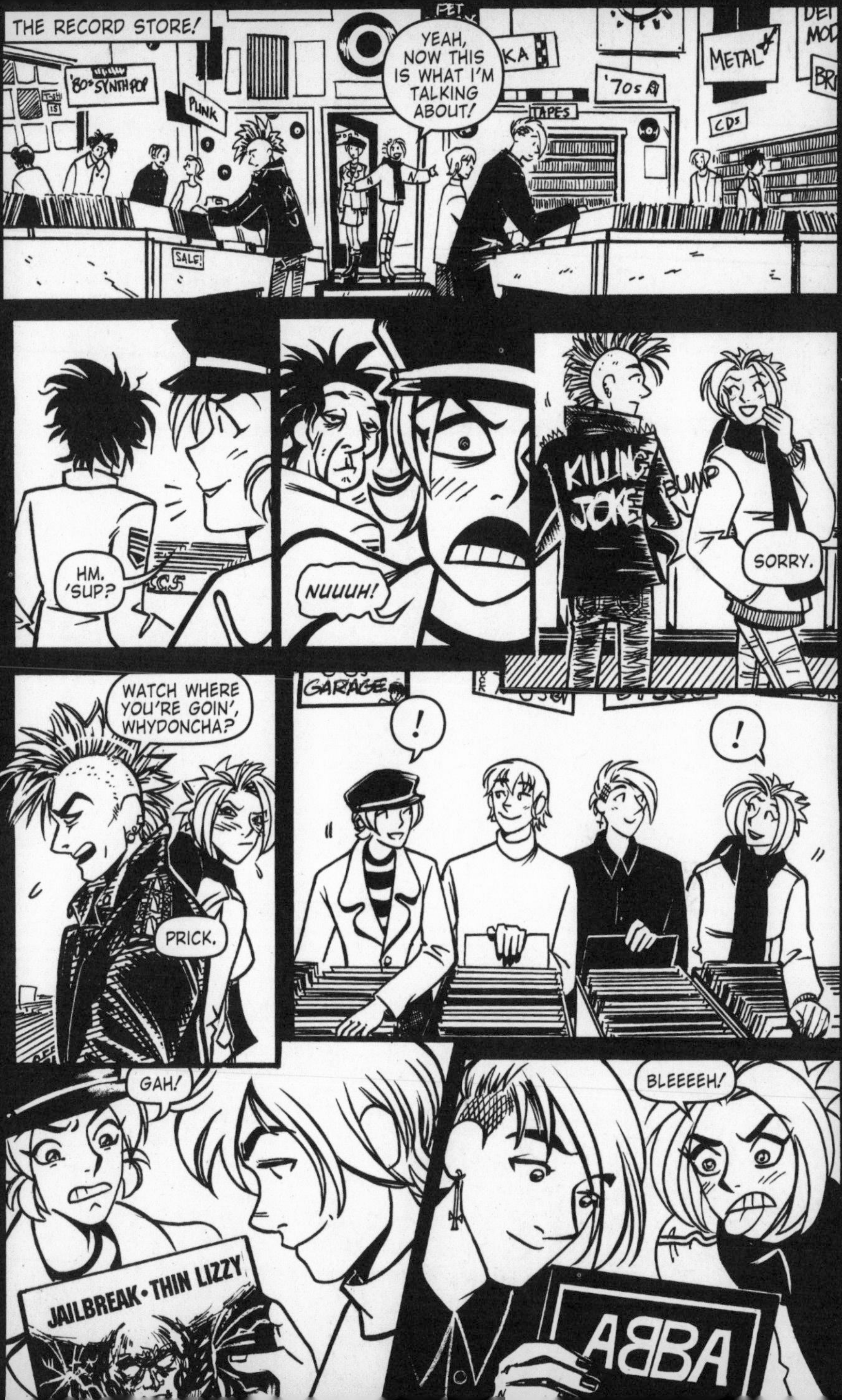
THE RECORD STORE!
'80s SYNTH POP
PUNK
YEAH, NOW THIS IS WHAT I'M TALKING ABOUT!
'70s
TAPES
METAL
CDs
SALE!
HM. 'SUP?
NUUUH!
KILLING JOKE
BUMP
SORRY.
WATCH WHERE YOU'RE GOIN', WHYDONCHA?
PRICK.
GARAGE
!
!
GAH!
JAILBREAK • THIN LIZZY
BLEEEEH!
ABBA

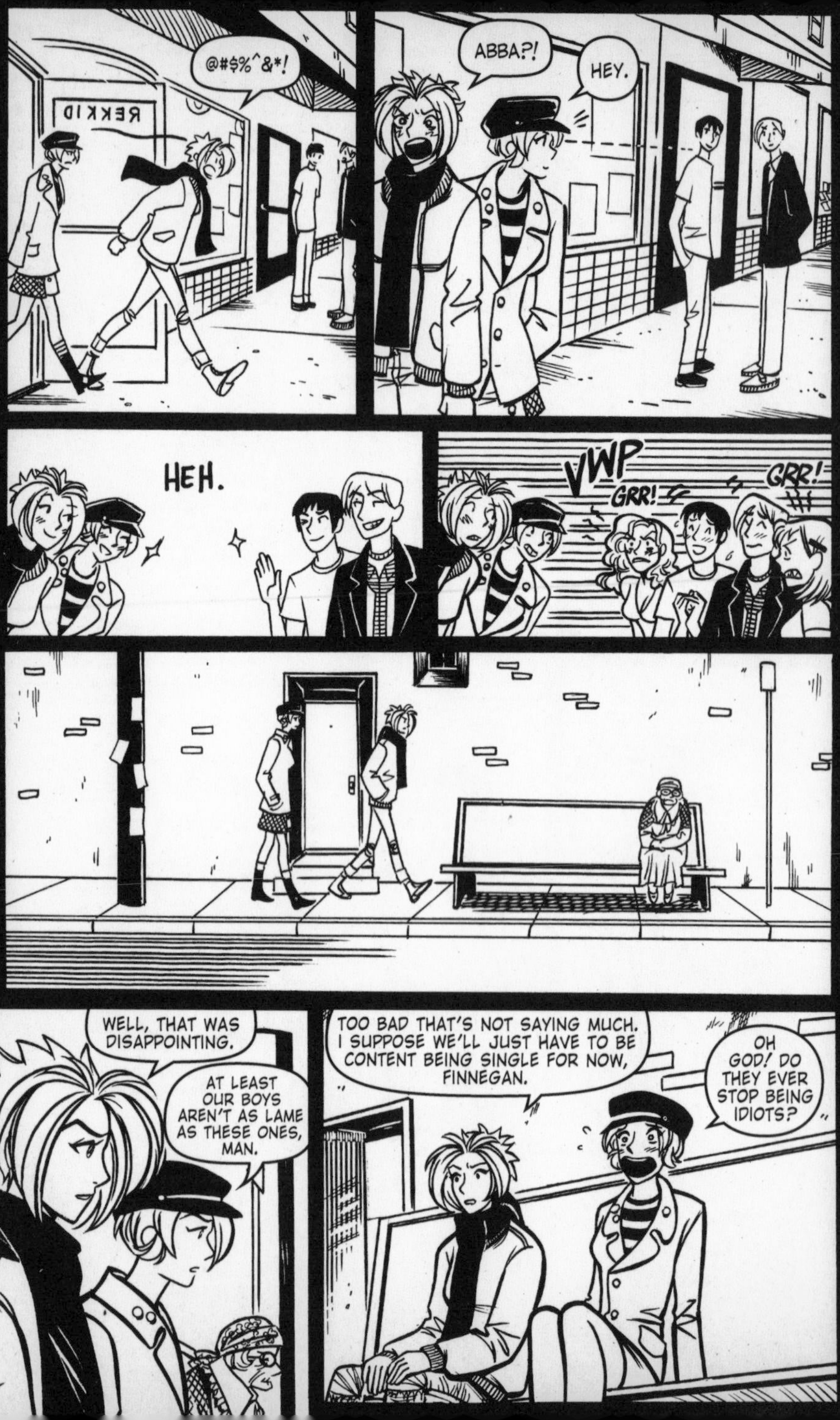

REKKID
@#$%^&*!
ABBA?!
HEY.
HEH.
VWP
GRR!
GRR!
WELL, THAT WAS DISAPPOINTING.
AT LEAST OUR BOYS AREN'T AS LAME AS THESE ONES, MAN.
TOO BAD THAT'S NOT SAYING MUCH. I SUPPOSE WE'LL JUST HAVE TO BE CONTENT BEING SINGLE FOR NOW, FINNEGAN.
OH GOD! DO THEY EVER STOP BEING IDIOTS?

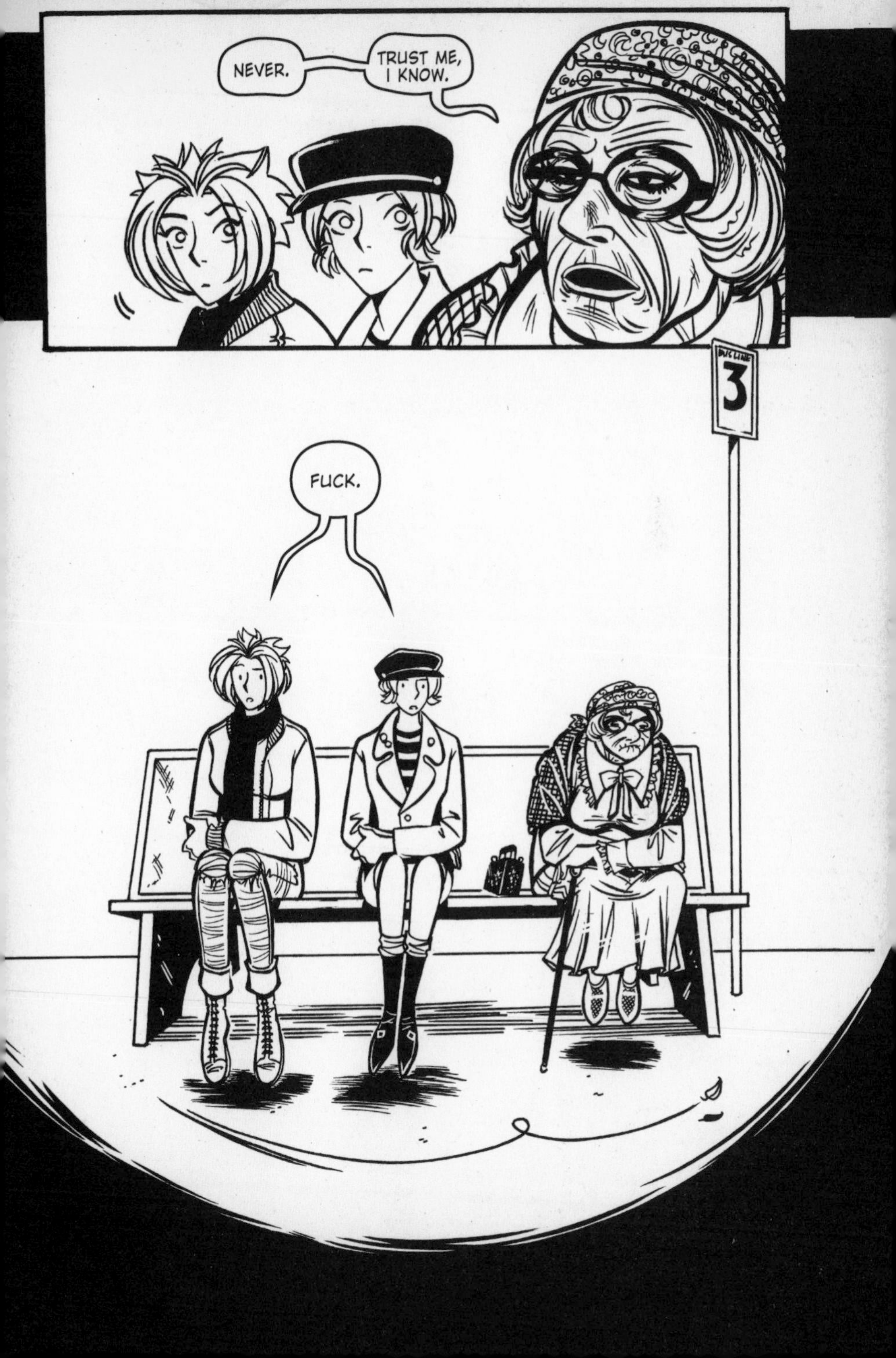
NEVER.
TRUST ME, I KNOW.
BUS LINE
3
FUCK.

chapter two:

"PICTURES OF LILY"

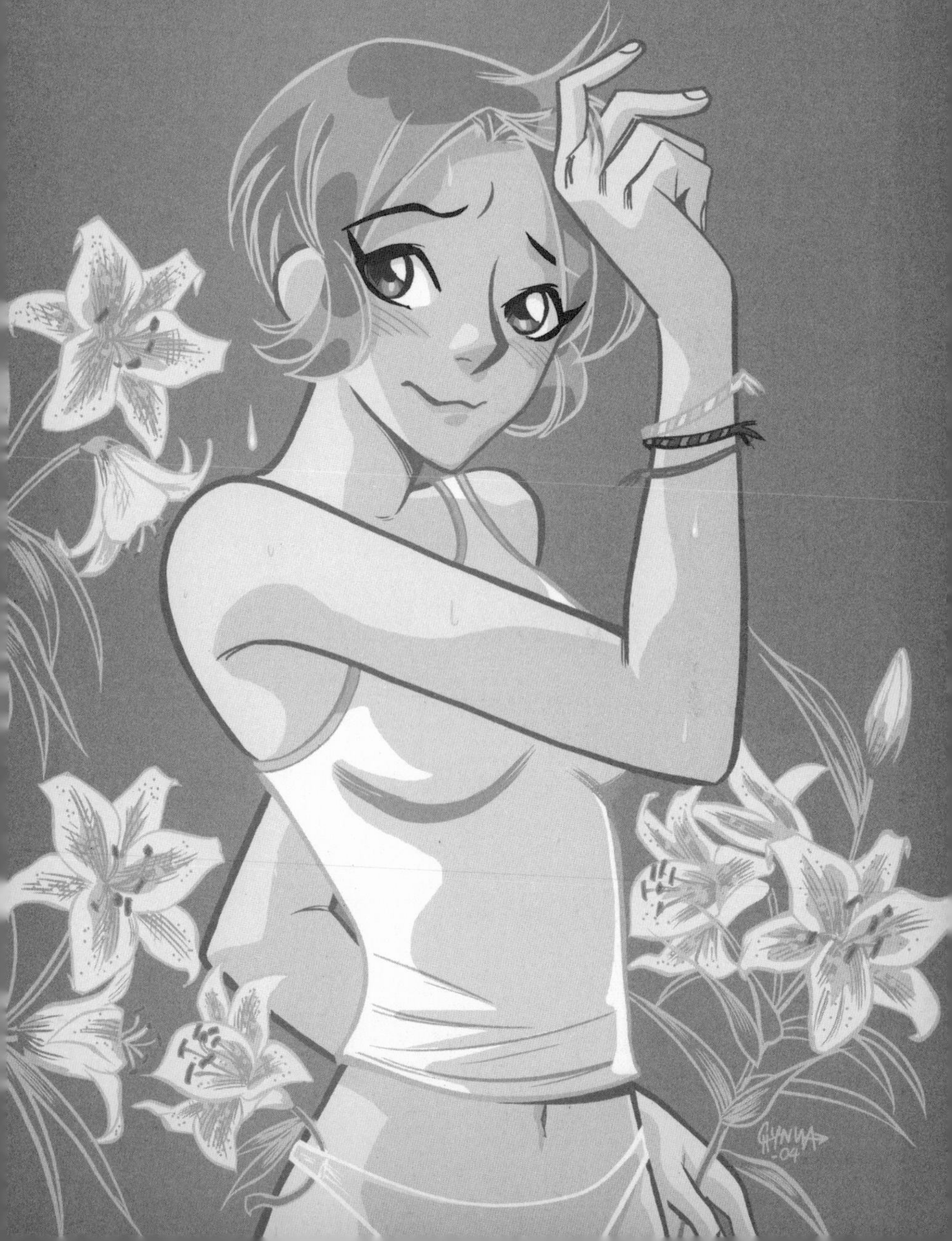

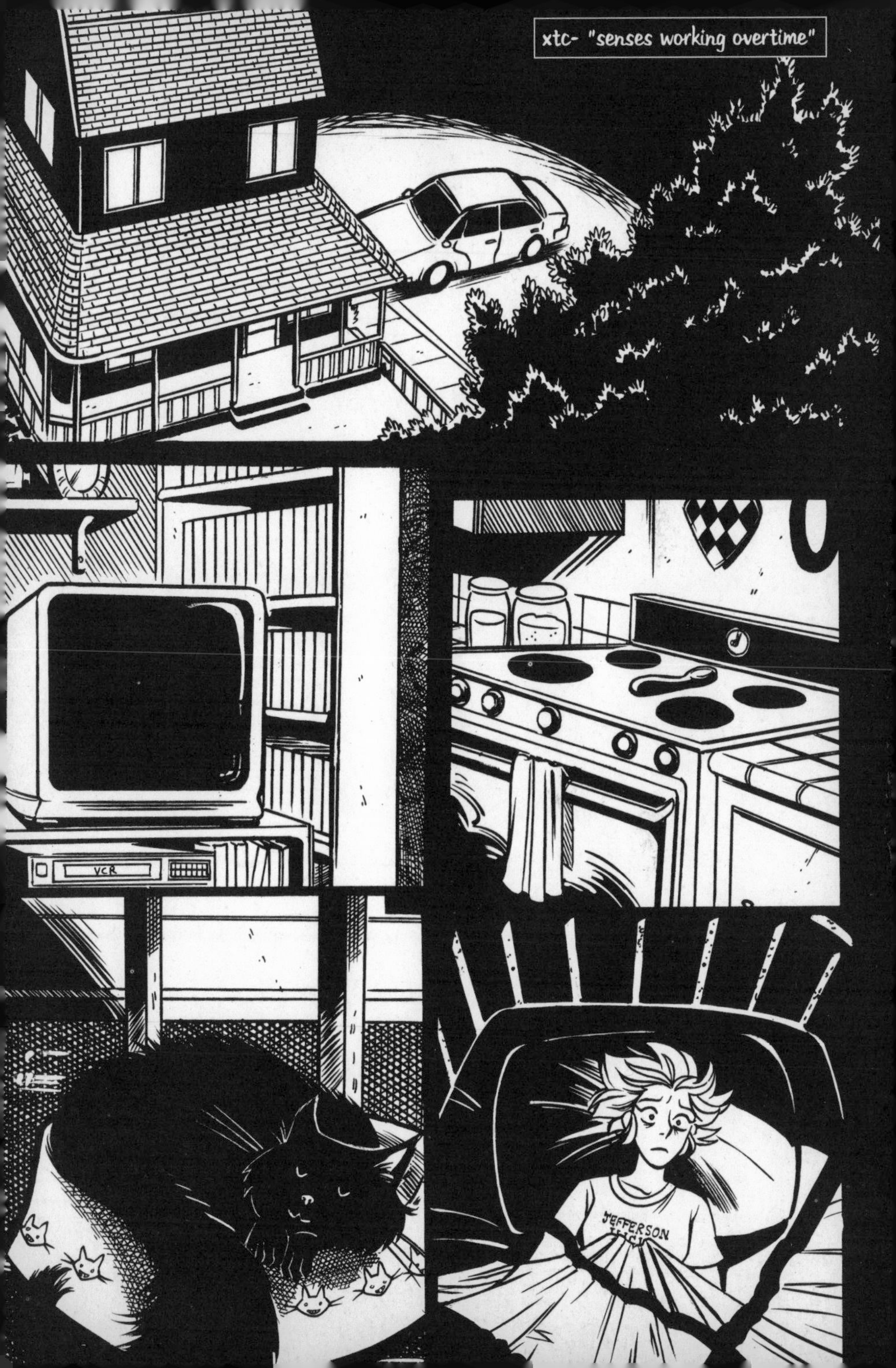
xtc- "senses working overtime"
VCR
JEFFERSON

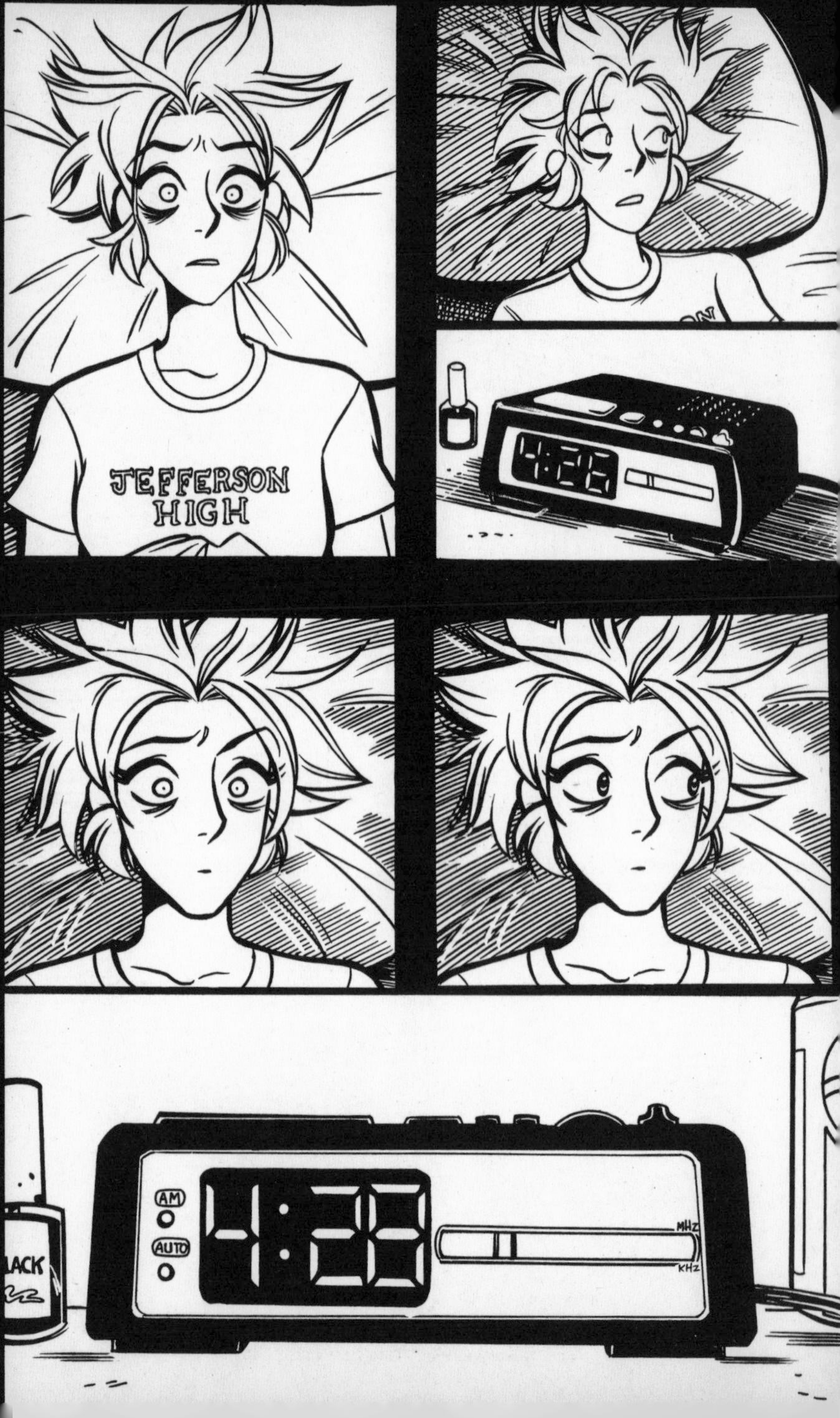
JEFFERSON HIGH
4:25
AM
AUTO
MHz
KHz
LACK

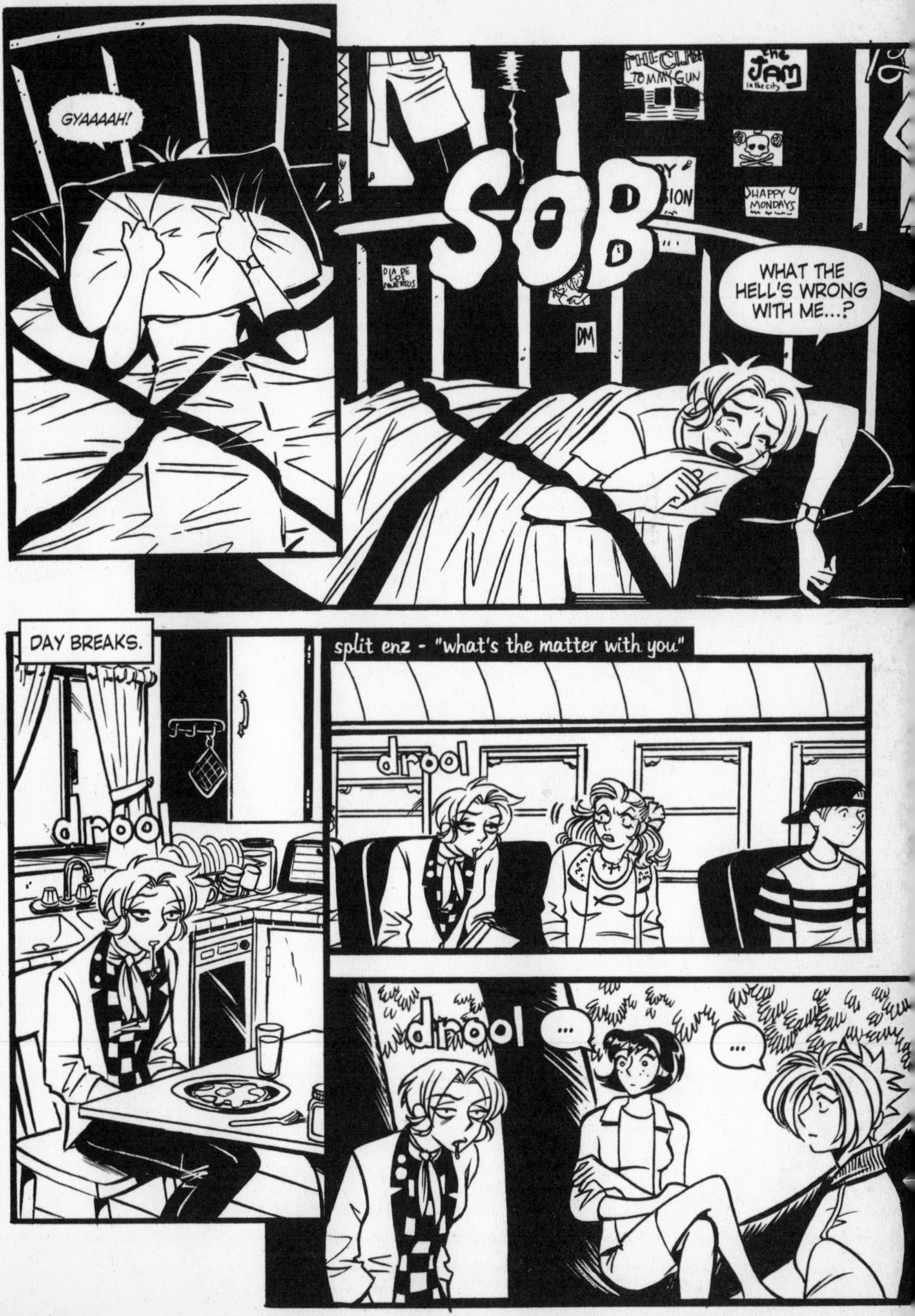
GYAAAAH!
TOMMY GUN
the JAM
HAPPY MONDAYS
SOB
WHAT THE HELL'S WRONG WITH ME...?
DAY BREAKS.
drool
split enz - "what's the matter with you"
drool
drool
...
...

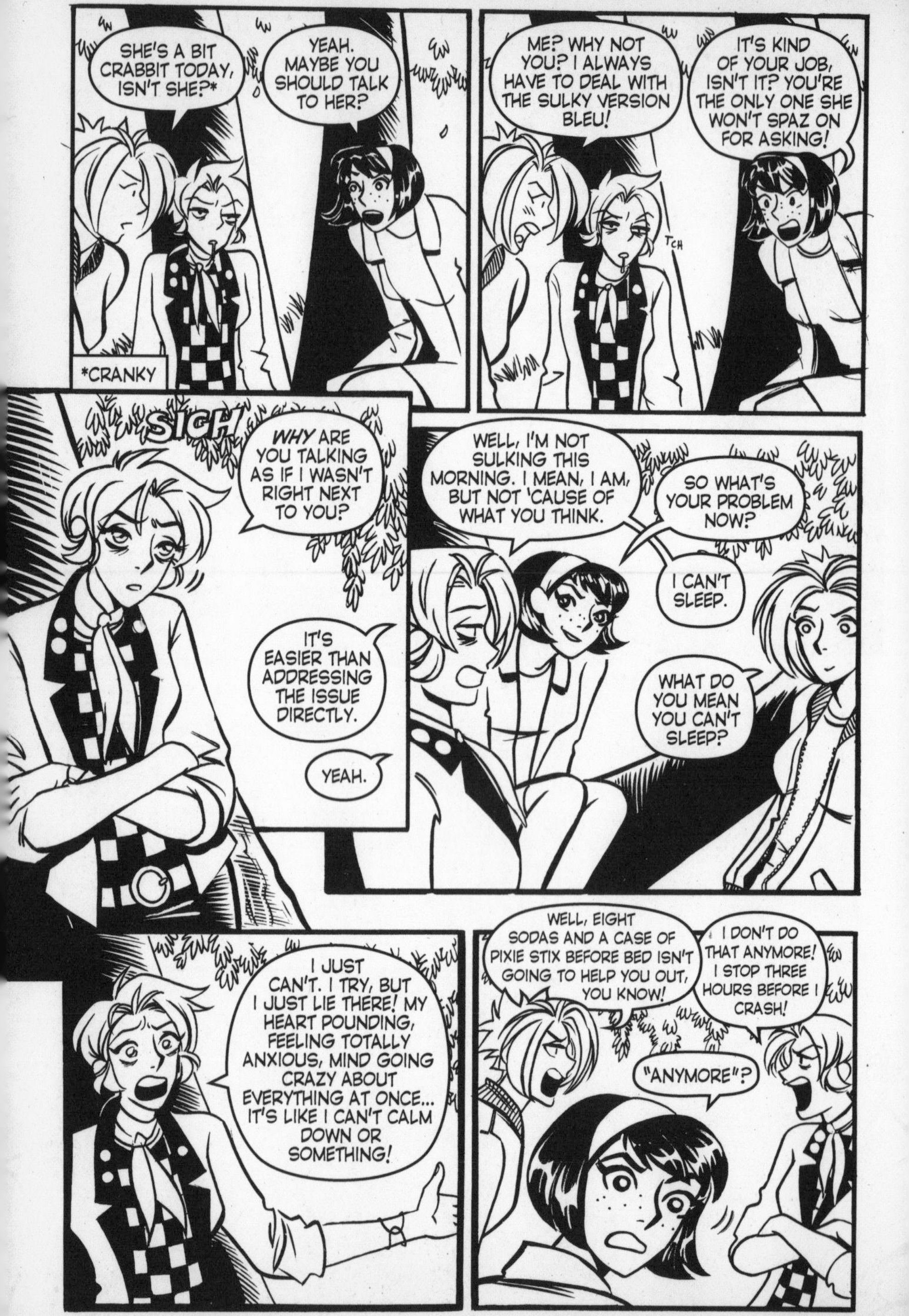
SHE'S A BIT CRABBIT TODAY, ISN'T SHE?*
YEAH. MAYBE YOU SHOULD TALK TO HER?
*CRANKY
ME? WHY NOT YOU? I ALWAYS HAVE TO DEAL WITH THE SULKY VERSION BLEU!
IT'S KIND OF YOUR JOB, ISN'T IT? YOU'RE THE ONLY ONE SHE WON'T SPAZ ON FOR ASKING!
TCH
SIGH
WHY ARE YOU TALKING AS IF I WASN'T RIGHT NEXT TO YOU?
IT'S EASIER THAN ADDRESSING THE ISSUE DIRECTLY.
YEAH.
WELL, I'M NOT SULKING THIS MORNING. I MEAN, I AM, BUT NOT 'CAUSE OF WHAT YOU THINK.
SO WHAT'S YOUR PROBLEM NOW?
I CAN'T SLEEP.
WHAT DO YOU MEAN YOU CAN'T SLEEP?
I JUST CAN'T. I TRY, BUT I JUST LIE THERE! MY HEART POUNDING, FEELING TOTALLY ANXIOUS, MIND GOING CRAZY ABOUT EVERYTHING AT ONCE... IT'S LIKE I CAN'T CALM DOWN OR SOMETHING!
WELL, EIGHT SODAS AND A CASE OF PIXIE STIX BEFORE BED ISN'T GOING TO HELP YOU OUT, YOU KNOW!
I DON'T DO THAT ANYMORE! I STOP THREE HOURS BEFORE I CRASH!
"ANYMORE"?

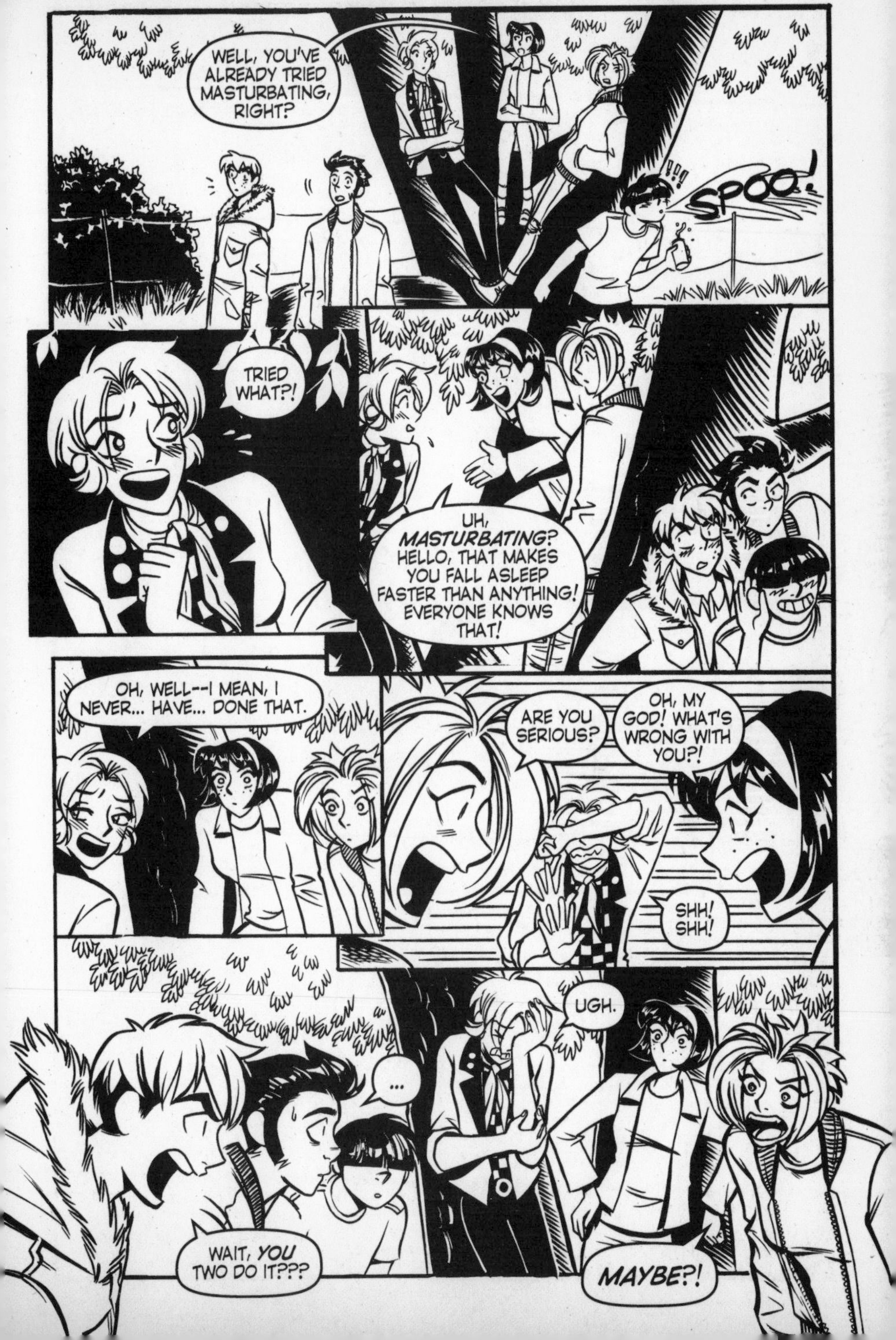

WELL, YOU'VE ALREADY TRIED MASTURBATING, RIGHT?
!!!
SPOO!
TRIED WHAT?!
UH, *MASTURBATING*? HELLO, THAT MAKES YOU FALL ASLEEP FASTER THAN ANYTHING! EVERYONE KNOWS THAT!
OH, WELL--I MEAN, I NEVER... HAVE... DONE THAT.
ARE YOU SERIOUS?
OH, MY GOD! WHAT'S WRONG WITH YOU?!
SHH! SHH!
UGH.
...
WAIT, *YOU* TWO DO IT???
MAYBE?!

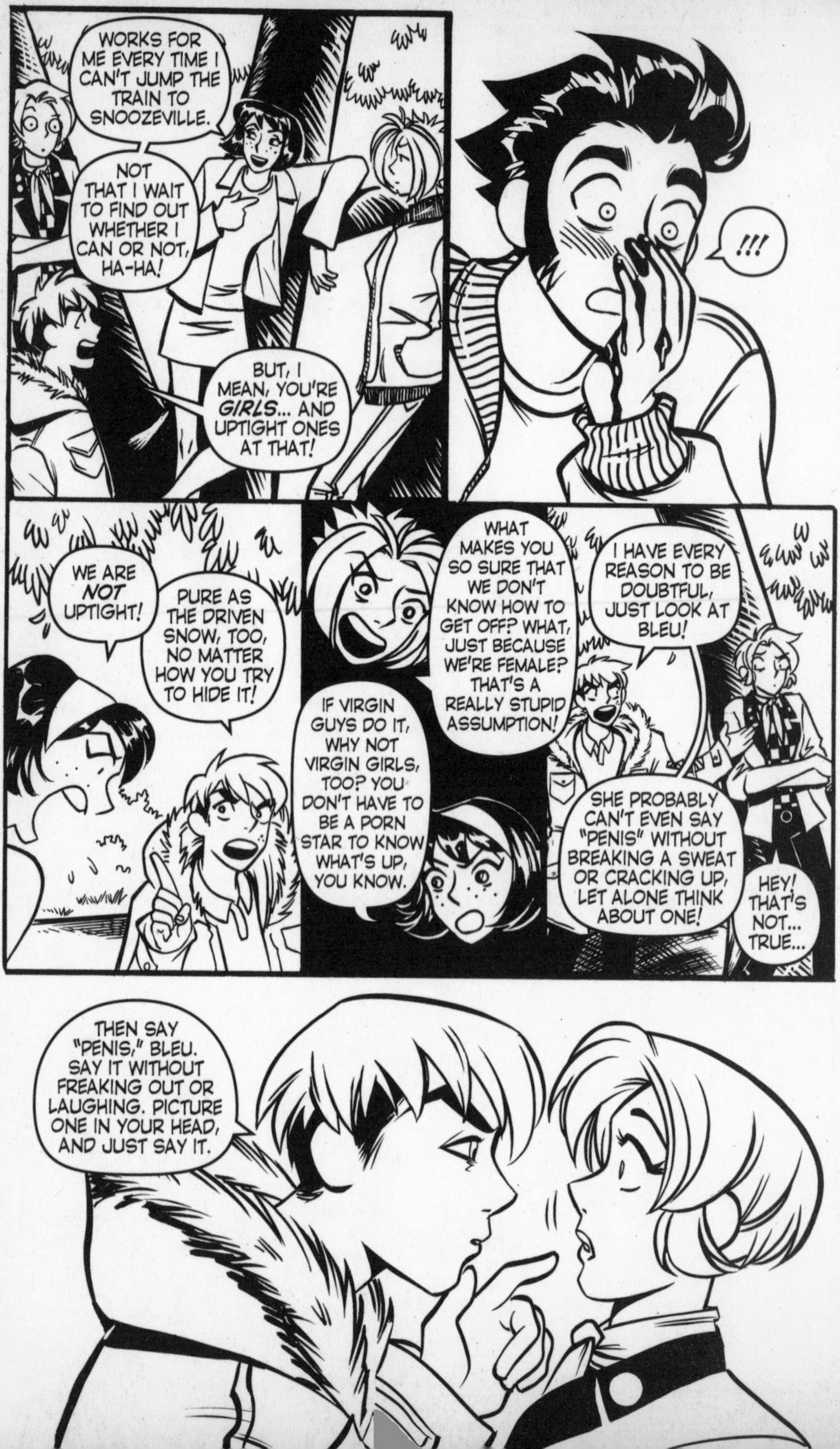
WORKS FOR ME EVERY TIME I CAN'T JUMP THE TRAIN TO SNOOZEVILLE.
NOT THAT I WAIT TO FIND OUT WHETHER I CAN OR NOT, HA-HA!
BUT, I MEAN, YOU'RE GIRLS... AND UPTIGHT ONES AT THAT!
!!!
WE ARE NOT UPTIGHT!
PURE AS THE DRIVEN SNOW, TOO, NO MATTER HOW YOU TRY TO HIDE IT!
WHAT MAKES YOU SO SURE THAT WE DON'T KNOW HOW TO GET OFF? WHAT, JUST BECAUSE WE'RE FEMALE? THAT'S A REALLY STUPID ASSUMPTION!
IF VIRGIN GUYS DO IT, WHY NOT VIRGIN GIRLS, TOO? YOU DON'T HAVE TO BE A PORN STAR TO KNOW WHAT'S UP, YOU KNOW.
I HAVE EVERY REASON TO BE DOUBTFUL, JUST LOOK AT BLEU!
SHE PROBABLY CAN'T EVEN SAY "PENIS" WITHOUT BREAKING A SWEAT OR CRACKING UP, LET ALONE THINK ABOUT ONE!
HEY! THAT'S NOT... TRUE...
THEN SAY "PENIS," BLEU. SAY IT WITHOUT FREAKING OUT OR LAUGHING. PICTURE ONE IN YOUR HEAD, AND JUST SAY IT.

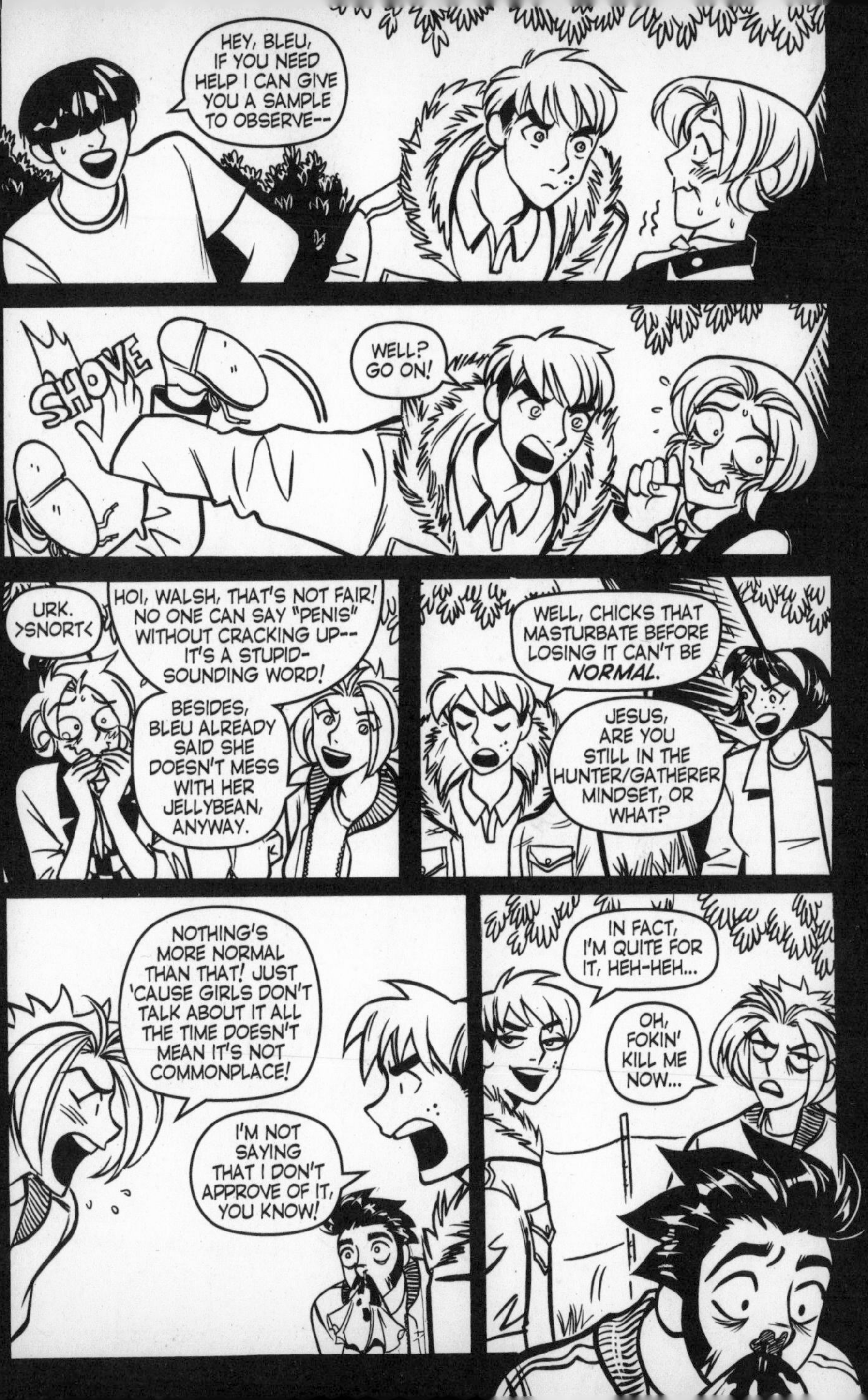

HEY, BLEU, IF YOU NEED HELP I CAN GIVE YOU A SAMPLE TO OBSERVE--
SHOVE
WELL? GO ON!
URK. >SNORT<
HOI, WALSH, THAT'S NOT FAIR! NO ONE CAN SAY "PENIS" WITHOUT CRACKING UP-- IT'S A STUPID-SOUNDING WORD!
BESIDES, BLEU ALREADY SAID SHE DOESN'T MESS WITH HER JELLYBEAN, ANYWAY.
WELL, CHICKS THAT MASTURBATE BEFORE LOSING IT CAN'T BE *NORMAL*.
JESUS, ARE YOU STILL IN THE HUNTER/GATHERER MINDSET, OR WHAT?
NOTHING'S MORE NORMAL THAN THAT! JUST 'CAUSE GIRLS DON'T TALK ABOUT IT ALL THE TIME DOESN'T MEAN IT'S NOT COMMONPLACE!
I'M NOT SAYING THAT I DON'T APPROVE OF IT, YOU KNOW!
IN FACT, I'M QUITE FOR IT, HEH-HEH...
OH, FOKIN' KILL ME NOW...

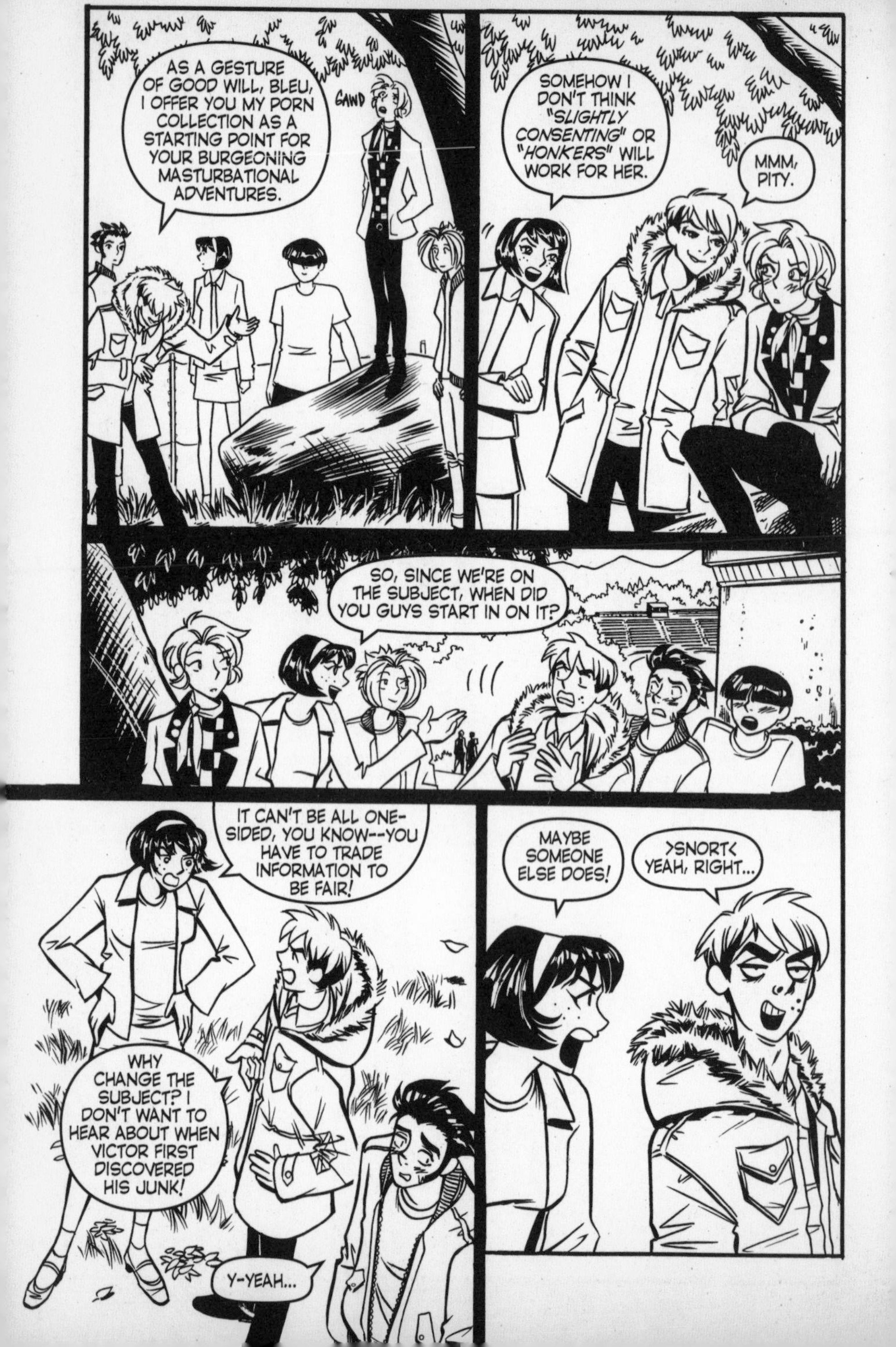
AS A GESTURE OF GOOD WILL, BLEU, I OFFER YOU MY PORN COLLECTION AS A STARTING POINT FOR YOUR BURGEONING MASTURBATIONAL ADVENTURES.
GAWD
SOMEHOW I DON'T THINK "SLIGHTLY CONSENTING" OR "HONKERS" WILL WORK FOR HER.
MMM, PITY.
SO, SINCE WE'RE ON THE SUBJECT, WHEN DID YOU GUYS START IN ON IT?
IT CAN'T BE ALL ONE-SIDED, YOU KNOW--YOU HAVE TO TRADE INFORMATION TO BE FAIR!
WHY CHANGE THE SUBJECT? I DON'T WANT TO HEAR ABOUT WHEN VICTOR FIRST DISCOVERED HIS JUNK!
Y-YEAH...
MAYBE SOMEONE ELSE DOES!
>SNORT< YEAH, RIGHT...

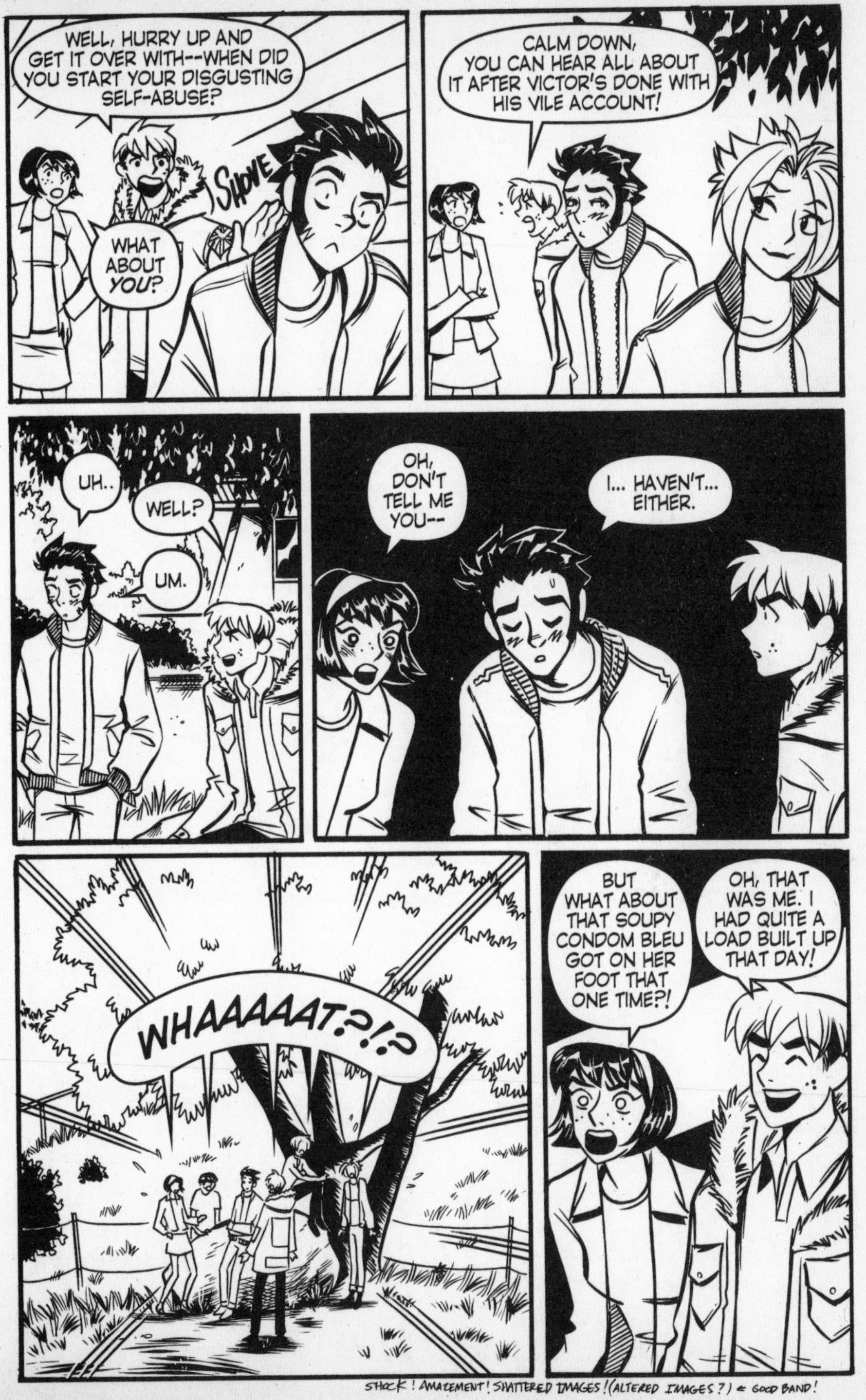
WELL, HURRY UP AND GET IT OVER WITH--WHEN DID YOU START YOUR DISGUSTING SELF-ABUSE?
SHOVE
WHAT ABOUT *YOU*?
CALM DOWN, YOU CAN HEAR ALL ABOUT IT AFTER VICTOR'S DONE WITH HIS VILE ACCOUNT!
UH..
WELL?
UM.
OH, DON'T TELL ME YOU--
I... HAVEN'T... EITHER.
WHAAAAAT?!?
BUT WHAT ABOUT THAT SOUPY CONDOM BLEU GOT ON HER FOOT THAT ONE TIME?!
OH, THAT WAS ME. I HAD QUITE A LOAD BUILT UP THAT DAY!

SHOCK! AMAZEMENT! SHATTERED IMAGES! (ALTERED IMAGES?) ← GOOD BAND!

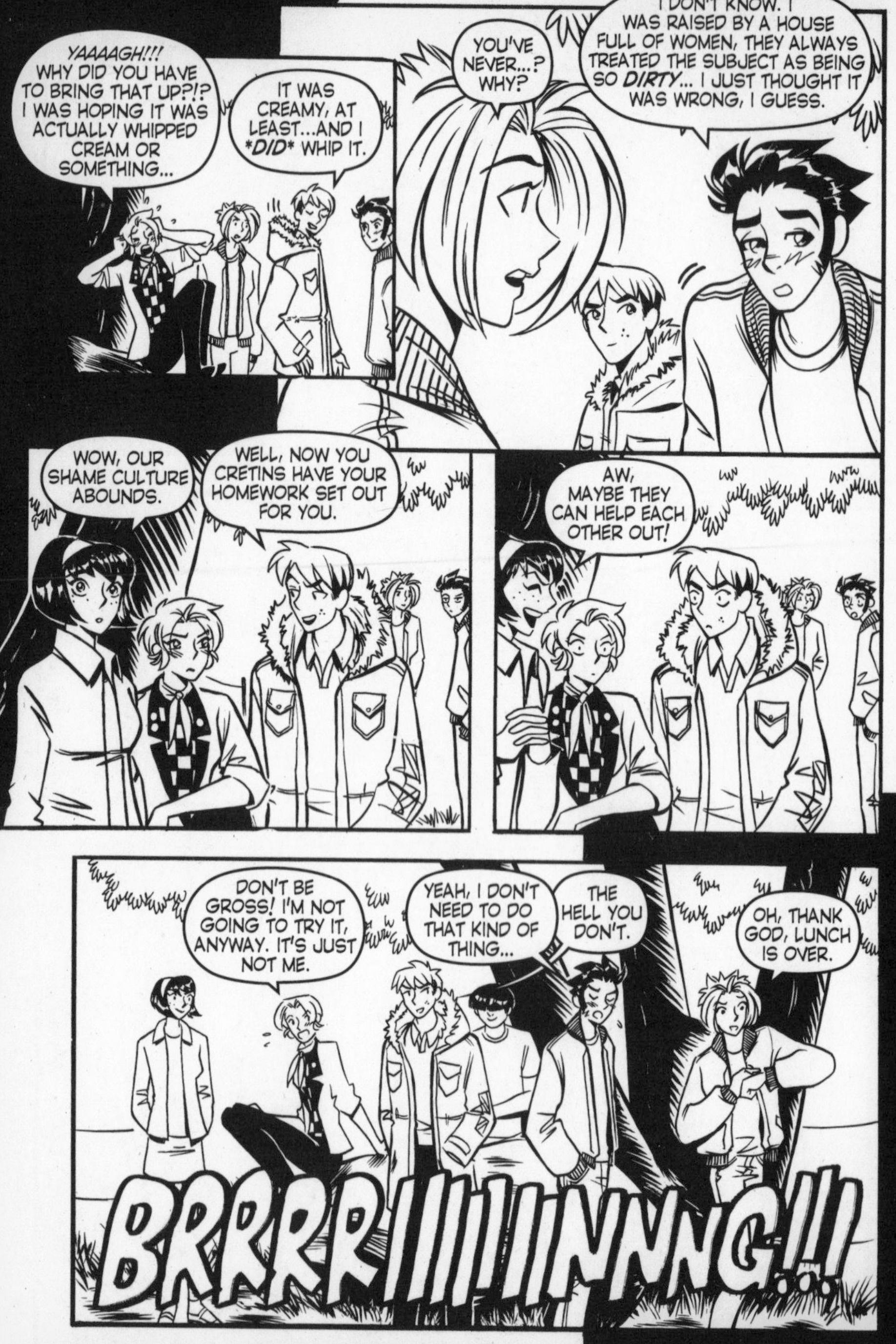
YAAAAGH!!! WHY DID YOU HAVE TO BRING THAT UP?!? I WAS HOPING IT WAS ACTUALLY WHIPPED CREAM OR SOMETHING...
IT WAS CREAMY, AT LEAST...AND I *DID* WHIP IT.
YOU'VE NEVER...? WHY?
I DON'T KNOW. I WAS RAISED BY A HOUSE FULL OF WOMEN, THEY ALWAYS TREATED THE SUBJECT AS BEING SO DIRTY... I JUST THOUGHT IT WAS WRONG, I GUESS.
WOW, OUR SHAME CULTURE ABOUNDS.
WELL, NOW YOU CRETINS HAVE YOUR HOMEWORK SET OUT FOR YOU.
AW, MAYBE THEY CAN HELP EACH OTHER OUT!
DON'T BE GROSS! I'M NOT GOING TO TRY IT, ANYWAY. IT'S JUST NOT ME.
YEAH, I DON'T NEED TO DO THAT KIND OF THING...
THE HELL YOU DON'T.
OH, THANK GOD, LUNCH IS OVER.
BRRRRIIIIIINNNG!!

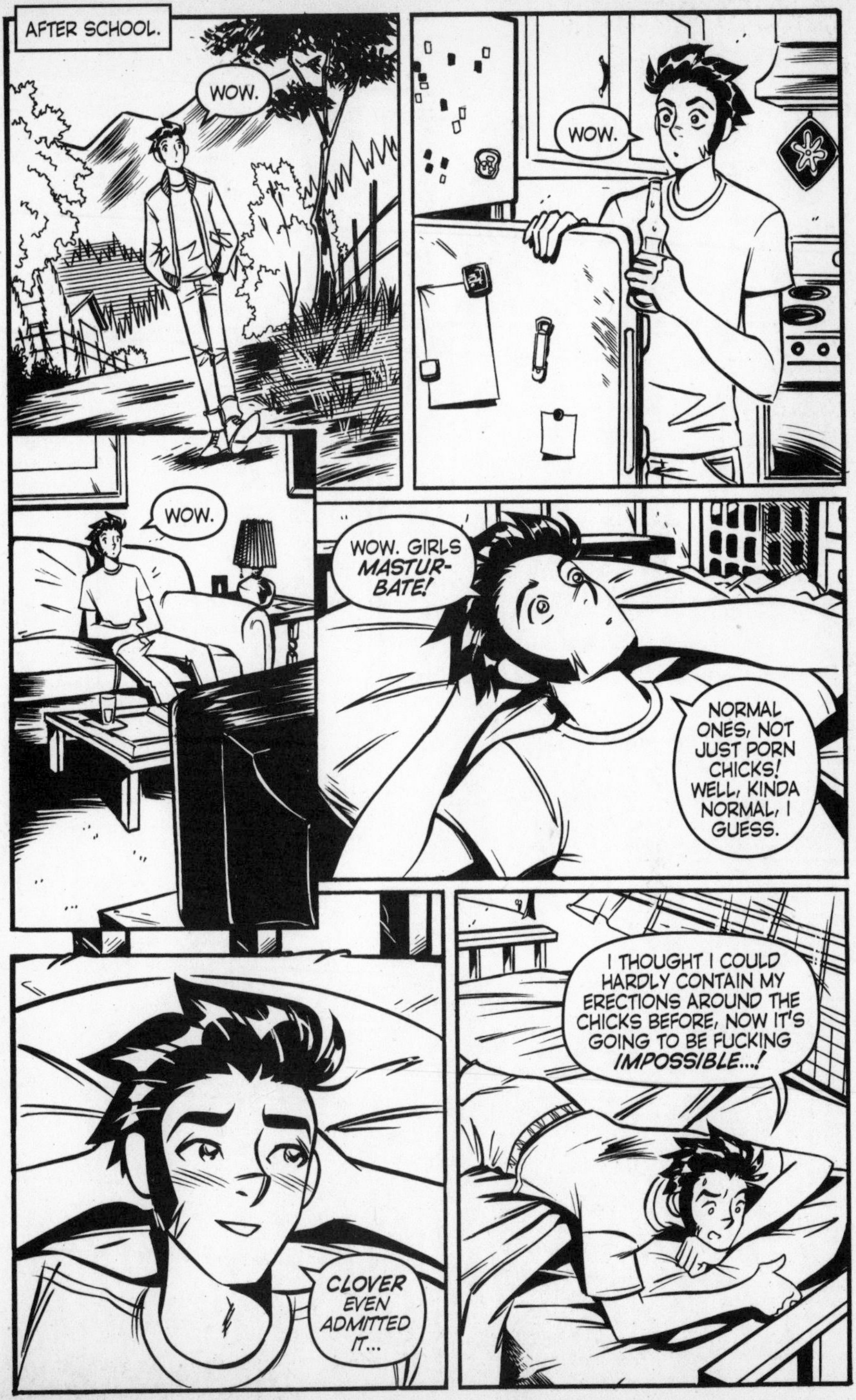
AFTER SCHOOL.
WOW.
WOW.
WOW.
WOW. GIRLS MASTURBATE!
NORMAL ONES, NOT JUST PORN CHICKS! WELL, KINDA NORMAL, I GUESS.
CLOVER EVEN ADMITTED IT...
I THOUGHT I COULD HARDLY CONTAIN MY ERECTIONS AROUND THE CHICKS BEFORE, NOW IT'S GOING TO BE FUCKING IMPOSSIBLE...!

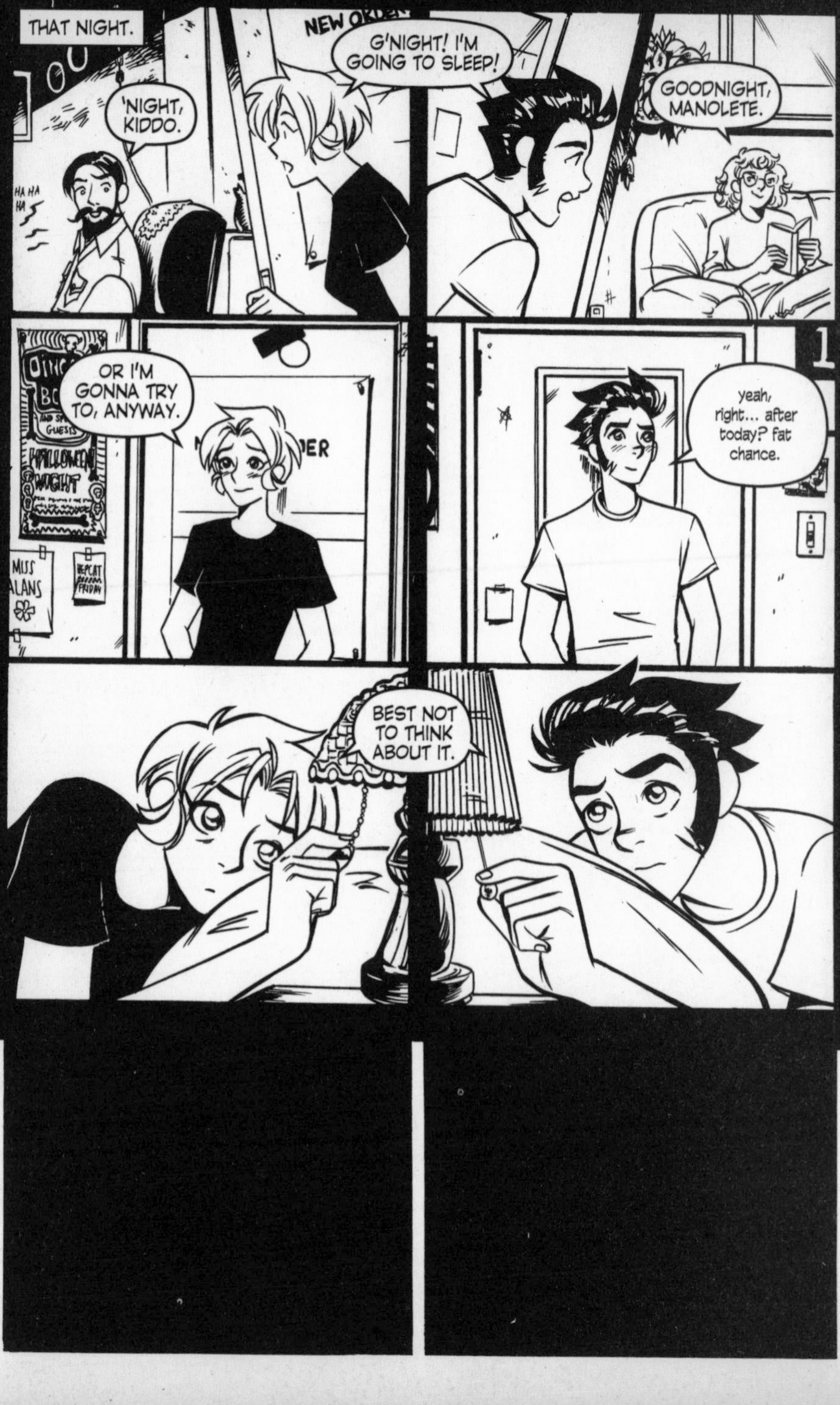
THAT NIGHT.
'NIGHT, KIDDO.
HA HA HA
G'NIGHT! I'M GOING TO SLEEP!
GOODNIGHT, MANOLETE.
OR I'M GONNA TRY TO, ANYWAY.
yeah, right... after today? fat chance.
BEST NOT TO THINK ABOUT IT.

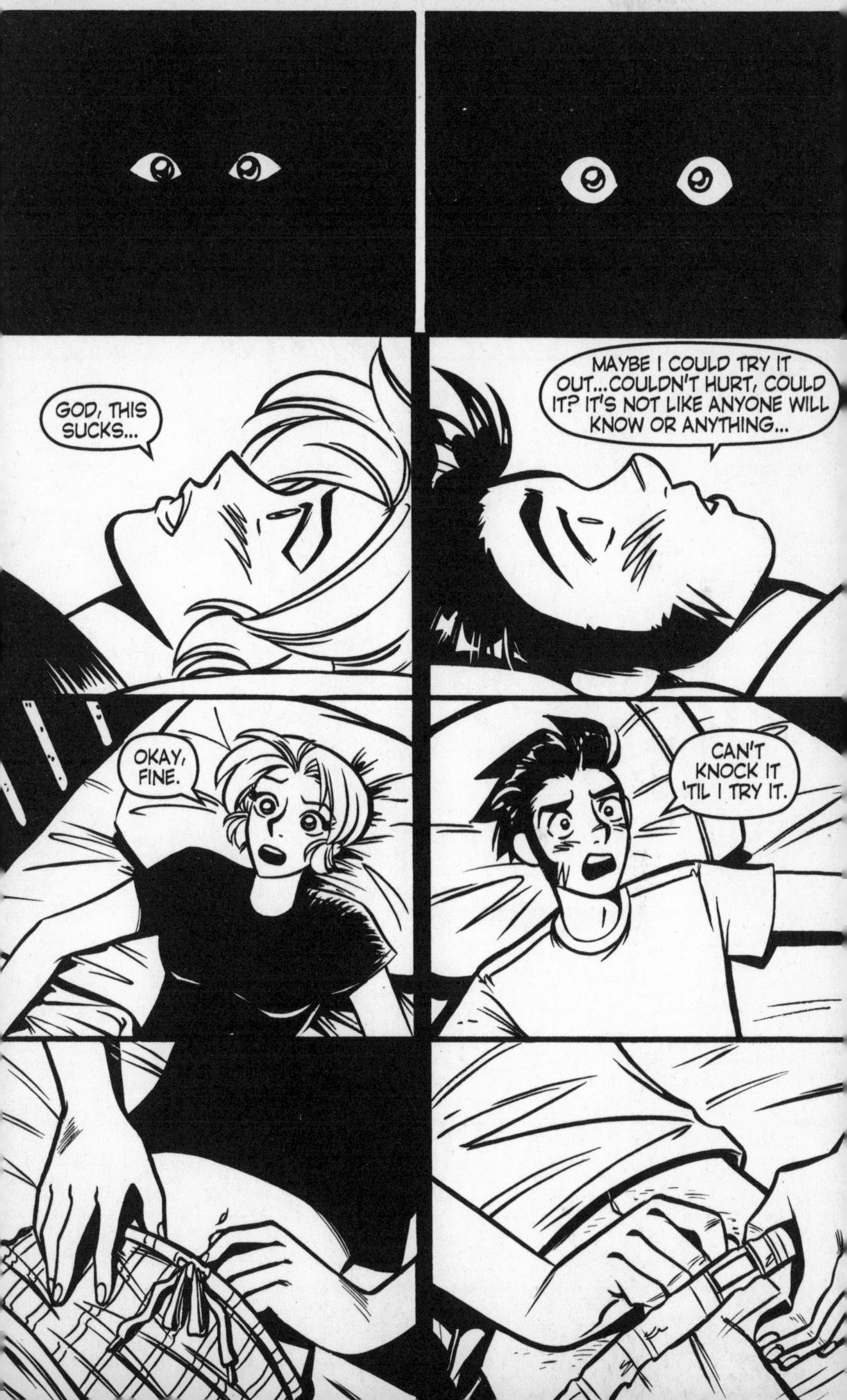
GOD, THIS SUCKS...
MAYBE I COULD TRY IT OUT...COULDN'T HURT, COULD IT? IT'S NOT LIKE ANYONE WILL KNOW OR ANYTHING...
OKAY, FINE.
CAN'T KNOCK IT 'TIL I TRY IT.

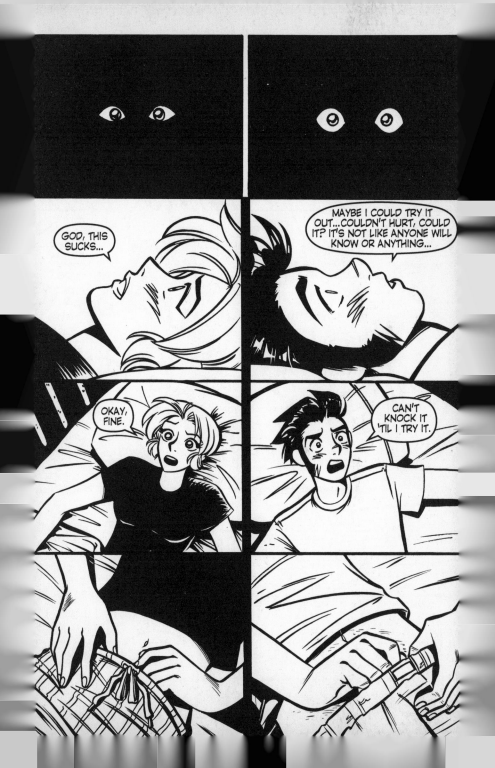

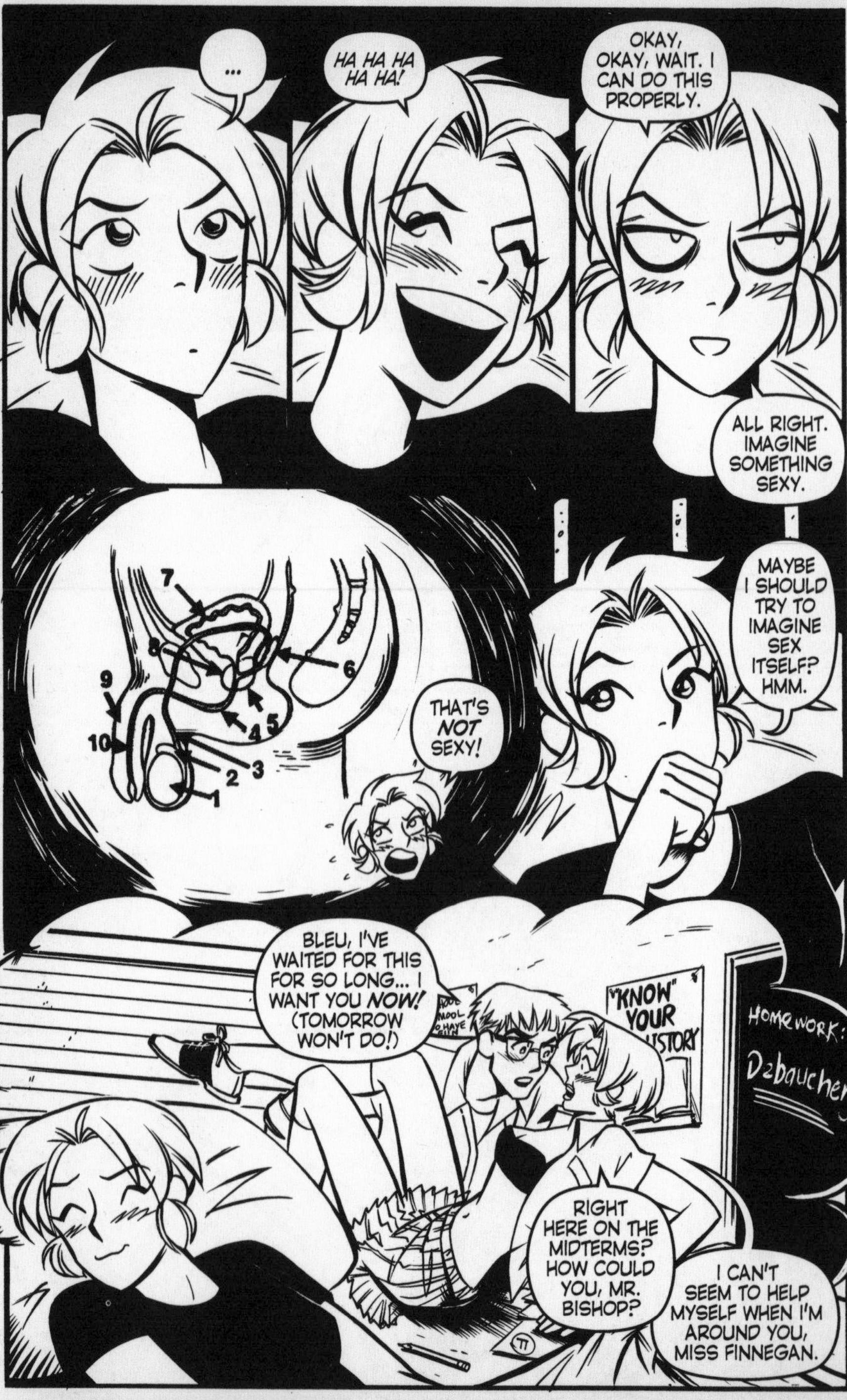
...
HA HA HA HA HA!
OKAY, OKAY, WAIT. I CAN DO THIS PROPERLY.
ALL RIGHT. IMAGINE SOMETHING SEXY.
MAYBE I SHOULD TRY TO IMAGINE SEX ITSELF? HMM.
7
8
6
9
5
4
10
3
2
1
THAT'S NOT SEXY!
BLEU, I'VE WAITED FOR THIS FOR SO LONG... I WANT YOU NOW! (TOMORROW WON'T DO!)
"KNOW" YOUR HISTORY
HOMEWORK: Debauchery!
RIGHT HERE ON THE MIDTERMS? HOW COULD YOU, MR. BISHOP?
I CAN'T SEEM TO HELP MYSELF WHEN I'M AROUND YOU, MISS FINNEGAN.

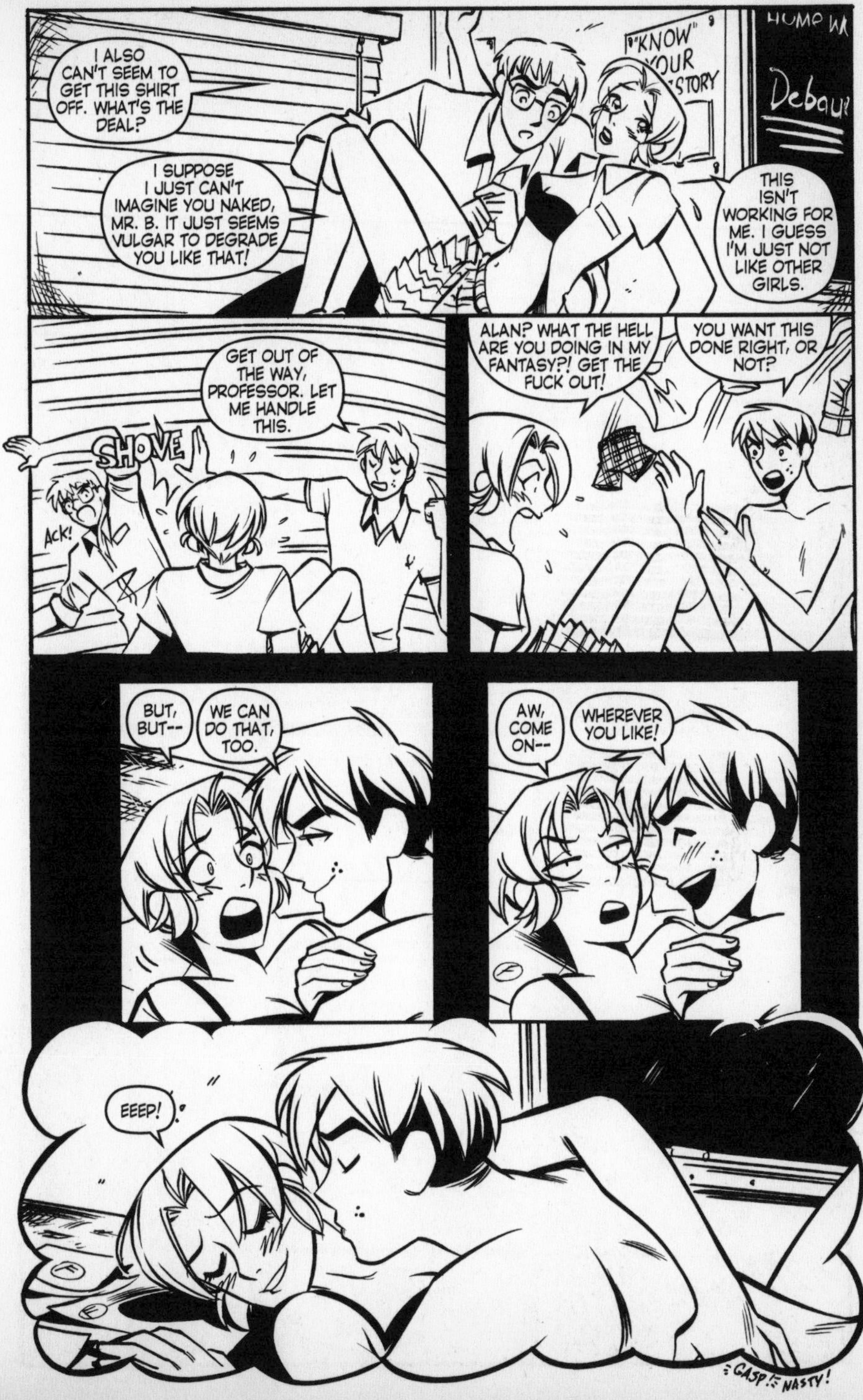
HUMEWR
"KNOW" YOUR ...STORY
Debau
I ALSO CAN'T SEEM TO GET THIS SHIRT OFF. WHAT'S THE DEAL?
I SUPPOSE I JUST CAN'T IMAGINE YOU NAKED, MR. B. IT JUST SEEMS VULGAR TO DEGRADE YOU LIKE THAT!
THIS ISN'T WORKING FOR ME. I GUESS I'M JUST NOT LIKE OTHER GIRLS.
GET OUT OF THE WAY, PROFESSOR. LET ME HANDLE THIS.
SHOVE
ACK!
ALAN? WHAT THE HELL ARE YOU DOING IN MY FANTASY?! GET THE FUCK OUT!
YOU WANT THIS DONE RIGHT, OR NOT?
BUT, BUT--
WE CAN DO THAT, TOO.
AW, COME ON--
WHEREVER YOU LIKE!
EEEP!
GASP! NASTY!

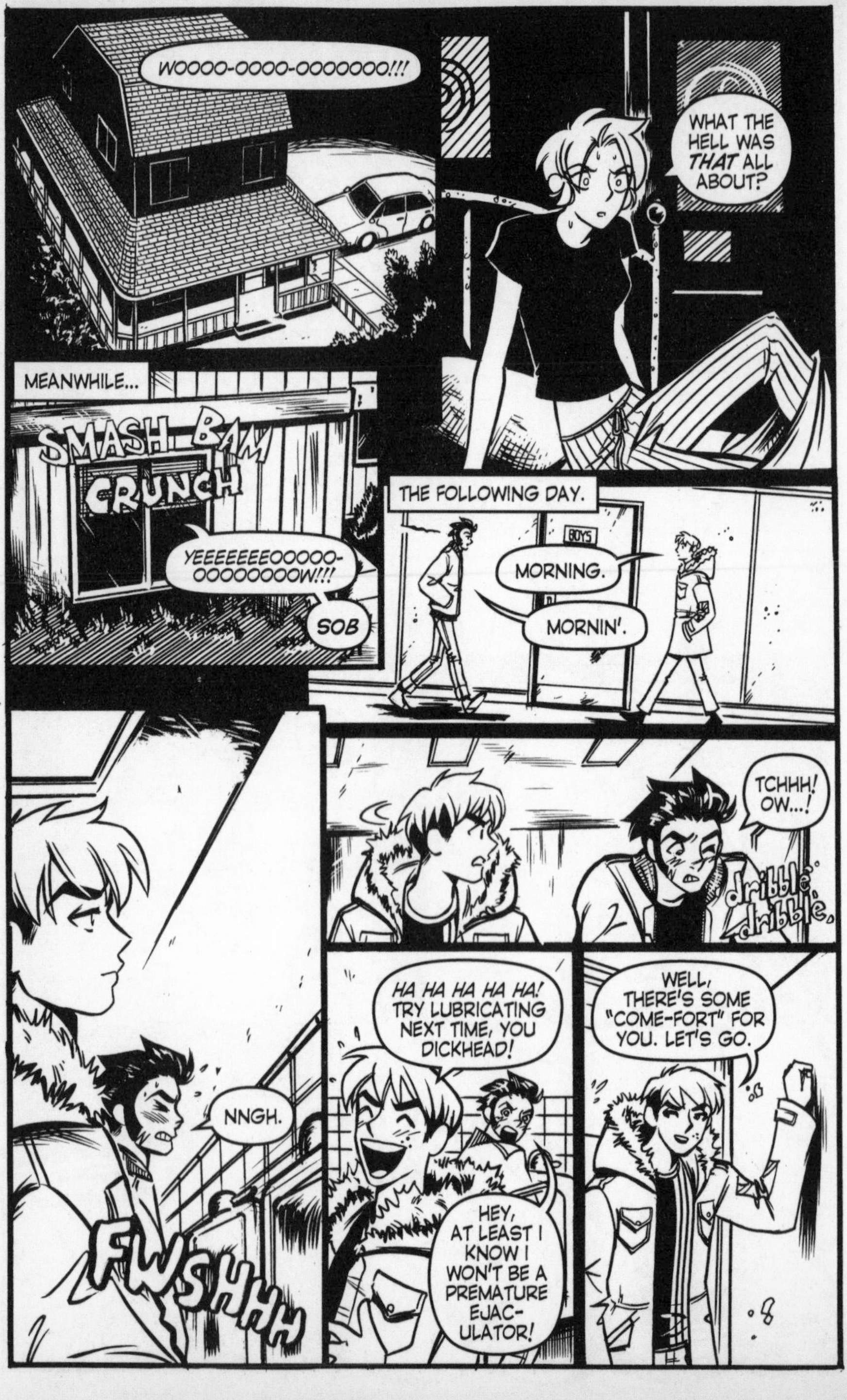
WOOOO-OOOO-OOOOOOO!!!
WHAT THE HELL WAS THAT ALL ABOUT?
MEANWHILE...
SMASH BAM CRUNCH
YEEEEEEEOOOOO-OOOOOOOOW!!!
SOB
THE FOLLOWING DAY.
BOYS
MORNING.
MORNIN'.
TCHHH! OW...!
dribble dribble
NNGH.
FWSHHH
HA HA HA HA HA! TRY LUBRICATING NEXT TIME, YOU DICKHEAD!
HEY, AT LEAST I KNOW I WON'T BE A PREMATURE EJAC-ULATOR!
WELL, THERE'S SOME "COME-FORT" FOR YOU. LET'S GO.

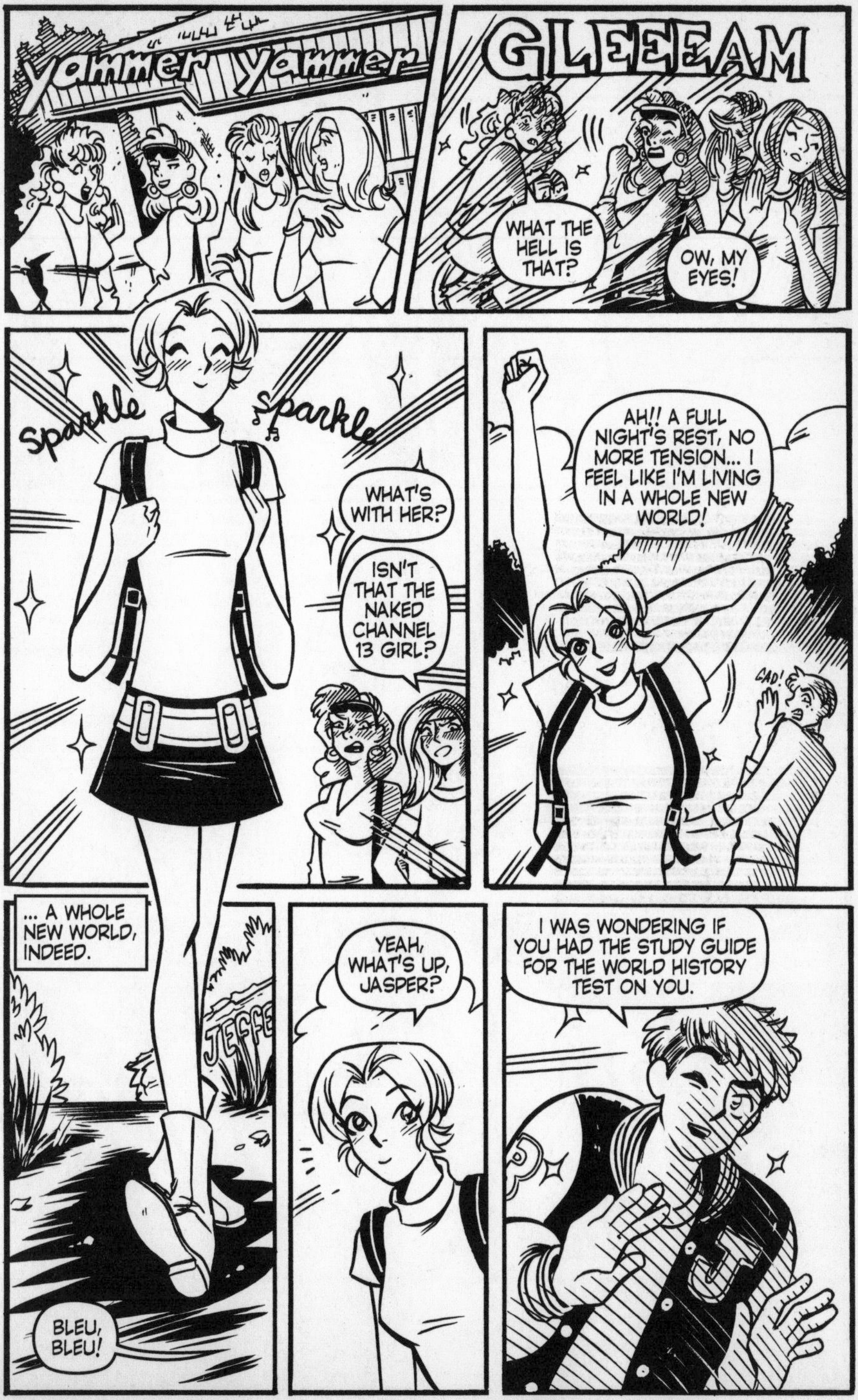
yammer yammer
GLEEEAM
WHAT THE HELL IS THAT?
OW, MY EYES!
sparkle sparkle
WHAT'S WITH HER?
ISN'T THAT THE NAKED CHANNEL 13 GIRL?
AH!! A FULL NIGHT'S REST, NO MORE TENSION... I FEEL LIKE I'M LIVING IN A WHOLE NEW WORLD!
... A WHOLE NEW WORLD, INDEED.
BLEU, BLEU!
YEAH, WHAT'S UP, JASPER?
I WAS WONDERING IF YOU HAD THE STUDY GUIDE FOR THE WORLD HISTORY TEST ON YOU.

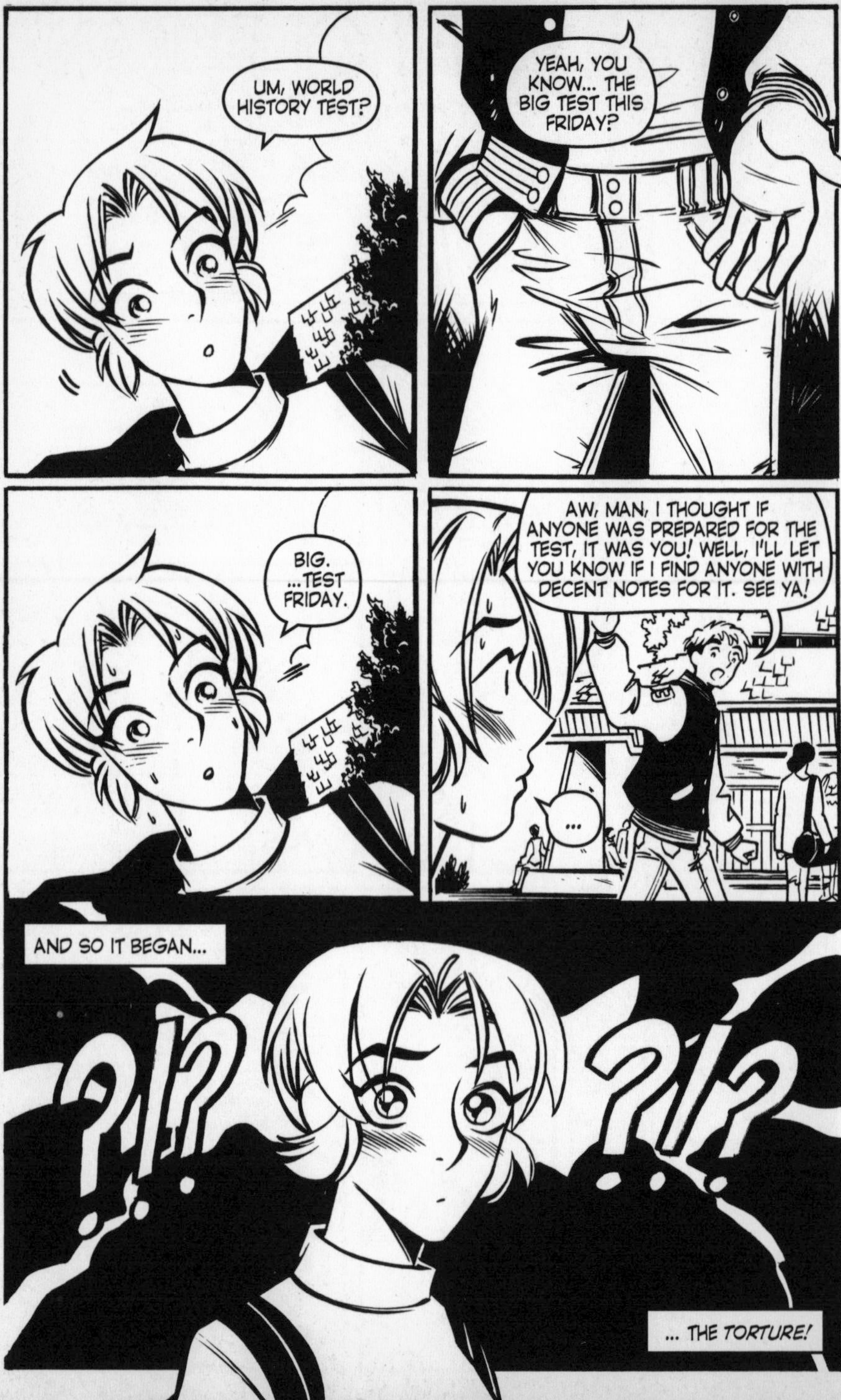
UM, WORLD HISTORY TEST?
YEAH, YOU KNOW... THE BIG TEST THIS FRIDAY?
BIG. ...TEST FRIDAY.
AW, MAN, I THOUGHT IF ANYONE WAS PREPARED FOR THE TEST, IT WAS YOU! WELL, I'LL LET YOU KNOW IF I FIND ANYONE WITH DECENT NOTES FOR IT. SEE YA!
...
AND SO IT BEGAN...
?!?
?!?
... THE *TORTURE!*

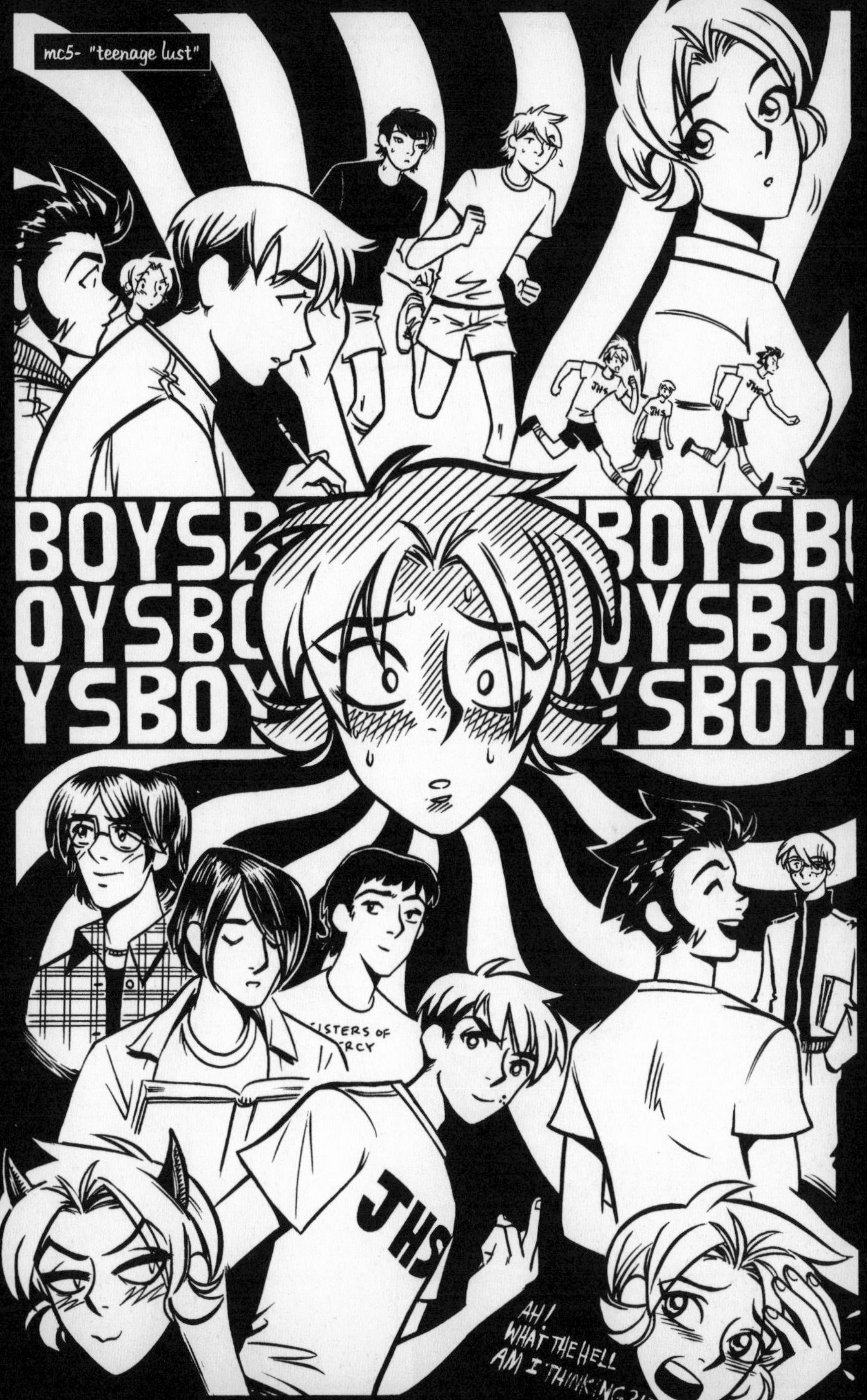
mc5- "teenage lust"
BOYSB
OYSBO
YSBOY
BOYSBO
BOYSBOY
YSBOYS
SISTERS OF
RCY
JHS
AH!
WHAT THE HELL
AM I THINKING?!?

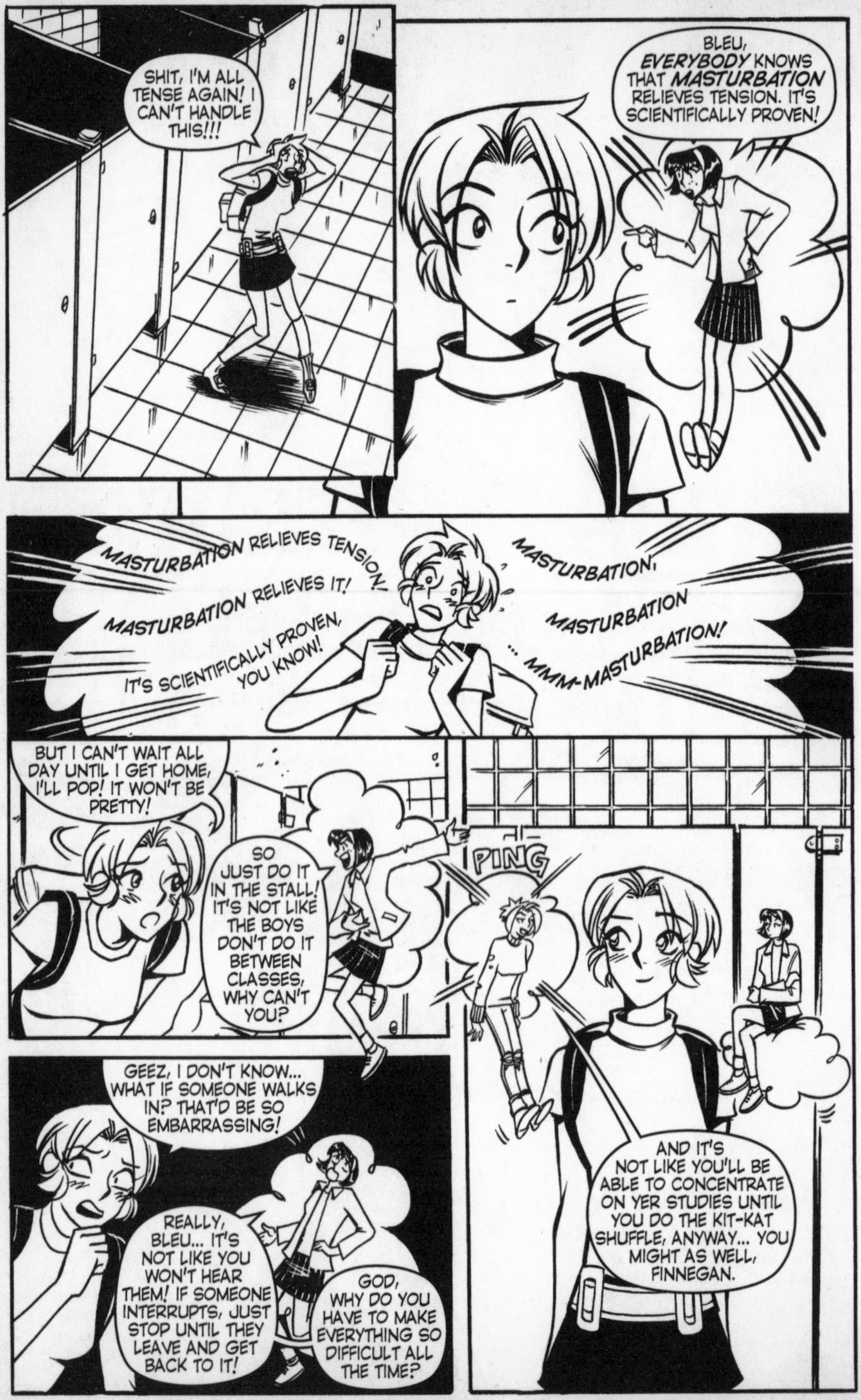
SHIT, I'M ALL TENSE AGAIN! I CAN'T HANDLE THIS!!!
BLEU, EVERYBODY KNOWS THAT MASTURBATION RELIEVES TENSION. IT'S SCIENTIFICALLY PROVEN!
MASTURBATION RELIEVES TENSION!
MASTURBATION RELIEVES IT!
IT'S SCIENTIFICALLY PROVEN, YOU KNOW!
MASTURBATION,
MASTURBATION
... MMM-MASTURBATION!
BUT I CAN'T WAIT ALL DAY UNTIL I GET HOME, I'LL POP! IT WON'T BE PRETTY!
SO JUST DO IT IN THE STALL! IT'S NOT LIKE THE BOYS DON'T DO IT BETWEEN CLASSES, WHY CAN'T YOU?
PING
AND IT'S NOT LIKE YOU'LL BE ABLE TO CONCENTRATE ON YER STUDIES UNTIL YOU DO THE KIT-KAT SHUFFLE, ANYWAY... YOU MIGHT AS WELL, FINNEGAN.
GEEZ, I DON'T KNOW... WHAT IF SOMEONE WALKS IN? THAT'D BE SO EMBARRASSING!
REALLY, BLEU... IT'S NOT LIKE YOU WON'T HEAR THEM! IF SOMEONE INTERRUPTS, JUST STOP UNTIL THEY LEAVE AND GET BACK TO IT!
GOD, WHY DO YOU HAVE TO MAKE EVERYTHING SO DIFFICULT ALL THE TIME?

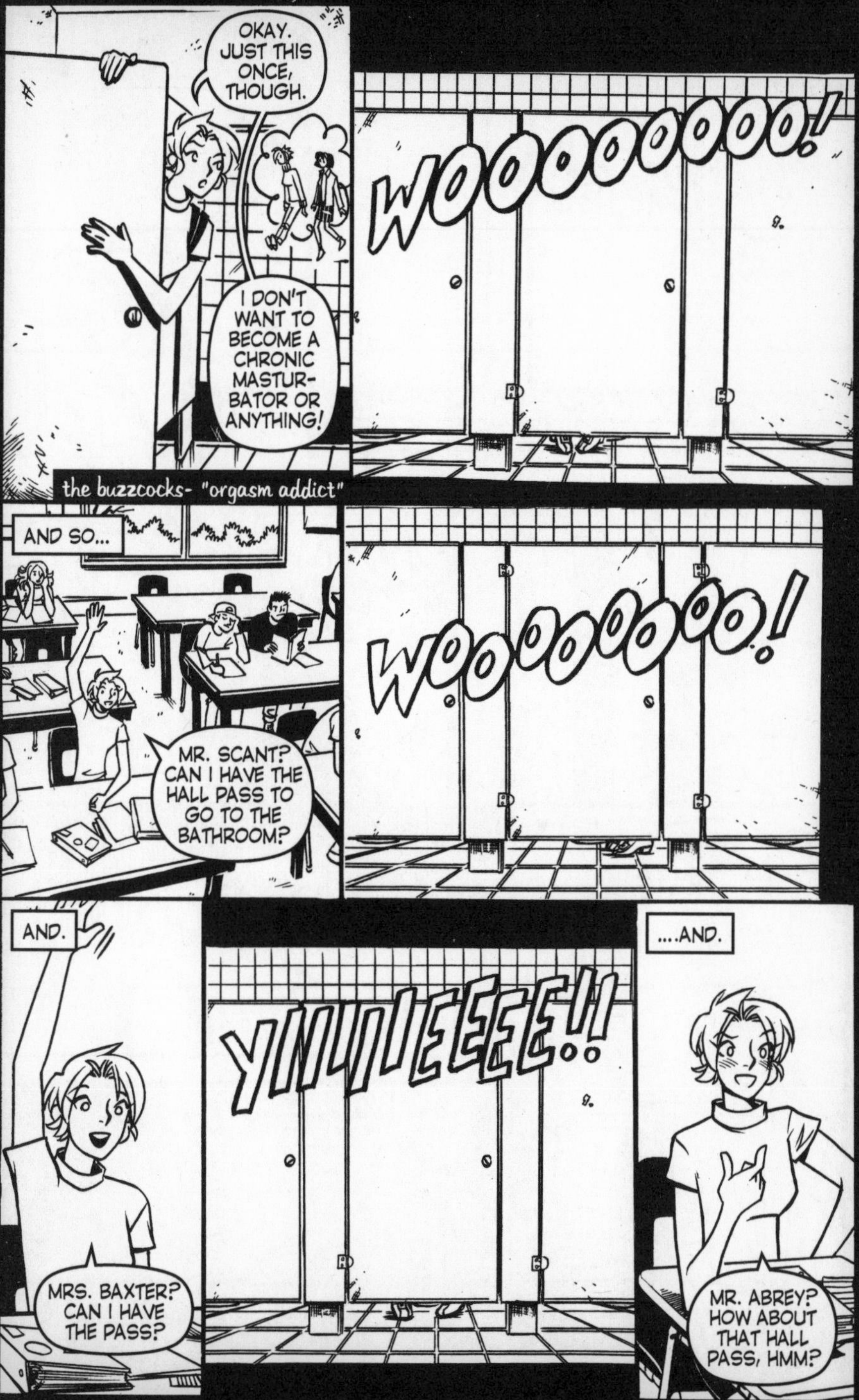
OKAY. JUST THIS ONCE, THOUGH.
I DON'T WANT TO BECOME A CHRONIC MASTUR-BATOR OR ANYTHING!
the buzzcocks- "orgasm addict"
WOOOOOOOO!
AND SO...
MR. SCANT? CAN I HAVE THE HALL PASS TO GO TO THE BATHROOM?
WOOOOOOOO!
AND.
MRS. BAXTER? CAN I HAVE THE PASS?
YIIIIIEEEE!!
....AND.
MR. ABREY? HOW ABOUT THAT HALL PASS, HMM?

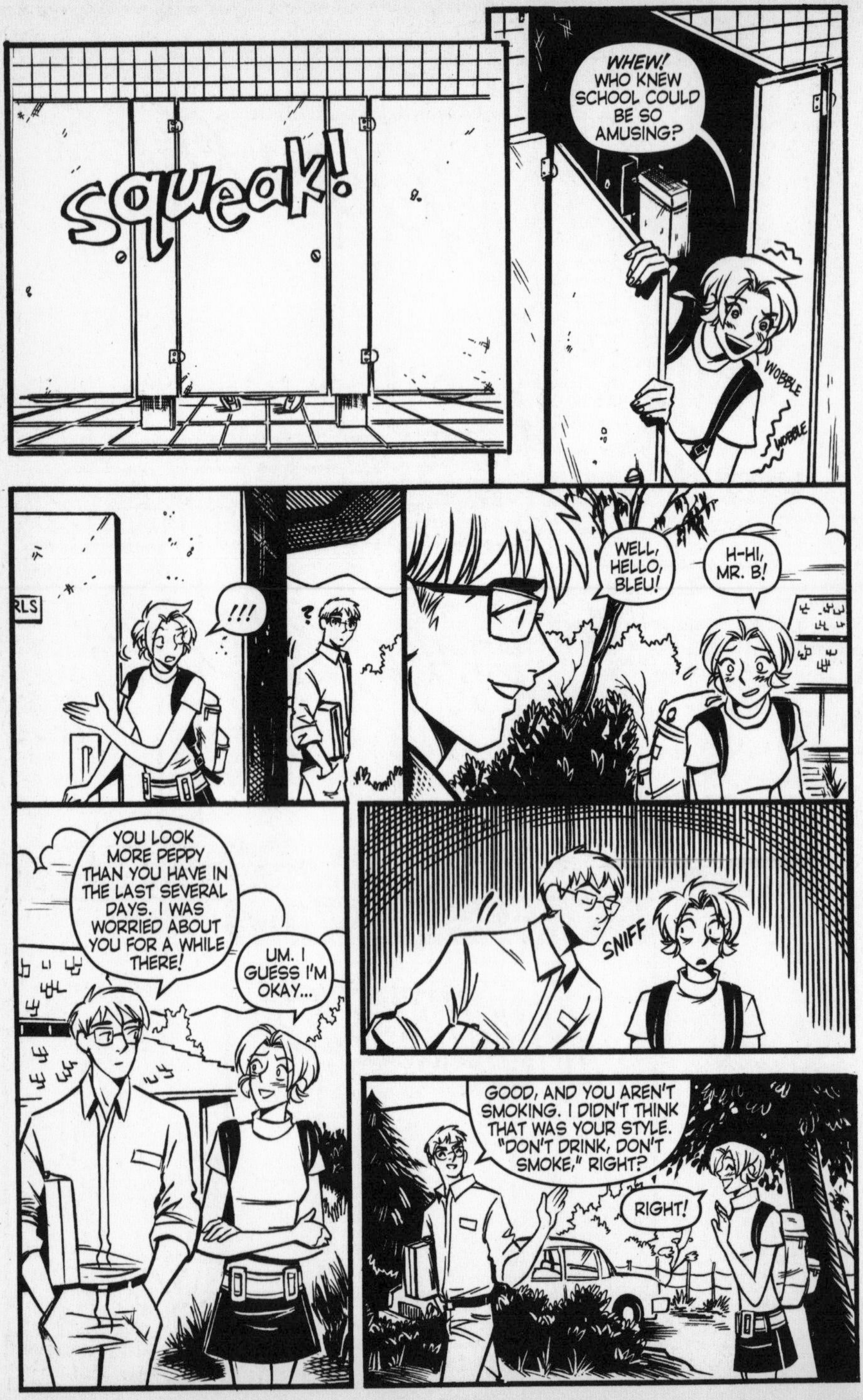
squeak!
WHEW! WHO KNEW SCHOOL COULD BE SO AMUSING?
WOBBLE
WOBBLE
RLS
!!!
?
WELL, HELLO, BLEU!
H-HI, MR. B!
YOU LOOK MORE PEPPY THAN YOU HAVE IN THE LAST SEVERAL DAYS. I WAS WORRIED ABOUT YOU FOR A WHILE THERE!
UM. I GUESS I'M OKAY...
SNIFF
GOOD, AND YOU AREN'T SMOKING. I DIDN'T THINK THAT WAS YOUR STYLE. "DON'T DRINK, DON'T SMOKE," RIGHT?
RIGHT!

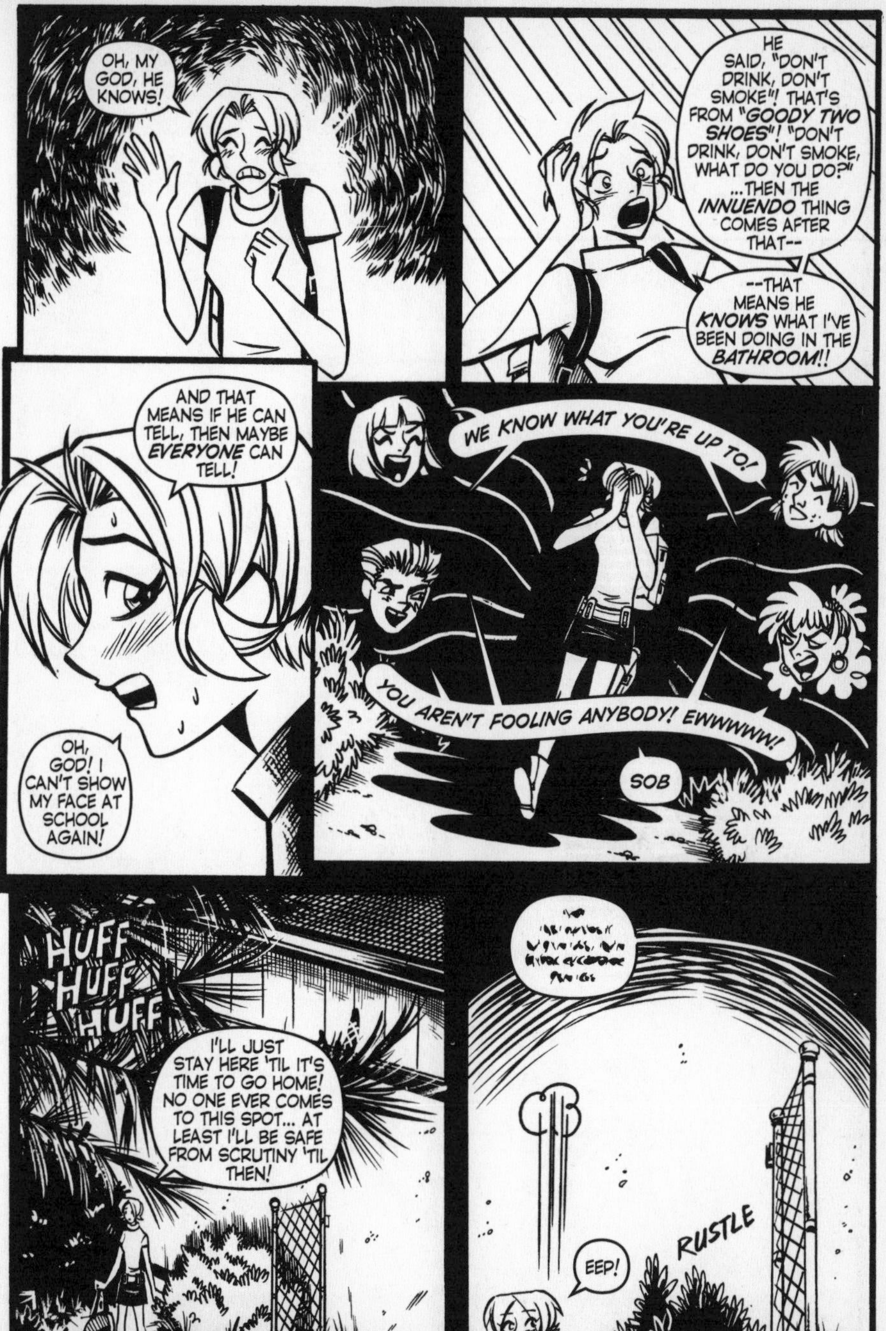
OH, MY GOD, HE KNOWS!
HE SAID, "DON'T DRINK, DON'T SMOKE"! THAT'S FROM "GOODY TWO SHOES"! "DON'T DRINK, DON'T SMOKE, WHAT DO YOU DO?" ...THEN THE INNUENDO THING COMES AFTER THAT--
--THAT MEANS HE KNOWS WHAT I'VE BEEN DOING IN THE BATHROOM!!
AND THAT MEANS IF HE CAN TELL, THEN MAYBE EVERYONE CAN TELL!
OH, GOD! I CAN'T SHOW MY FACE AT SCHOOL AGAIN!
WE KNOW WHAT YOU'RE UP TO!
YOU AREN'T FOOLING ANYBODY! EWWWWW!
SOB
HUFF
HUFF
HUFF
I'LL JUST STAY HERE 'TIL IT'S TIME TO GO HOME! NO ONE EVER COMES TO THIS SPOT... AT LEAST I'LL BE SAFE FROM SCRUTINY 'TIL THEN!
RUSTLE
EEP!

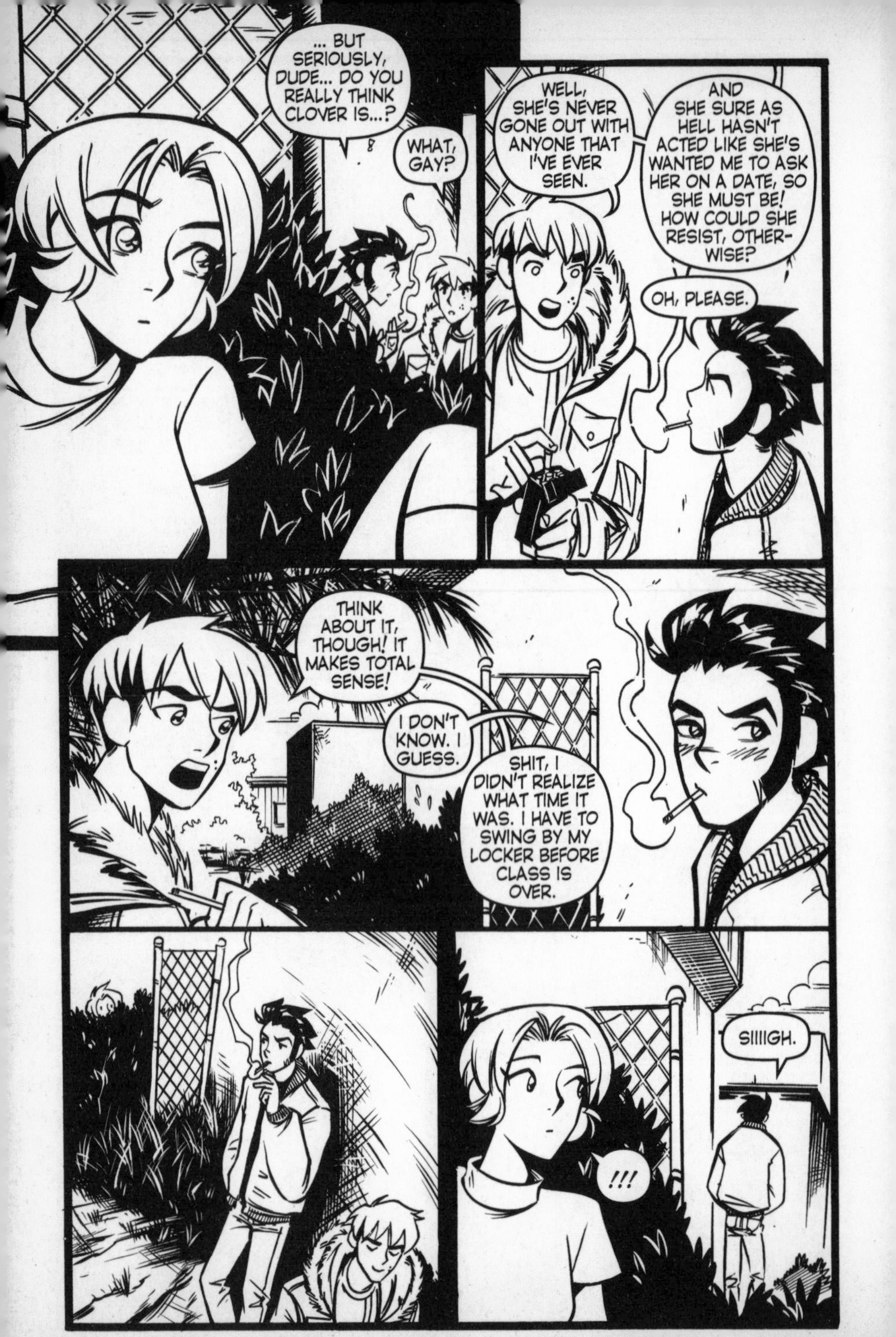
... BUT SERIOUSLY, DUDE... DO YOU REALLY THINK CLOVER IS...?
WHAT, GAY?
WELL, SHE'S NEVER GONE OUT WITH ANYONE THAT I'VE EVER SEEN.
AND SHE SURE AS HELL HASN'T ACTED LIKE SHE'S WANTED ME TO ASK HER ON A DATE, SO SHE MUST BE! HOW COULD SHE RESIST, OTHER-WISE?
OH, PLEASE.
THINK ABOUT IT, THOUGH! IT MAKES TOTAL SENSE!
I DON'T KNOW. I GUESS.
SHIT, I DIDN'T REALIZE WHAT TIME IT WAS. I HAVE TO SWING BY MY LOCKER BEFORE CLASS IS OVER.
SIIIIGH.
!!!

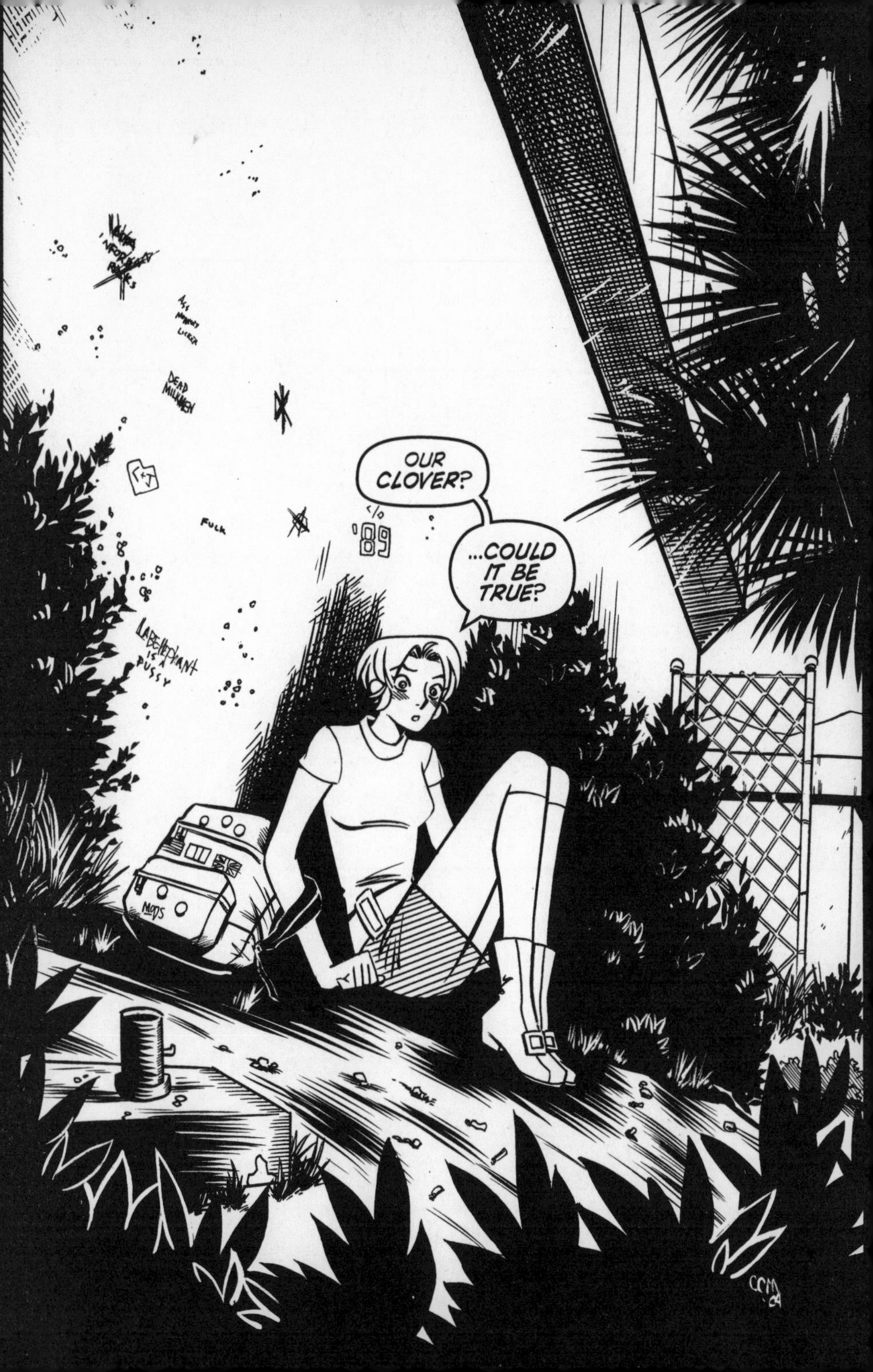
OUR CLOVER?
...COULD IT BE TRUE?

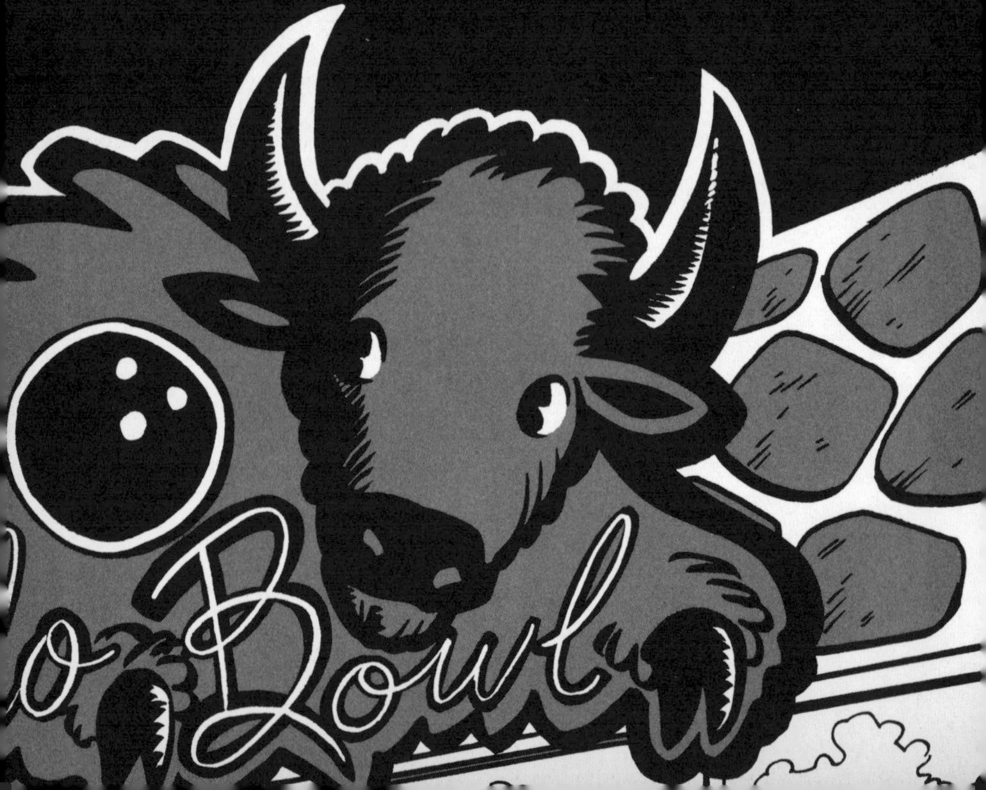
o Bowl

chapter three:
"BLUES BEFORE AND AFTER"

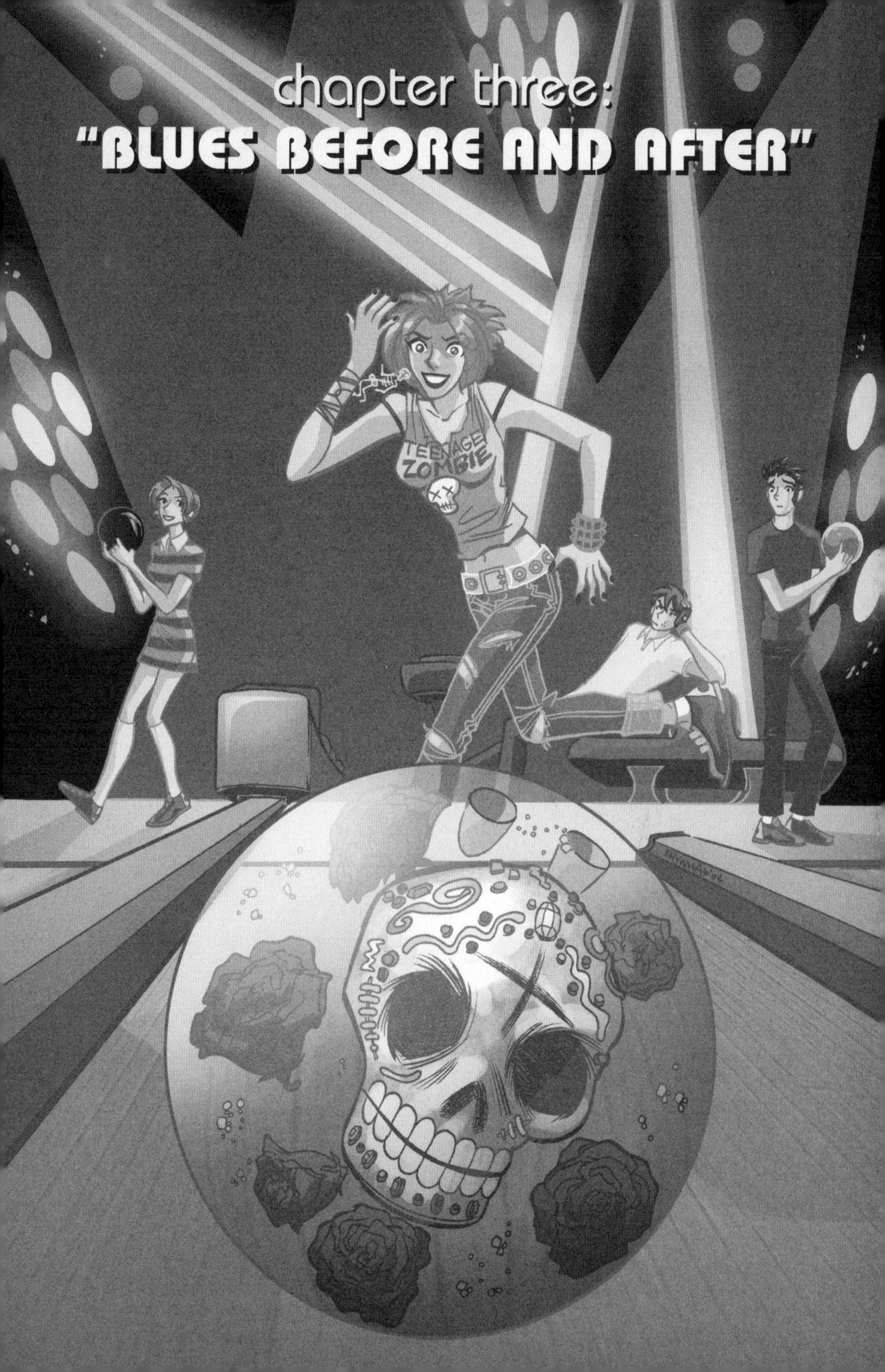
TEENAGE ZOMBIE

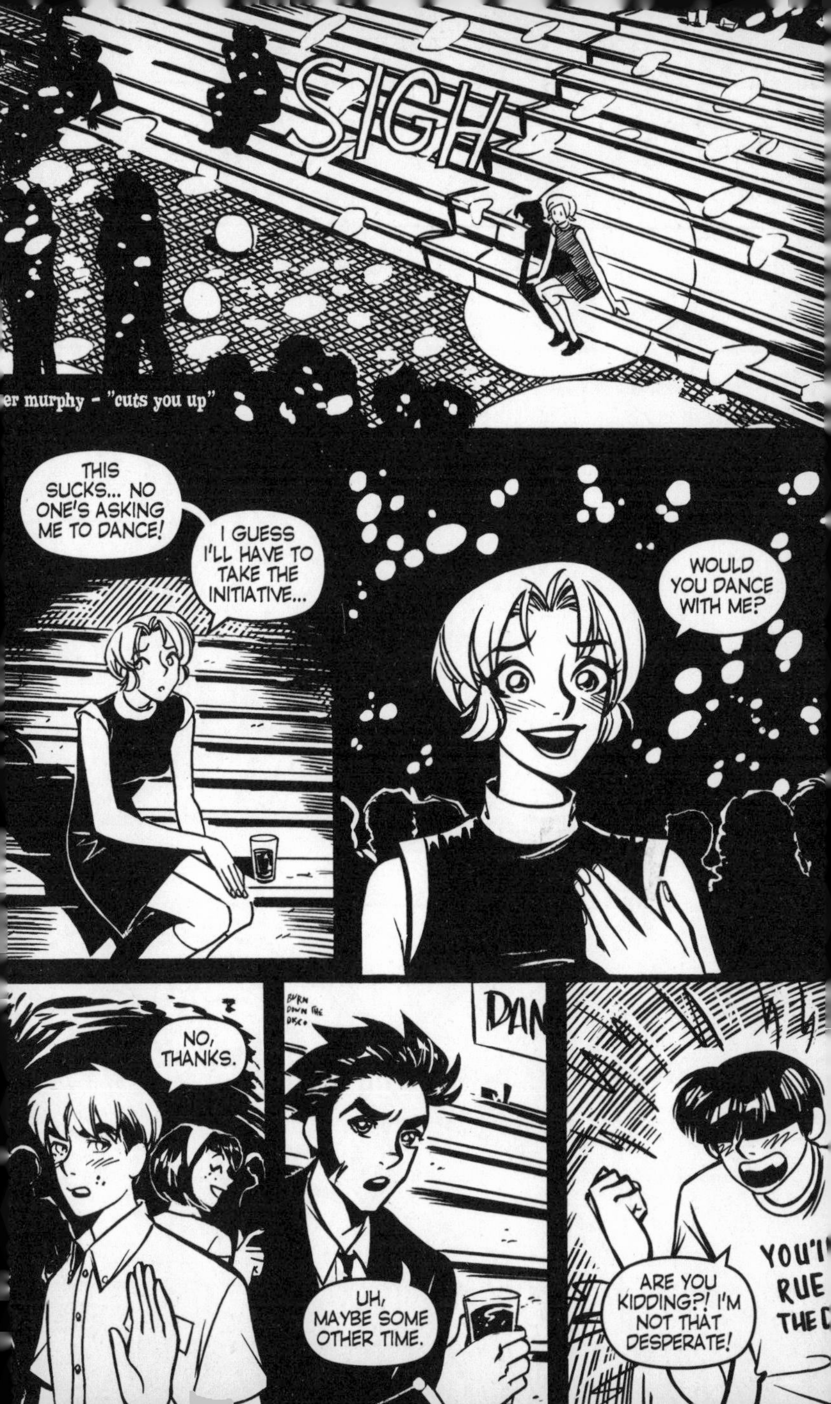
SIGH
er murphy - "cuts you up"
THIS SUCKS... NO ONE'S ASKING ME TO DANCE!
I GUESS I'LL HAVE TO TAKE THE INITIATIVE...
WOULD YOU DANCE WITH ME?
NO, THANKS.
BURN DOWN THE DISCO
DAN
UH, MAYBE SOME OTHER TIME.
ARE YOU KIDDING?! I'M NOT THAT DESPERATE!
YOU'I
RUE
THE D

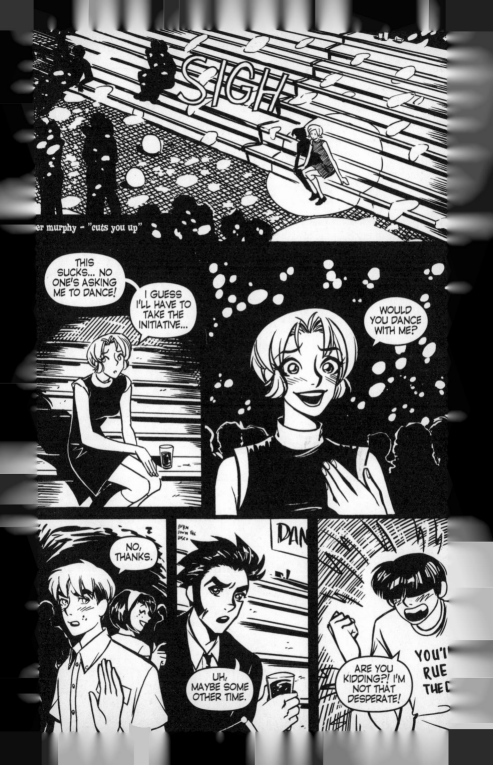

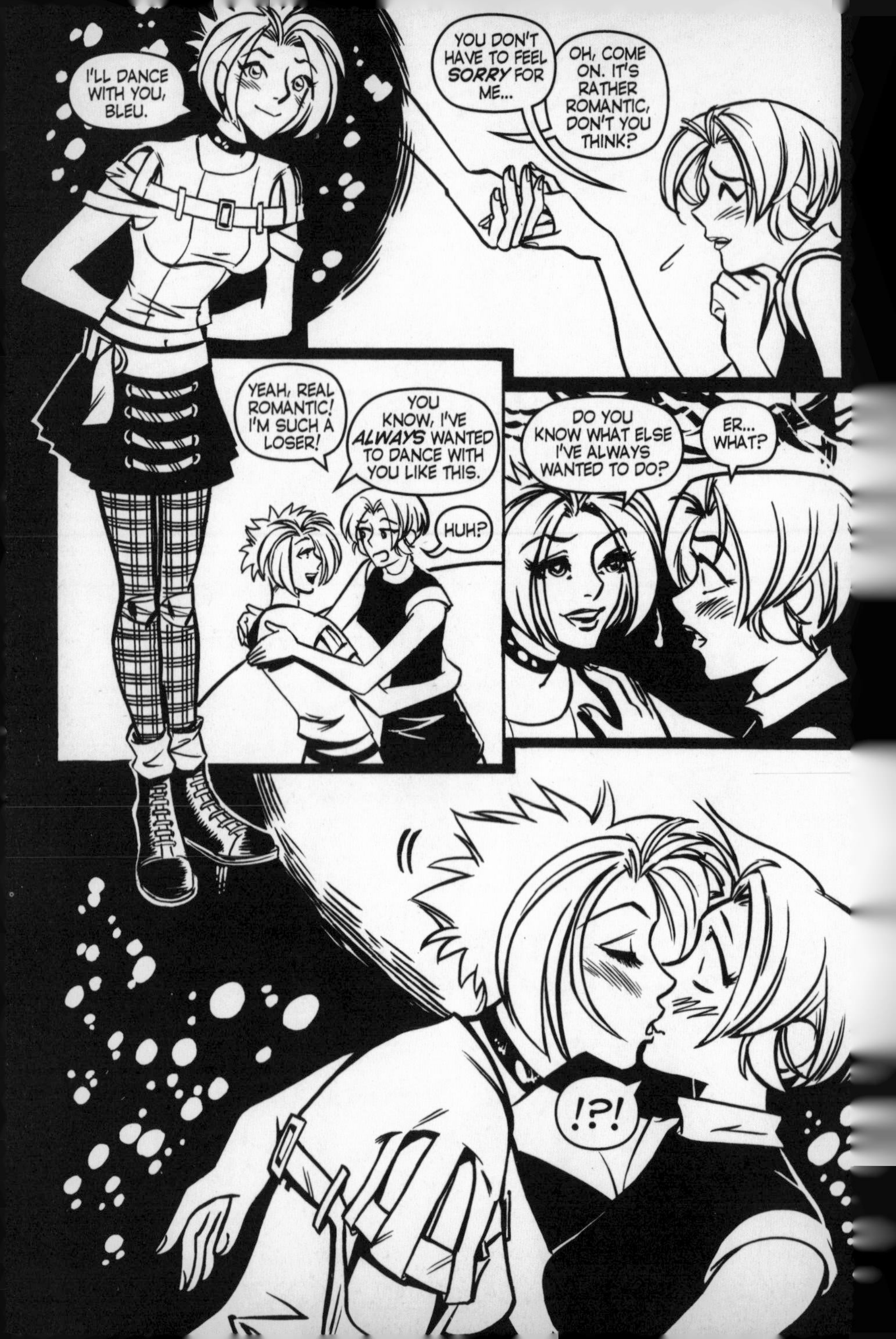
I'LL DANCE WITH YOU, BLEU.
YOU DON'T HAVE TO FEEL SORRY FOR ME...
OH, COME ON. IT'S RATHER ROMANTIC, DON'T YOU THINK?
YEAH, REAL ROMANTIC! I'M SUCH A LOSER!
YOU KNOW, I'VE ALWAYS WANTED TO DANCE WITH YOU LIKE THIS.
HUH?
DO YOU KNOW WHAT ELSE I'VE ALWAYS WANTED TO DO?
ER... WHAT?
!?!

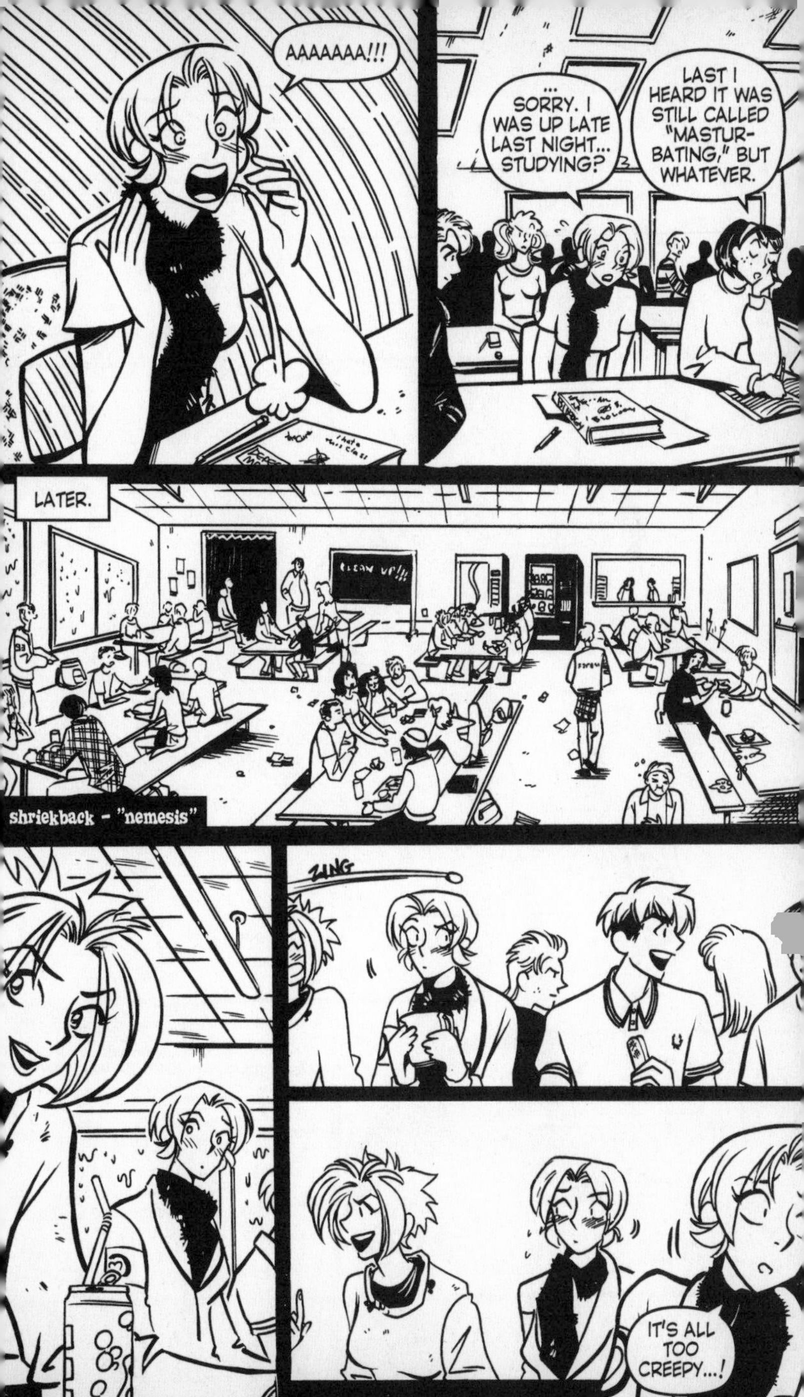
AAAAAAA!!!
... SORRY. I WAS UP LATE LAST NIGHT... STUDYING?
LAST I HEARD IT WAS STILL CALLED "MASTUR-BATING," BUT WHATEVER.
LATER.
CLEAN UP!!!
shriekback - "nemesis"
ZING
IT'S ALL TOO CREEPY...!
RRRRIIING!

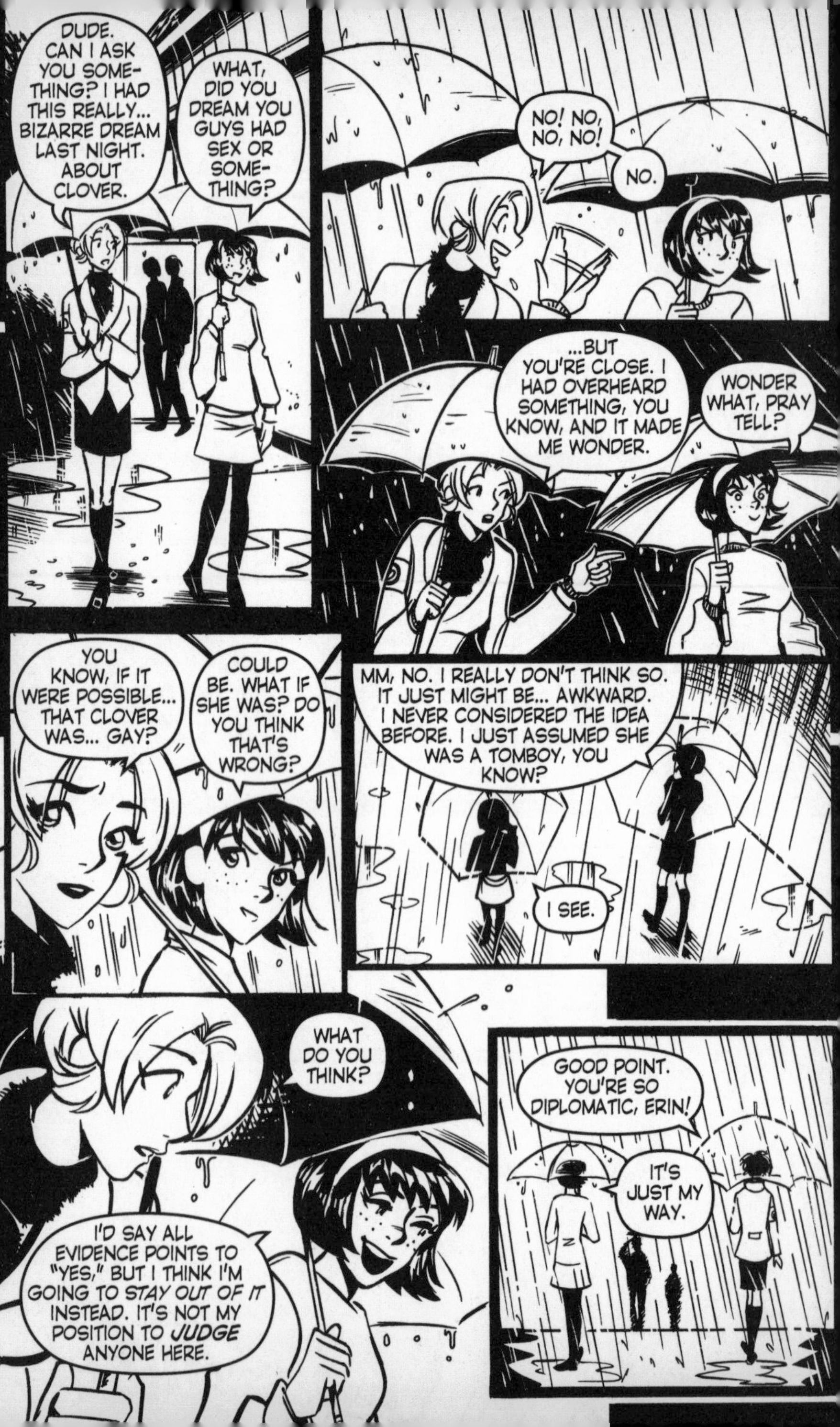
DUDE. CAN I ASK YOU SOMETHING? I HAD THIS REALLY... BIZARRE DREAM LAST NIGHT. ABOUT CLOVER.
WHAT, DID YOU DREAM YOU GUYS HAD SEX OR SOMETHING?
NO! NO, NO, NO!
NO.
...BUT YOU'RE CLOSE. I HAD OVERHEARD SOMETHING, YOU KNOW, AND IT MADE ME WONDER.
WONDER WHAT, PRAY TELL?
YOU KNOW, IF IT WERE POSSIBLE... THAT CLOVER WAS... GAY?
COULD BE. WHAT IF SHE WAS? DO YOU THINK THAT'S WRONG?
MM, NO. I REALLY DON'T THINK SO. IT JUST MIGHT BE... AWKWARD. I NEVER CONSIDERED THE IDEA BEFORE. I JUST ASSUMED SHE WAS A TOMBOY, YOU KNOW?
I SEE.
WHAT DO YOU THINK?
I'D SAY ALL EVIDENCE POINTS TO "YES," BUT I THINK I'M GOING TO STAY OUT OF IT INSTEAD. IT'S NOT MY POSITION TO JUDGE ANYONE HERE.
GOOD POINT. YOU'RE SO DIPLOMATIC, ERIN!
IT'S JUST MY WAY.

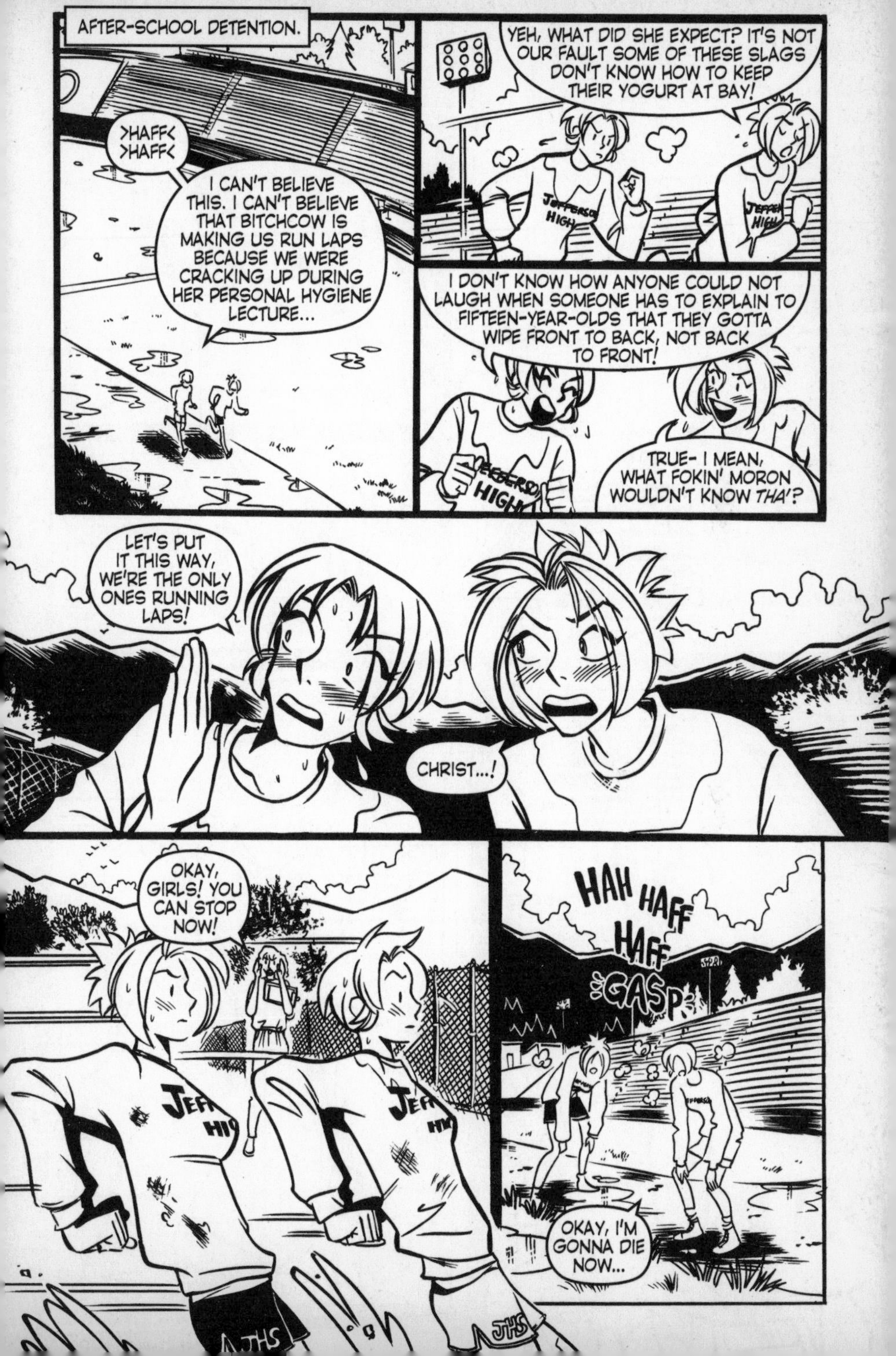
AFTER-SCHOOL DETENTION.
>HAFF< >HAFF<
I CAN'T BELIEVE THIS. I CAN'T BELIEVE THAT BITCHCOW IS MAKING US RUN LAPS BECAUSE WE WERE CRACKING UP DURING HER PERSONAL HYGIENE LECTURE...
YEH, WHAT DID SHE EXPECT? IT'S NOT OUR FAULT SOME OF THESE SLAGS DON'T KNOW HOW TO KEEP THEIR YOGURT AT BAY!
I DON'T KNOW HOW ANYONE COULD NOT LAUGH WHEN SOMEONE HAS TO EXPLAIN TO FIFTEEN-YEAR-OLDS THAT THEY GOTTA WIPE FRONT TO BACK, NOT BACK TO FRONT!
TRUE- I MEAN, WHAT FOKIN' MORON WOULDN'T KNOW *THA'*?
LET'S PUT IT THIS WAY, WE'RE THE ONLY ONES RUNNING LAPS!
CHRIST...!
OKAY, GIRLS! YOU CAN STOP NOW!
HAH HAFF HAFF GASP
OKAY, I'M GONNA DIE NOW...

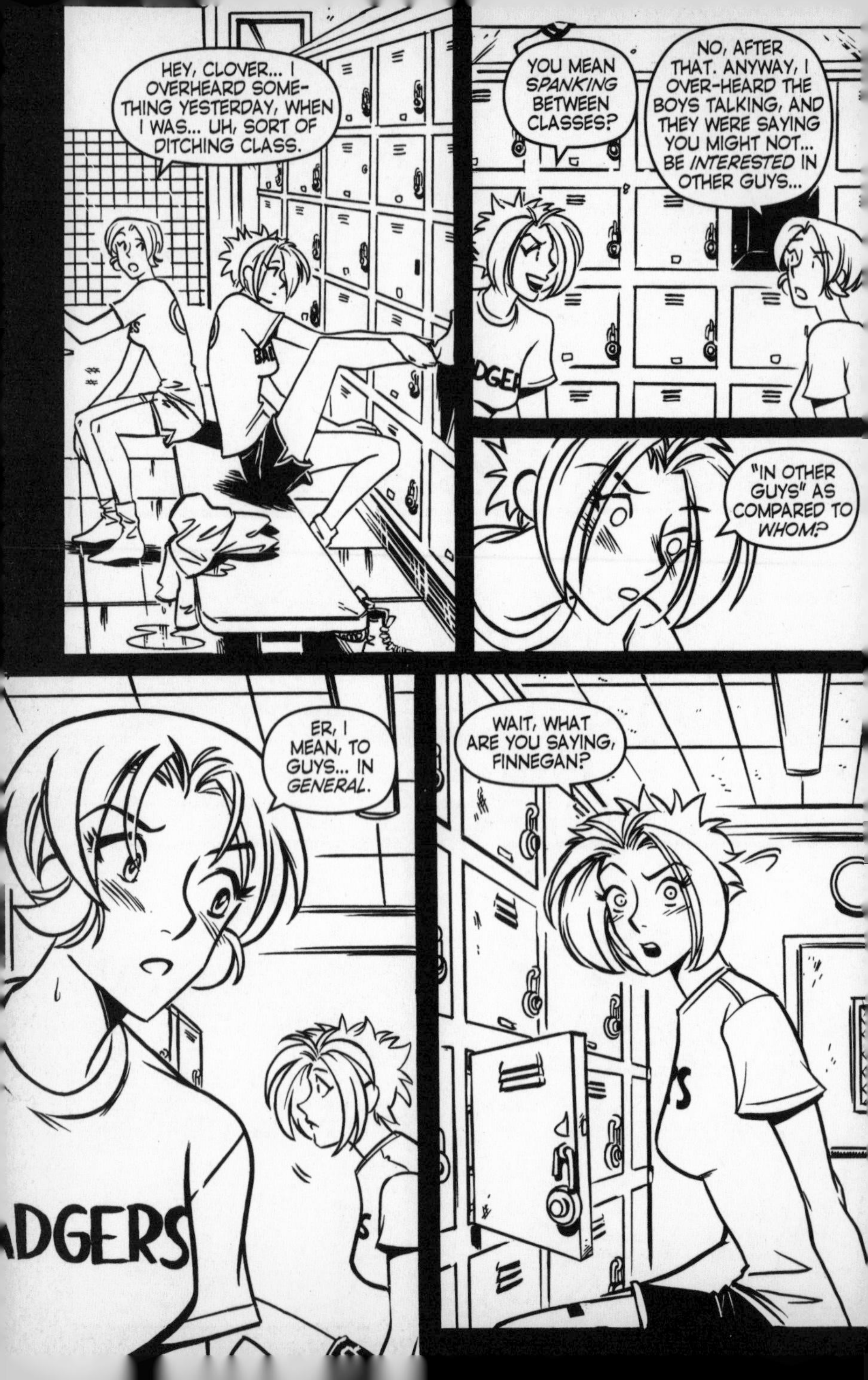
HEY, CLOVER... I OVERHEARD SOME-THING YESTERDAY, WHEN I WAS... UH, SORT OF DITCHING CLASS.
YOU MEAN *SPANKING* BETWEEN CLASSES?
NO, AFTER THAT. ANYWAY, I OVER-HEARD THE BOYS TALKING, AND THEY WERE SAYING YOU MIGHT NOT... BE *INTERESTED* IN OTHER GUYS...
"IN OTHER GUYS" AS COMPARED TO *WHOM?*
ER, I MEAN, TO GUYS... IN *GENERAL*.
WAIT, WHAT ARE YOU SAYING, FINNEGAN?

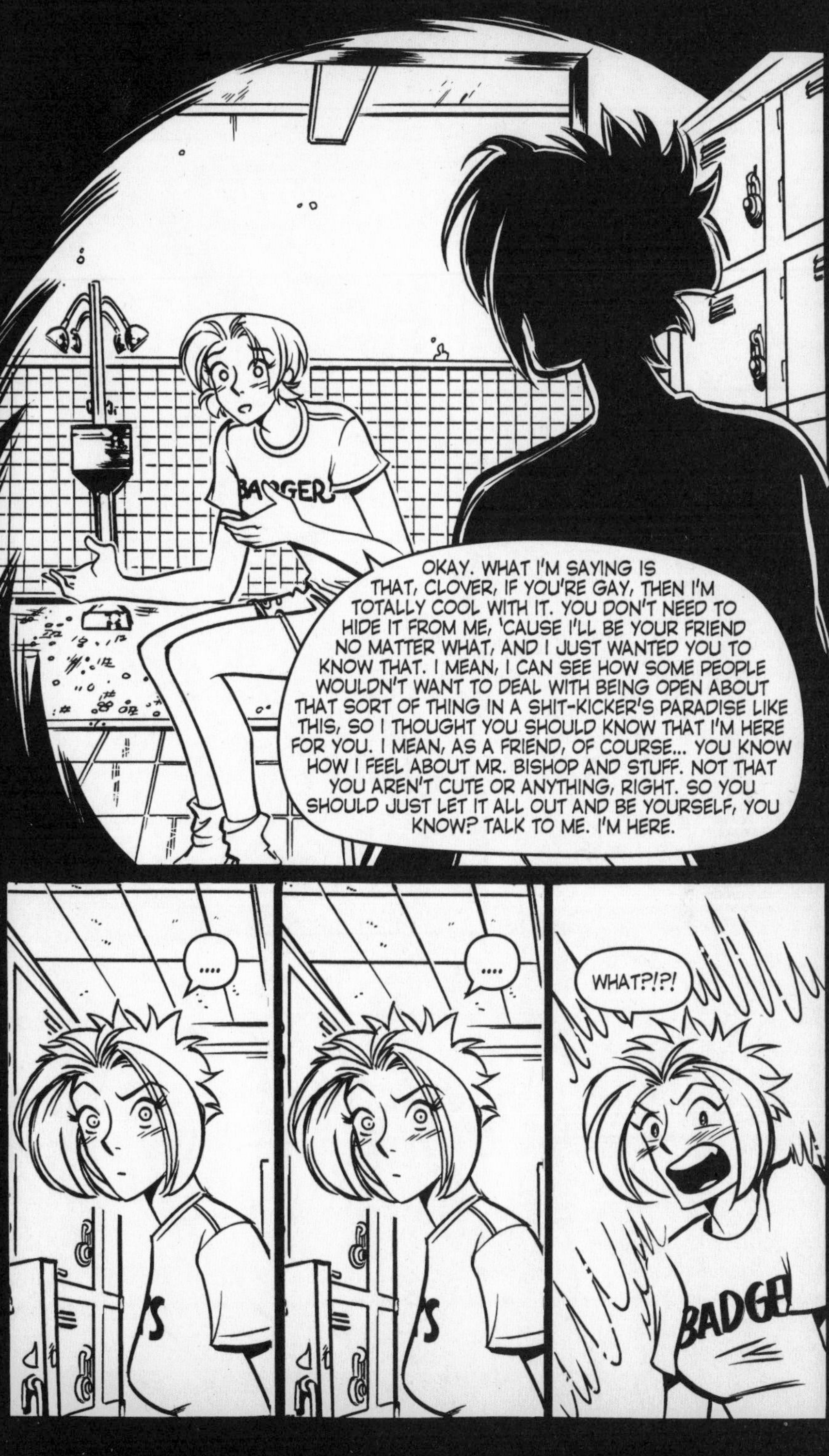
OKAY. WHAT I'M SAYING IS THAT, CLOVER, IF YOU'RE GAY, THEN I'M TOTALLY COOL WITH IT. YOU DON'T NEED TO HIDE IT FROM ME, 'CAUSE I'LL BE YOUR FRIEND NO MATTER WHAT, AND I JUST WANTED YOU TO KNOW THAT. I MEAN, I CAN SEE HOW SOME PEOPLE WOULDN'T WANT TO DEAL WITH BEING OPEN ABOUT THAT SORT OF THING IN A SHIT-KICKER'S PARADISE LIKE THIS, SO I THOUGHT YOU SHOULD KNOW THAT I'M HERE FOR YOU. I MEAN, AS A FRIEND, OF COURSE... YOU KNOW HOW I FEEL ABOUT MR. BISHOP AND STUFF. NOT THAT YOU AREN'T CUTE OR ANYTHING, RIGHT. SO YOU SHOULD JUST LET IT ALL OUT AND BE YOURSELF, YOU KNOW? TALK TO ME. I'M HERE.
....
....
WHAT?!?!

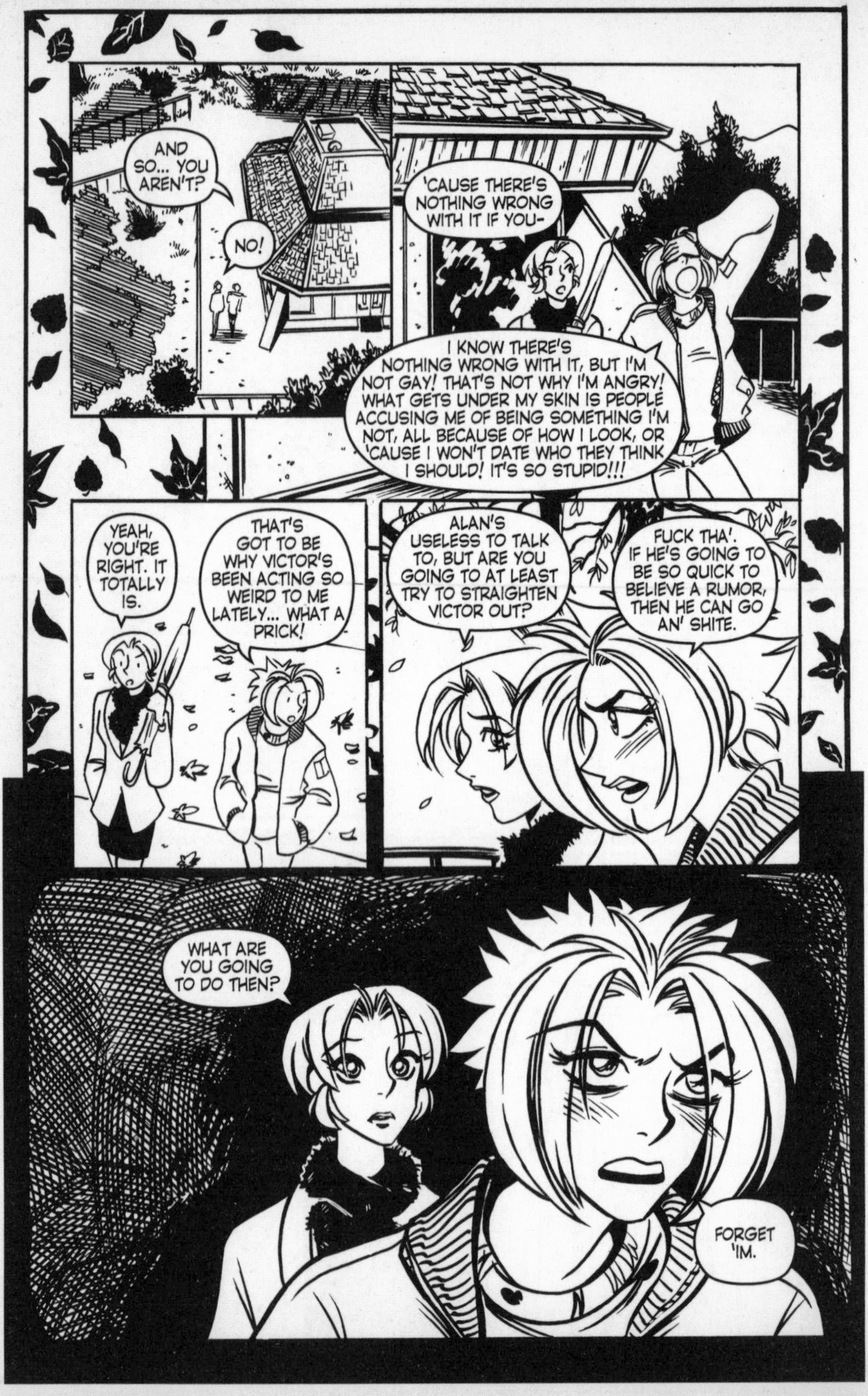
AND SO... YOU AREN'T?
NO!
'CAUSE THERE'S NOTHING WRONG WITH IT IF YOU-
I KNOW THERE'S NOTHING WRONG WITH IT, BUT I'M NOT GAY! THAT'S NOT WHY I'M ANGRY! WHAT GETS UNDER MY SKIN IS PEOPLE ACCUSING ME OF BEING SOMETHING I'M NOT, ALL BECAUSE OF HOW I LOOK, OR 'CAUSE I WON'T DATE WHO THEY THINK I SHOULD! IT'S SO STUPID!!!
THAT'S GOT TO BE WHY VICTOR'S BEEN ACTING SO WEIRD TO ME LATELY... WHAT A PRICK!
YEAH, YOU'RE RIGHT. IT TOTALLY IS.
ALAN'S USELESS TO TALK TO, BUT ARE YOU GOING TO AT LEAST TRY TO STRAIGHTEN VICTOR OUT?
FUCK THA'. IF HE'S GOING TO BE SO QUICK TO BELIEVE A RUMOR, THEN HE CAN GO AN' SHITE.
WHAT ARE YOU GOING TO DO THEN?
FORGET 'IM.

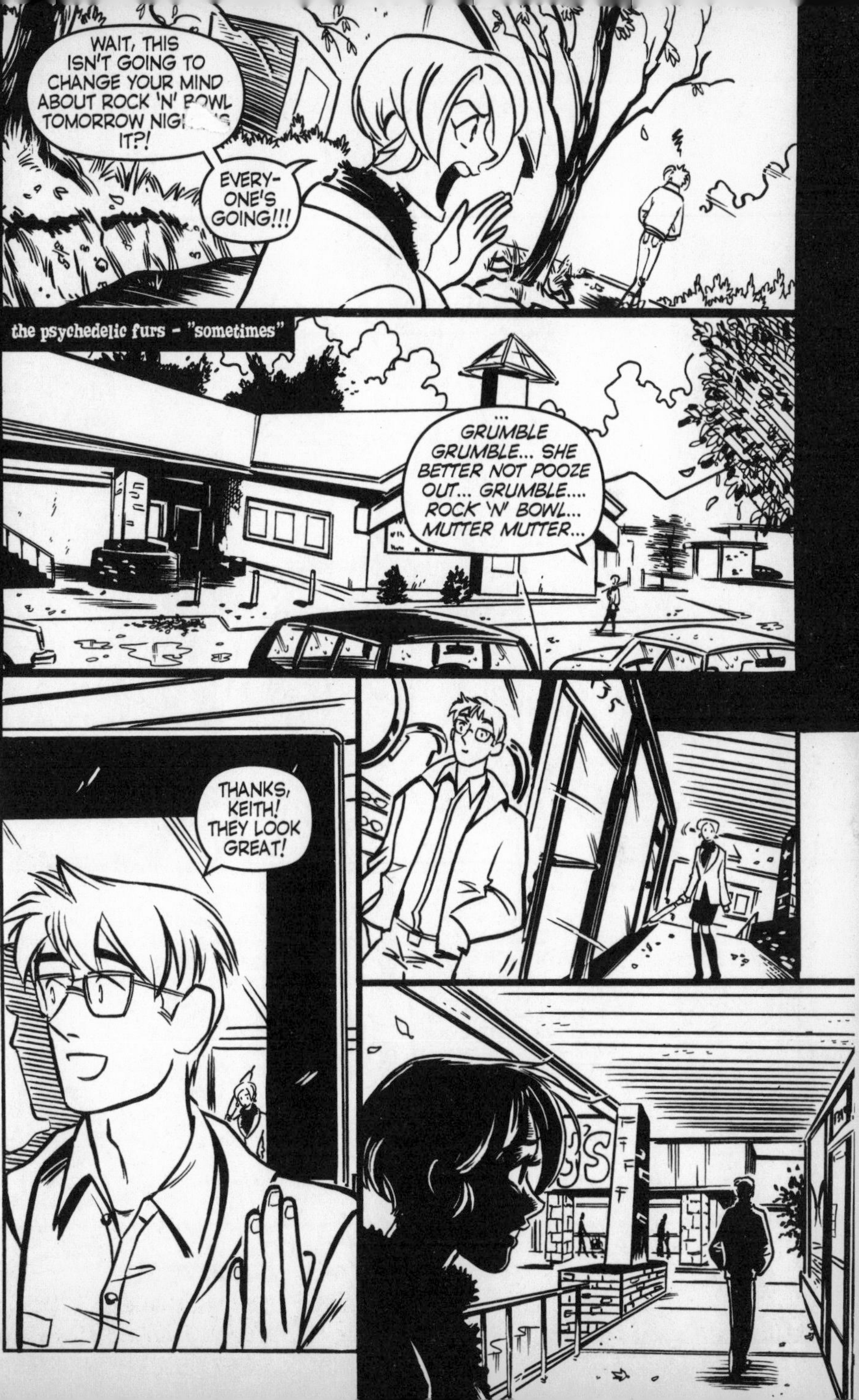
WAIT, THIS ISN'T GOING TO CHANGE YOUR MIND ABOUT ROCK 'N' BOWL TOMORROW NIG IT?!
EVERY-ONE'S GOING!!!
the psychedelic furs - "sometimes"
... GRUMBLE GRUMBLE... SHE BETTER NOT POOZE OUT... GRUMBLE.... ROCK 'N' BOWL... MUTTER MUTTER...
THANKS, KEITH! THEY LOOK GREAT!

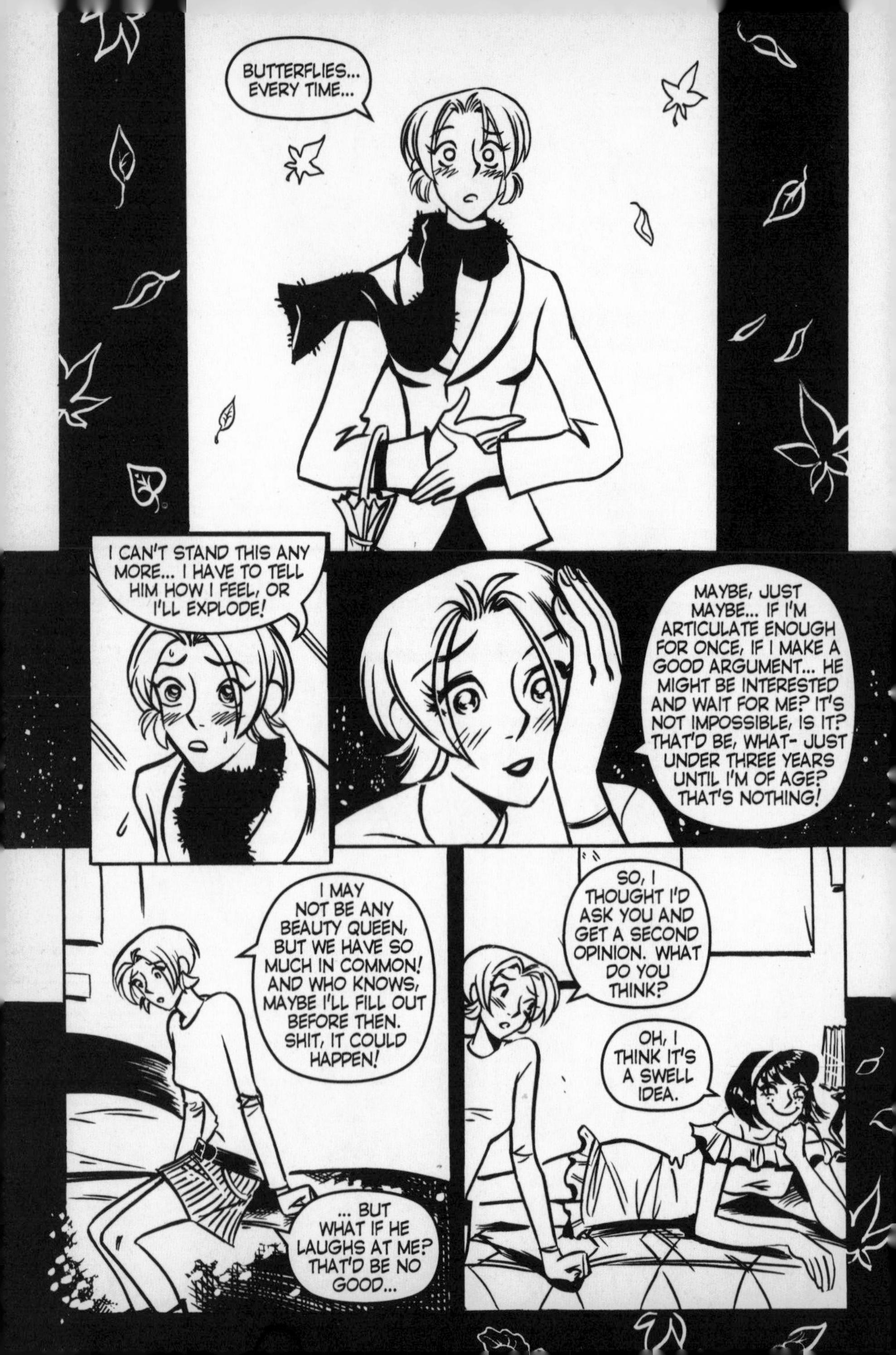
BUTTERFLIES... EVERY TIME...
I CAN'T STAND THIS ANY MORE... I HAVE TO TELL HIM HOW I FEEL, OR I'LL EXPLODE!
MAYBE, JUST MAYBE... IF I'M ARTICULATE ENOUGH FOR ONCE, IF I MAKE A GOOD ARGUMENT... HE MIGHT BE INTERESTED AND WAIT FOR ME? IT'S NOT IMPOSSIBLE, IS IT? THAT'D BE, WHAT- JUST UNDER THREE YEARS UNTIL I'M OF AGE? THAT'S NOTHING!
I MAY NOT BE ANY BEAUTY QUEEN, BUT WE HAVE SO MUCH IN COMMON! AND WHO KNOWS, MAYBE I'LL FILL OUT BEFORE THEN. SHIT, IT COULD HAPPEN!
... BUT WHAT IF HE LAUGHS AT ME? THAT'D BE NO GOOD...
SO, I THOUGHT I'D ASK YOU AND GET A SECOND OPINION. WHAT DO YOU THINK?
OH, I THINK IT'S A SWELL IDEA.

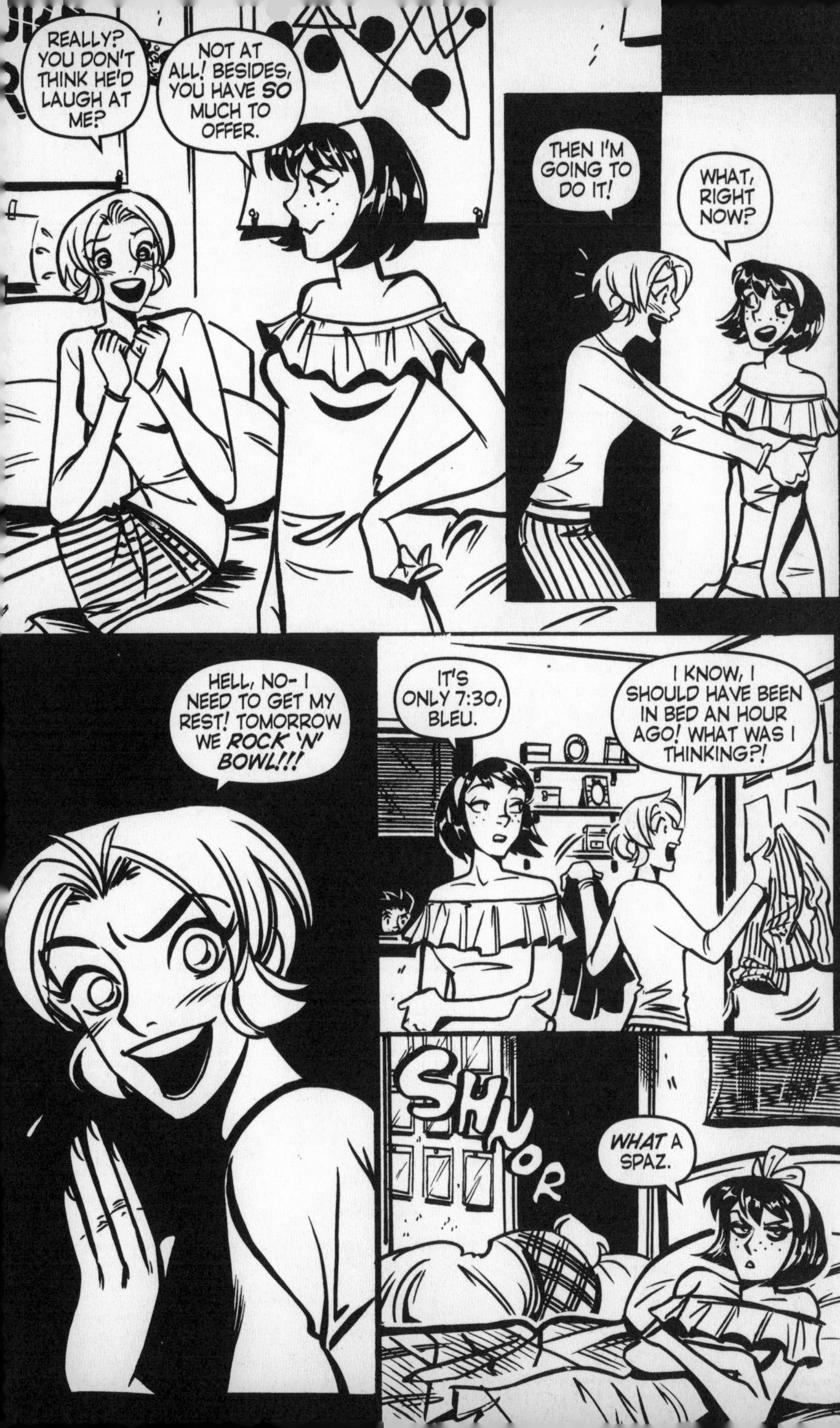
REALLY? YOU DON'T THINK HE'D LAUGH AT ME?
NOT AT ALL! BESIDES, YOU HAVE SO MUCH TO OFFER.
THEN I'M GOING TO DO IT!
WHAT, RIGHT NOW?
HELL, NO- I NEED TO GET MY REST! TOMORROW WE ROCK 'N' BOWL!!!
IT'S ONLY 7:30, BLEU.
I KNOW, I SHOULD HAVE BEEN IN BED AN HOUR AGO! WHAT WAS I THINKING?!
SHNOR
WHAT A SPAZ.

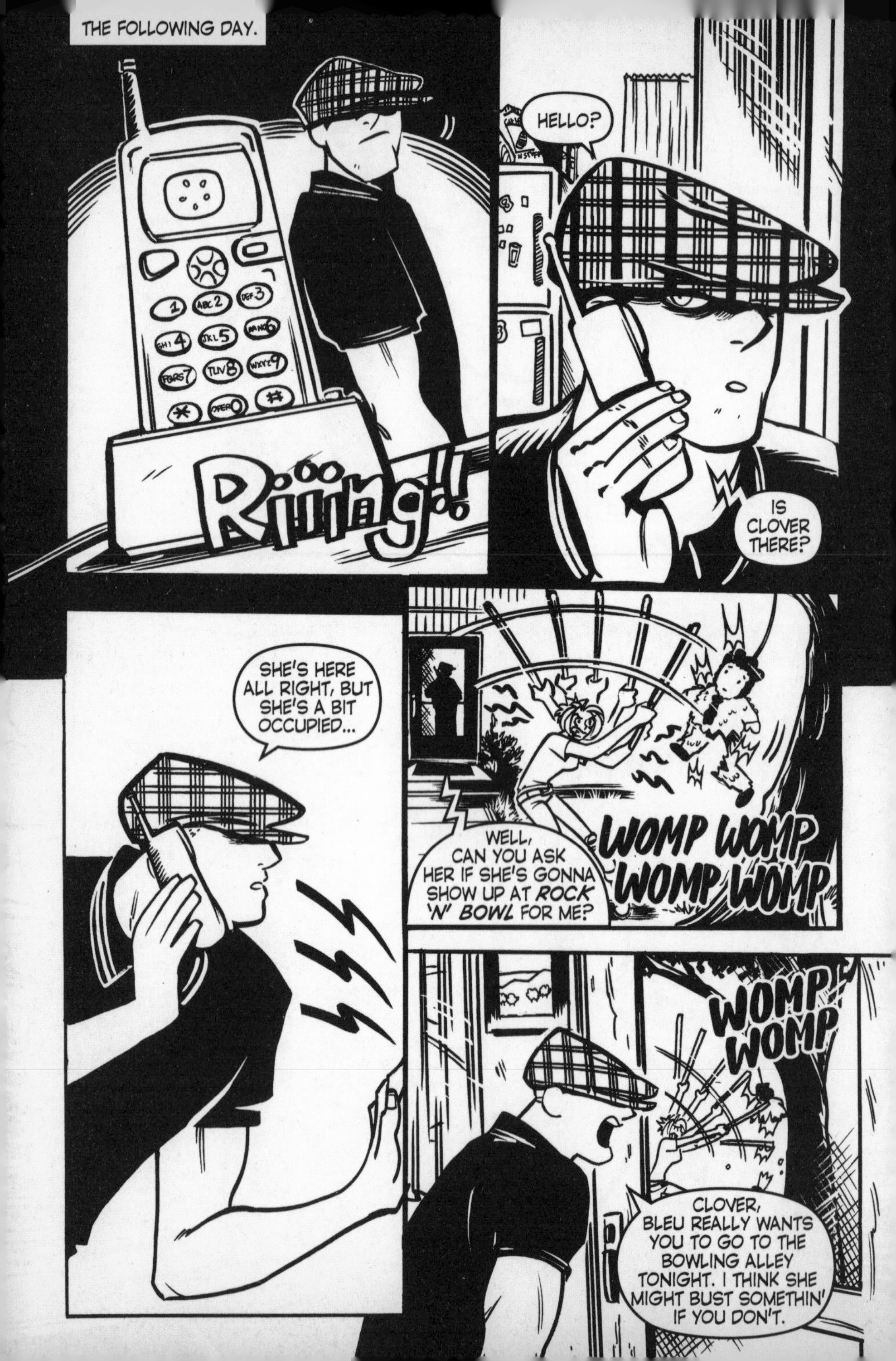
THE FOLLOWING DAY.
Riiing!!
HELLO?
IS CLOVER THERE?
SHE'S HERE ALL RIGHT, BUT SHE'S A BIT OCCUPIED...
WELL, CAN YOU ASK HER IF SHE'S GONNA SHOW UP AT ROCK 'N' BOWL FOR ME?
WOMP WOMP WOMP WOMP
WOMP WOMP
CLOVER, BLEU REALLY WANTS YOU TO GO TO THE BOWLING ALLEY TONIGHT. I THINK SHE MIGHT BUST SOMETHIN' IF YOU DON'T.

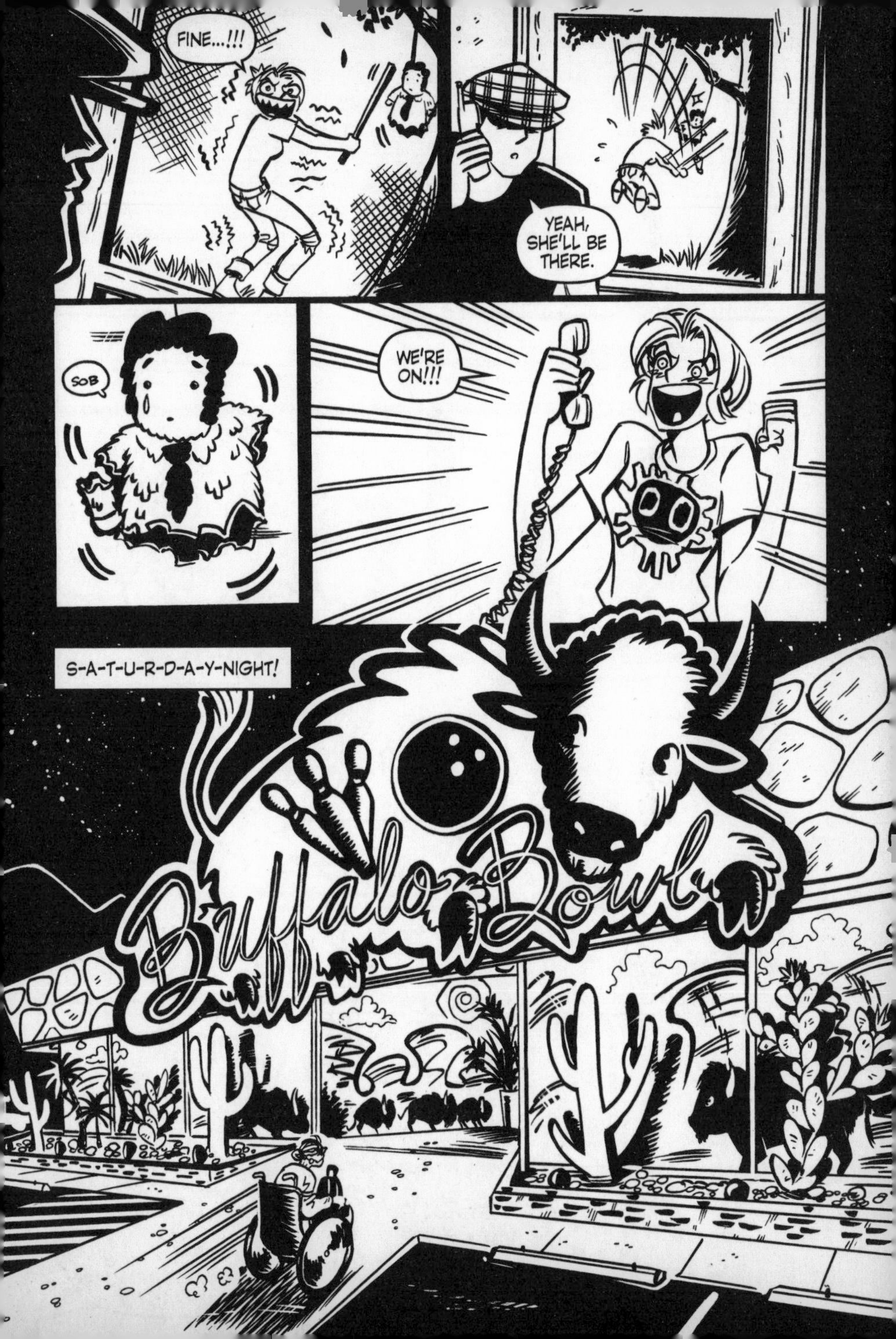
FINE...!!!
YEAH, SHE'LL BE THERE.
SOB
WE'RE ON!!!
S-A-T-U-R-D-A-Y-NIGHT!
Buffalo Bowl

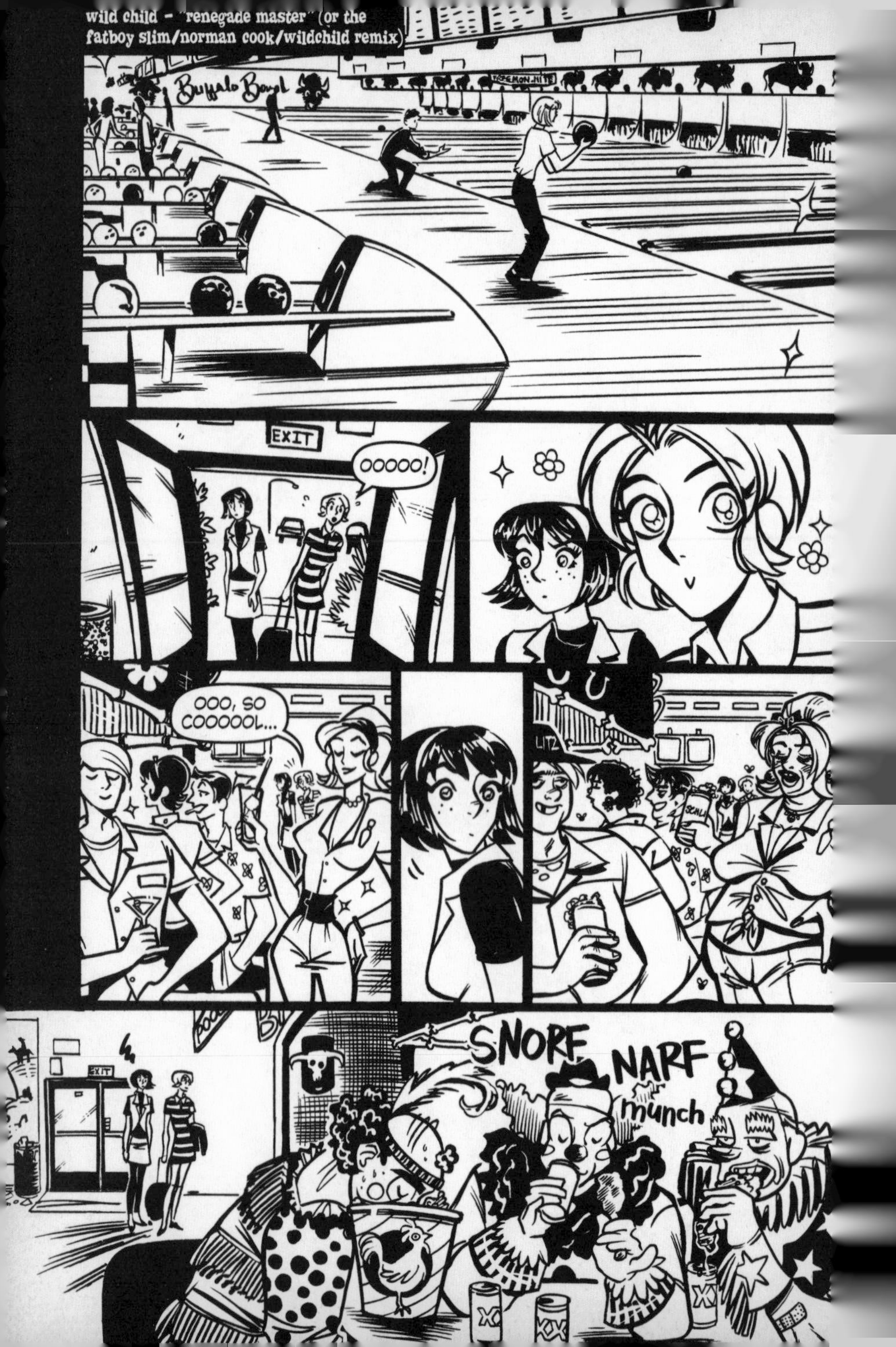
wild child - "renegade master" (or the fatboy slim/norman cook/wildchild remix)
Buffalo Bowl
EXIT
OOOOO!
OOO, SO COOOOOL...
SNORF
NARF
munch

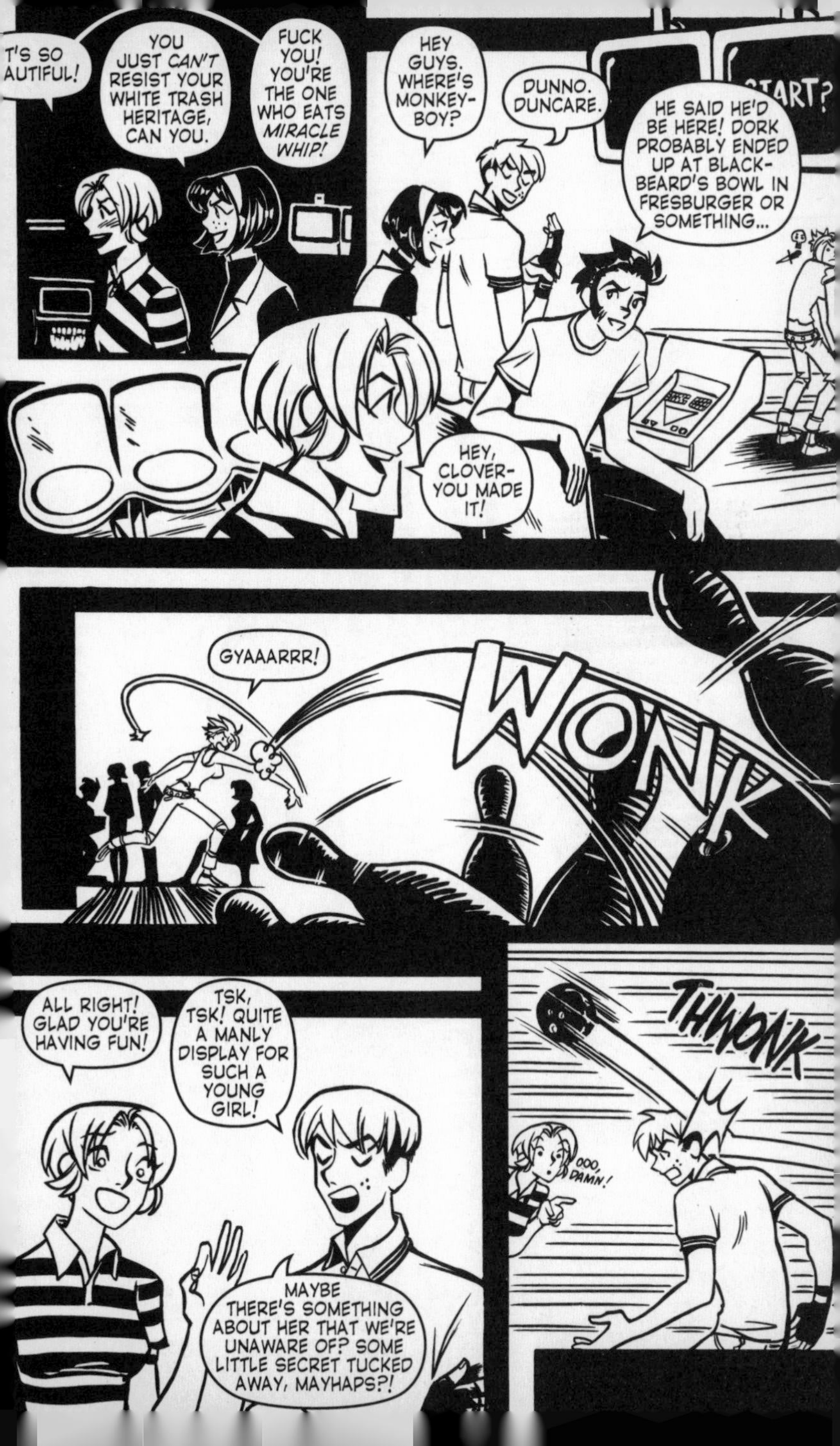
T'S SO AUTIFUL!
YOU JUST CAN'T RESIST YOUR WHITE TRASH HERITAGE, CAN YOU.
FUCK YOU! YOU'RE THE ONE WHO EATS MIRACLE WHIP!
HEY GUYS. WHERE'S MONKEY-BOY?
DUNNO. DUNCARE.
START?
HE SAID HE'D BE HERE! DORK PROBABLY ENDED UP AT BLACK-BEARD'S BOWL IN FRESBURGER OR SOMETHING...
HEY, CLOVER-YOU MADE IT!
GYAAARRR!
WONK
ALL RIGHT! GLAD YOU'RE HAVING FUN!
TSK, TSK! QUITE A MANLY DISPLAY FOR SUCH A YOUNG GIRL!
MAYBE THERE'S SOMETHING ABOUT HER THAT WE'RE UNAWARE OF? SOME LITTLE SECRET TUCKED AWAY, MAYHAPS?!
THWONK
OOO, DAMN!

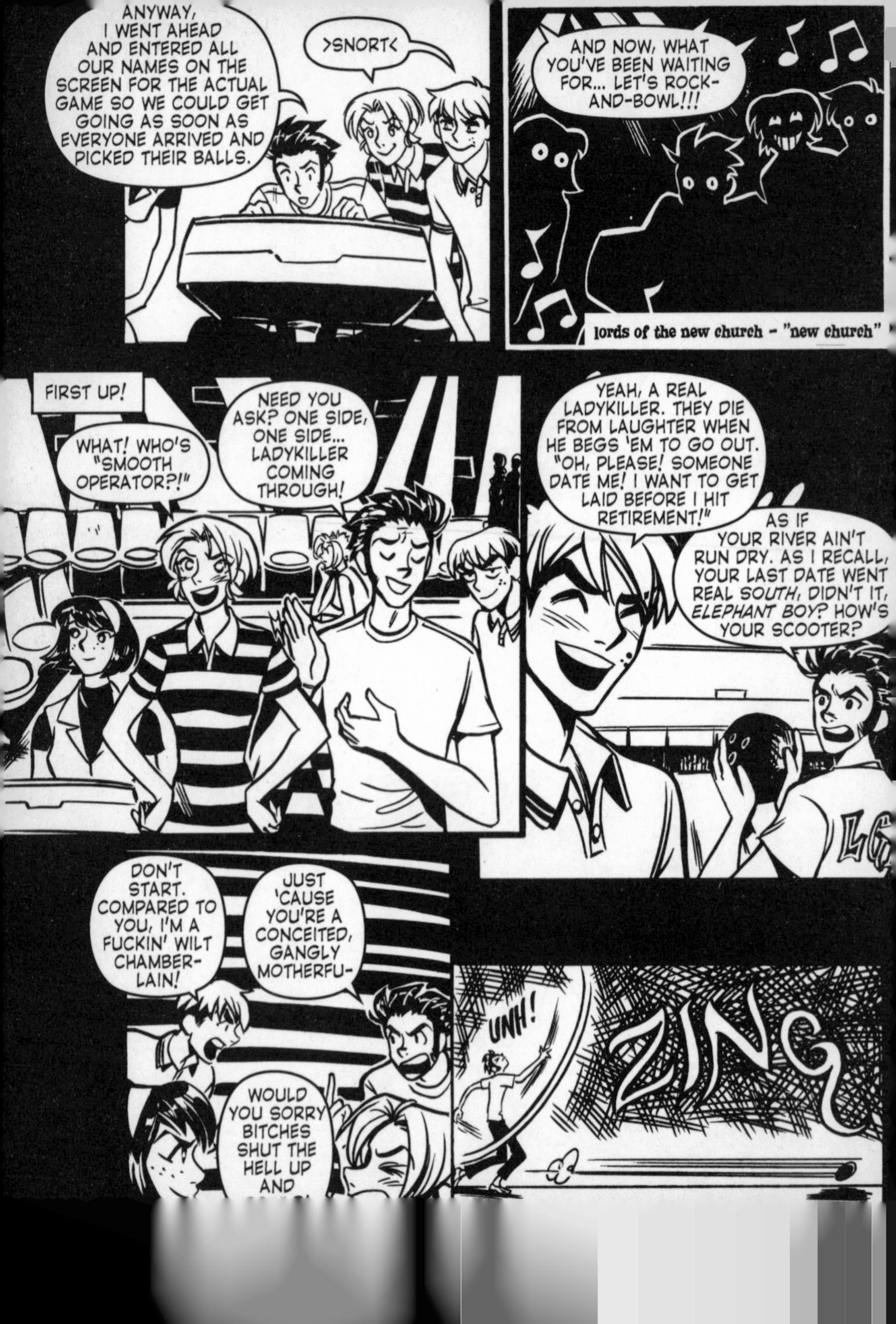

ANYWAY, I WENT AHEAD AND ENTERED ALL OUR NAMES ON THE SCREEN FOR THE ACTUAL GAME SO WE COULD GET GOING AS SOON AS EVERYONE ARRIVED AND PICKED THEIR BALLS.
>SNORT<
AND NOW, WHAT YOU'VE BEEN WAITING FOR... LET'S ROCK-AND-BOWL!!!
lords of the new church - "new church"
FIRST UP!
WHAT! WHO'S "SMOOTH OPERATOR?!"
NEED YOU ASK? ONE SIDE, ONE SIDE... LADYKILLER COMING THROUGH!
YEAH, A REAL LADYKILLER. THEY DIE FROM LAUGHTER WHEN HE BEGS 'EM TO GO OUT. "OH, PLEASE! SOMEONE DATE ME! I WANT TO GET LAID BEFORE I HIT RETIREMENT!"
AS IF YOUR RIVER AIN'T RUN DRY. AS I RECALL, YOUR LAST DATE WENT REAL *SOUTH*, DIDN'T IT, *ELEPHANT BOY*? HOW'S YOUR SCOOTER?
DON'T START. COMPARED TO YOU, I'M A FUCKIN' WILT CHAMBER-LAIN!
JUST 'CAUSE YOU'RE A CONCEITED, GANGLY MOTHERFU-
WOULD YOU SORRY BITCHES SHUT THE HELL UP AND
UNH!
ZING

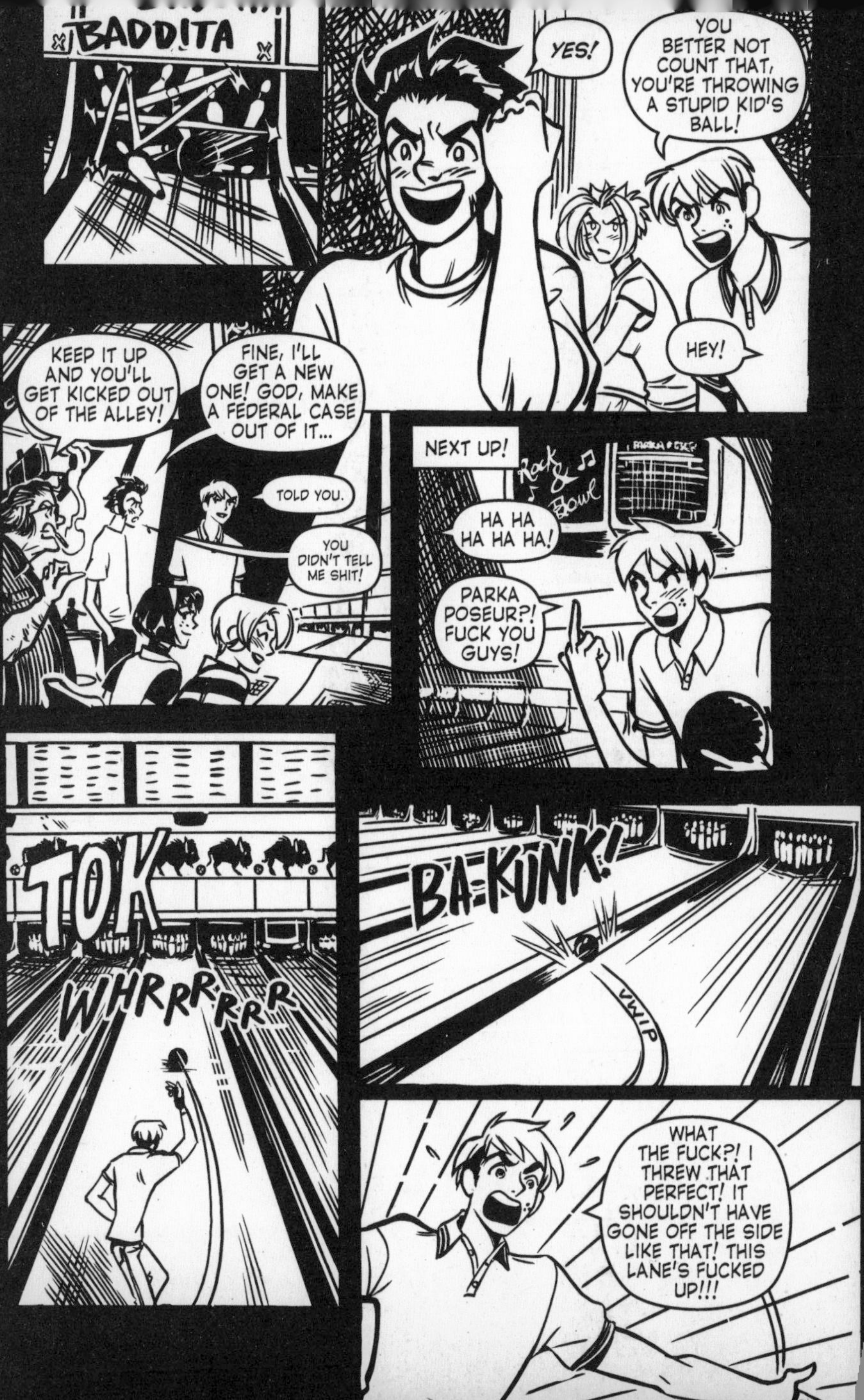
BADD!TA
YES!
YOU BETTER NOT COUNT THAT, YOU'RE THROWING A STUPID KID'S BALL!
HEY!
KEEP IT UP AND YOU'LL GET KICKED OUT OF THE ALLEY!
FINE, I'LL GET A NEW ONE! GOD, MAKE A FEDERAL CASE OUT OF IT...
TOLD YOU.
YOU DIDN'T TELL ME SHIT!
NEXT UP!
Rock & Bowl
HA HA HA HA HA!
PARKA POSEUR?! FUCK YOU GUYS!
TOK
WHRRRRRR
BA-KUNK!
WHAT THE FUCK?! I THREW THAT PERFECT! IT SHOULDN'T HAVE GONE OFF THE SIDE LIKE THAT! THIS LANE'S FUCKED UP!!!

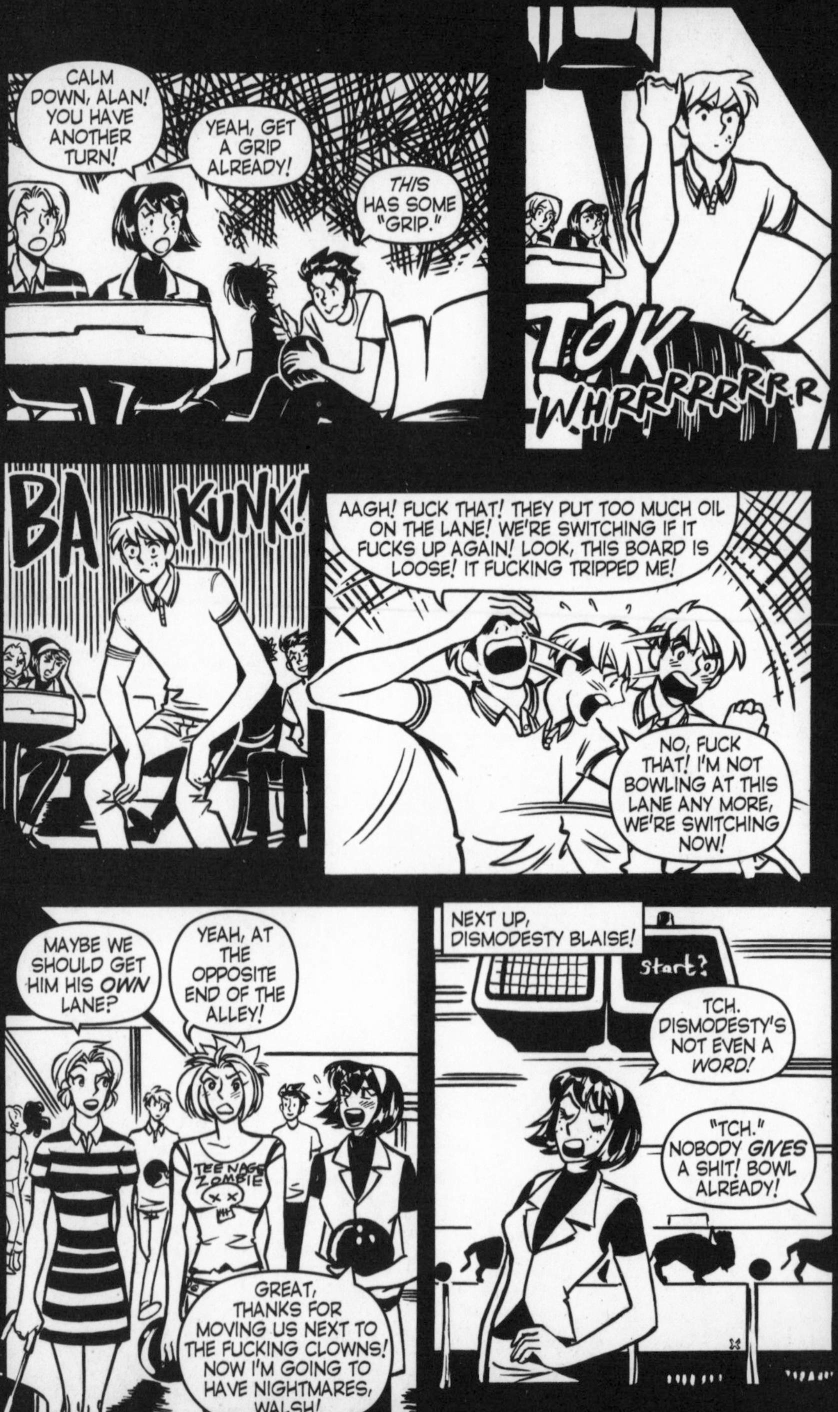
CALM DOWN, ALAN! YOU HAVE ANOTHER TURN!
YEAH, GET A GRIP ALREADY!
THIS HAS SOME "GRIP."
TOK
WHRRRRRRRRR
BA KUNK!
AAGH! FUCK THAT! THEY PUT TOO MUCH OIL ON THE LANE! WE'RE SWITCHING IF IT FUCKS UP AGAIN! LOOK, THIS BOARD IS LOOSE! IT FUCKING TRIPPED ME!
NO, FUCK THAT! I'M NOT BOWLING AT THIS LANE ANY MORE, WE'RE SWITCHING NOW!
MAYBE WE SHOULD GET HIM HIS *OWN* LANE?
YEAH, AT THE OPPOSITE END OF THE ALLEY!
TEENAGE ZOMBIE
GREAT, THANKS FOR MOVING US NEXT TO THE FUCKING CLOWNS! NOW I'M GOING TO HAVE NIGHTMARES, WALSH!
NEXT UP, DISMODESTY BLAISE!
start?
TCH. DISMODESTY'S NOT EVEN A *WORD*!
"TCH." NOBODY *GIVES* A SHIT! BOWL ALREADY!

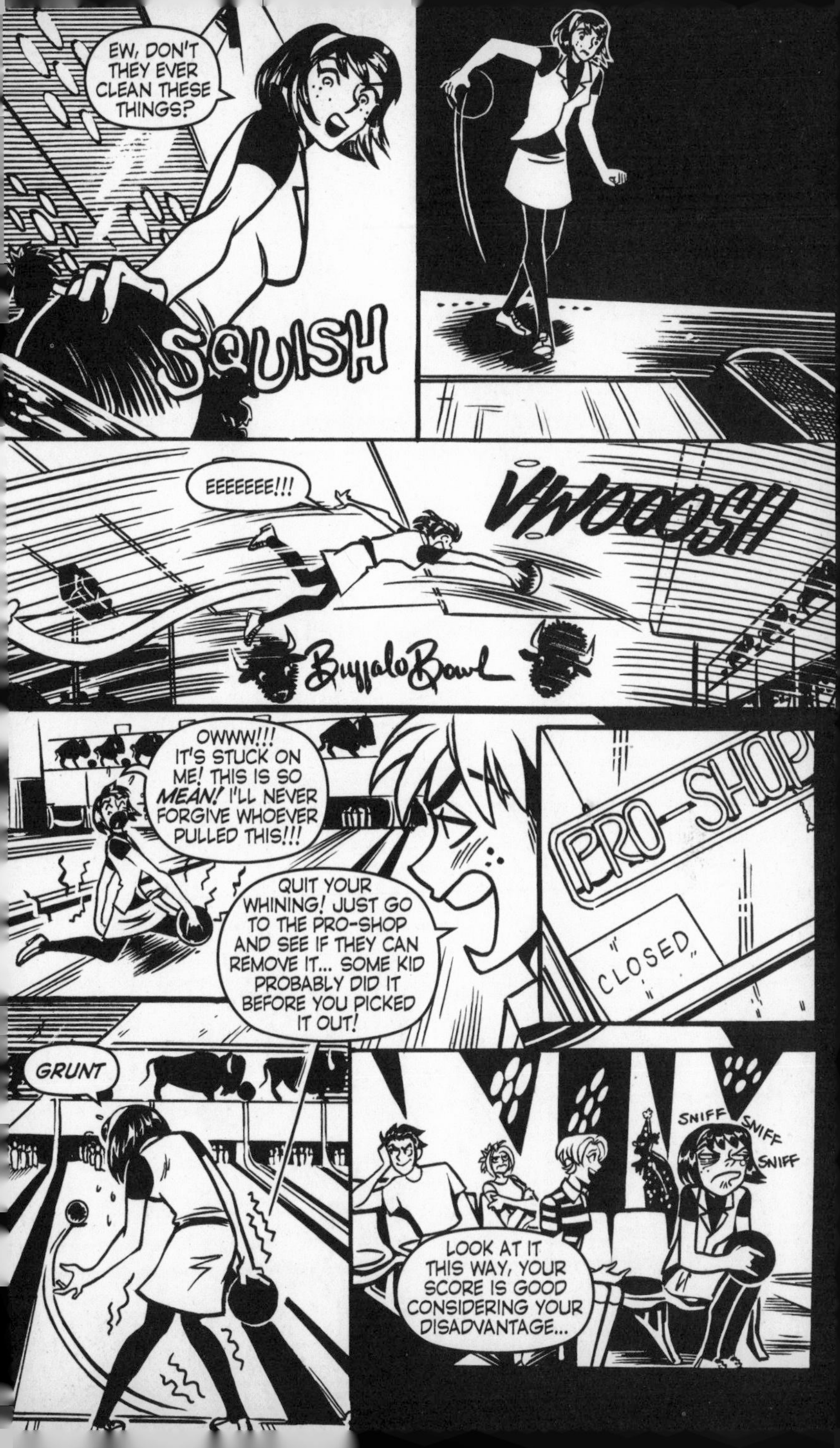
EW, DON'T THEY EVER CLEAN THESE THINGS?
SQUISH
EEEEEEE!!!
VWOOOSH
BuffaloBowl
OWWW!!! IT'S STUCK ON ME! THIS IS SO *MEAN!* I'LL NEVER FORGIVE WHOEVER PULLED THIS!!!
QUIT YOUR WHINING! JUST GO TO THE PRO-SHOP AND SEE IF THEY CAN REMOVE IT... SOME KID PROBABLY DID IT BEFORE YOU PICKED IT OUT!
PRO-SHOP
"CLOSED"
GRUNT
SNIFF SNIFF SNIFF
LOOK AT IT THIS WAY, YOUR SCORE IS GOOD CONSIDERING YOUR DISADVANTAGE...

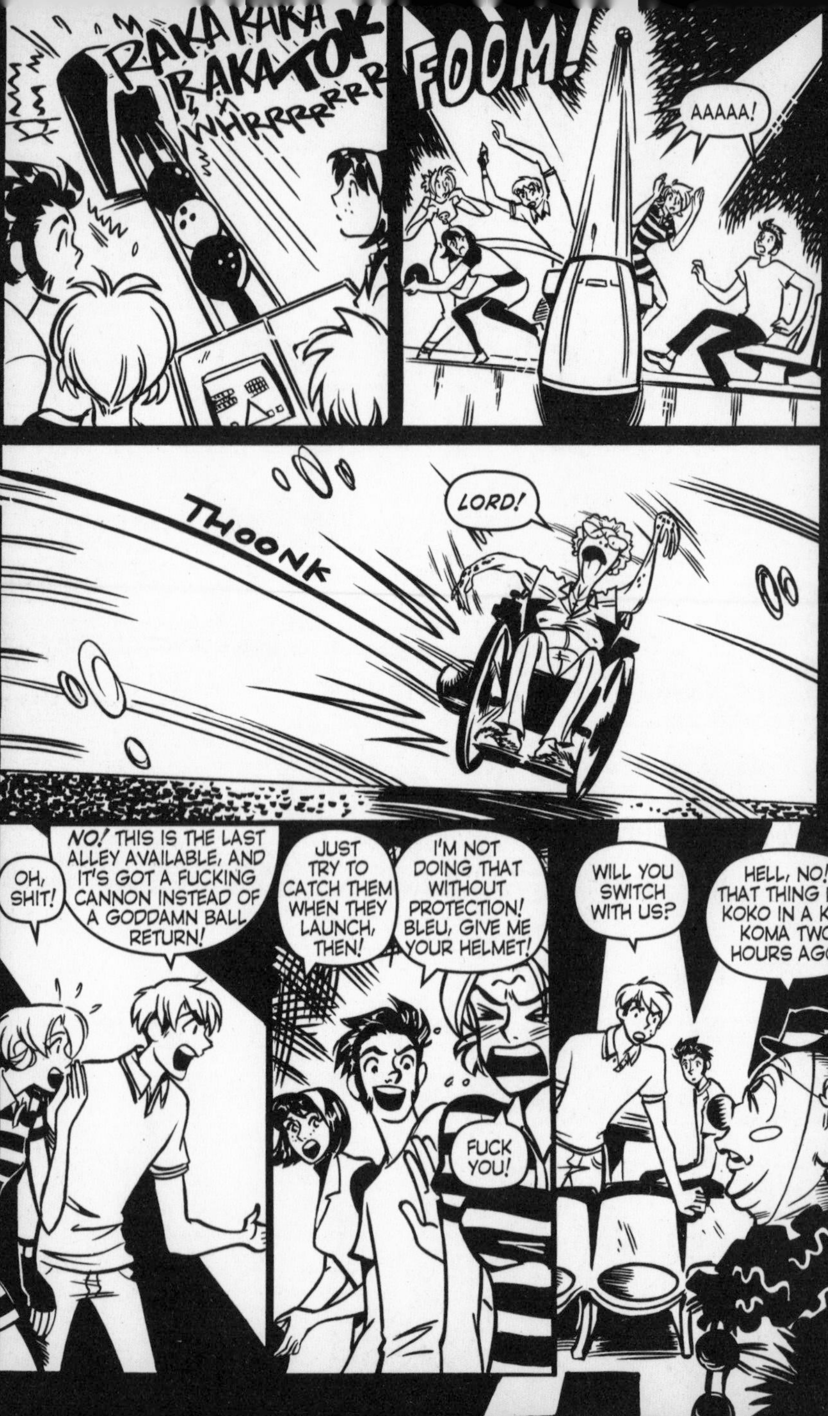
RAKA KAKA
RAKA TOK
WHRRRRRRRR
FOOM!
AAAAA!
LORD!
THOONK
OH, SHIT!
NO! THIS IS THE LAST ALLEY AVAILABLE, AND IT'S GOT A FUCKING CANNON INSTEAD OF A GODDAMN BALL RETURN!
JUST TRY TO CATCH THEM WHEN THEY LAUNCH, THEN!
I'M NOT DOING THAT WITHOUT PROTECTION! BLEU, GIVE ME YOUR HELMET!
FUCK YOU!
WILL YOU SWITCH WITH US?
HELL, NO! THAT THING PUT KOKO IN A KO-KOMA TWO HOURS AGO!

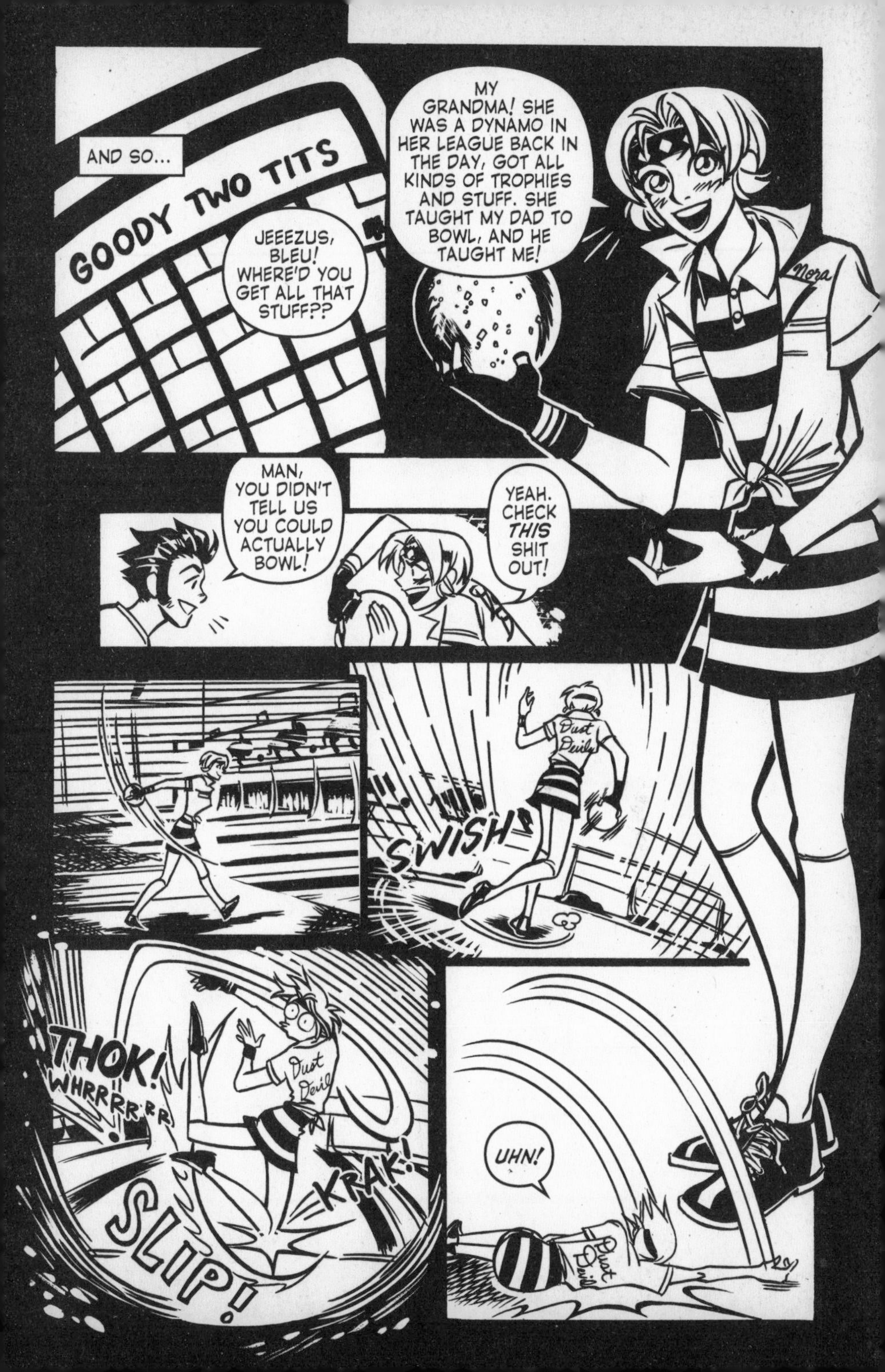
AND SO...
GOODY TWO TITS
JEEEZUS, BLEU! WHERE'D YOU GET ALL THAT STUFF??
MY GRANDMA! SHE WAS A DYNAMO IN HER LEAGUE BACK IN THE DAY, GOT ALL KINDS OF TROPHIES AND STUFF. SHE TAUGHT MY DAD TO BOWL, AND HE TAUGHT ME!
Nora
MAN, YOU DIDN'T TELL US YOU COULD ACTUALLY BOWL!
YEAH. CHECK *THIS* SHIT OUT!
Dust Devils
SWISH
THOK!
WHRRRRRR
Dust Devil
KRAK!
SLIP!
UHN!
Dust Devil

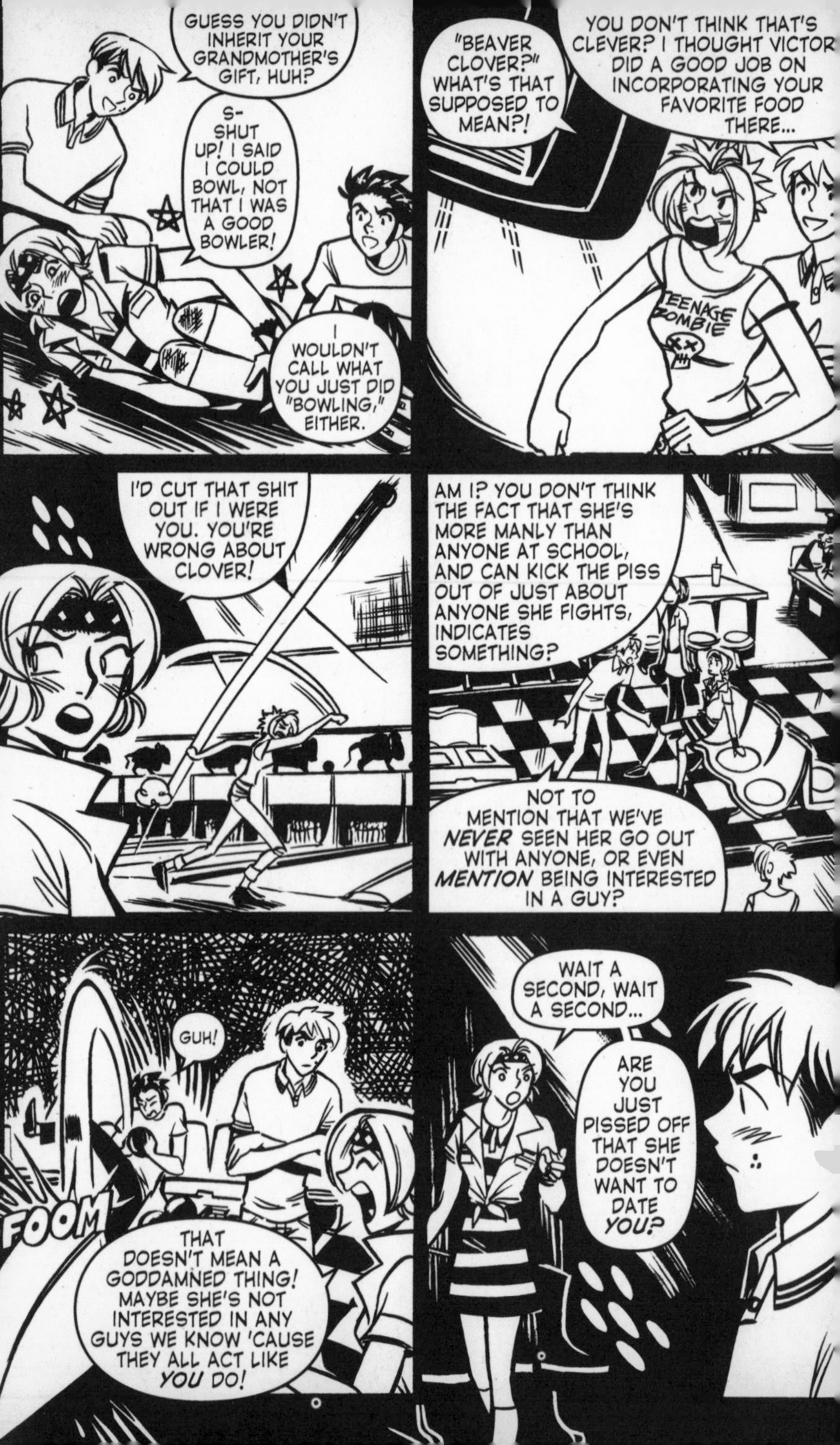
GUESS YOU DIDN'T INHERIT YOUR GRANDMOTHER'S GIFT, HUH?
S-SHUT UP! I SAID I COULD BOWL, NOT THAT I WAS A GOOD BOWLER!
I WOULDN'T CALL WHAT YOU JUST DID "BOWLING," EITHER.
"BEAVER CLOVER?" WHAT'S THAT SUPPOSED TO MEAN?!
YOU DON'T THINK THAT'S CLEVER? I THOUGHT VICTOR DID A GOOD JOB ON INCORPORATING YOUR FAVORITE FOOD THERE...
TEENAGE ZOMBIE
I'D CUT THAT SHIT OUT IF I WERE YOU. YOU'RE WRONG ABOUT CLOVER!
AM I? YOU DON'T THINK THE FACT THAT SHE'S MORE MANLY THAN ANYONE AT SCHOOL, AND CAN KICK THE PISS OUT OF JUST ABOUT ANYONE SHE FIGHTS, INDICATES SOMETHING?
NOT TO MENTION THAT WE'VE NEVER SEEN HER GO OUT WITH ANYONE, OR EVEN MENTION BEING INTERESTED IN A GUY?
GUH!
FOOM
THAT DOESN'T MEAN A GODDAMNED THING! MAYBE SHE'S NOT INTERESTED IN ANY GUYS WE KNOW 'CAUSE THEY ALL ACT LIKE YOU DO!
WAIT A SECOND, WAIT A SECOND...
ARE YOU JUST PISSED OFF THAT SHE DOESN'T WANT TO DATE YOU?

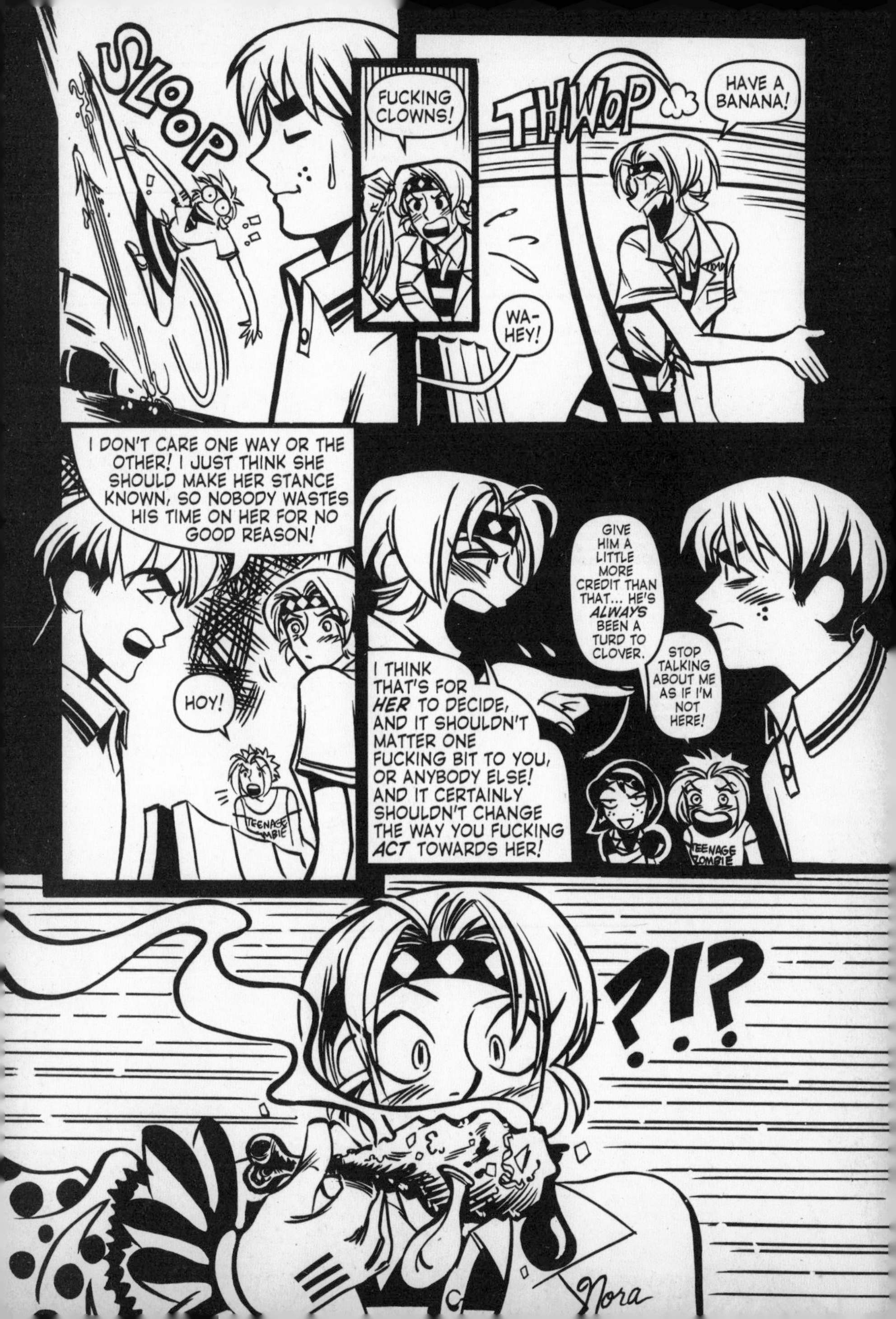
SLOOP
FUCKING CLOWNS!
THWOP
HAVE A BANANA!
WA-HEY!
I DON'T CARE ONE WAY OR THE OTHER! I JUST THINK SHE SHOULD MAKE HER STANCE KNOWN, SO NOBODY WASTES HIS TIME ON HER FOR NO GOOD REASON!
HOY!
TEENAGE ZOMBIE
I THINK THAT'S FOR HER TO DECIDE, AND IT SHOULDN'T MATTER ONE FUCKING BIT TO YOU, OR ANYBODY ELSE! AND IT CERTAINLY SHOULDN'T CHANGE THE WAY YOU FUCKING ACT TOWARDS HER!
GIVE HIM A LITTLE MORE CREDIT THAN THAT... HE'S ALWAYS BEEN A TURD TO CLOVER.
STOP TALKING ABOUT ME AS IF I'M NOT HERE!
TEENAGE ZOMBIE
?!?
Nora

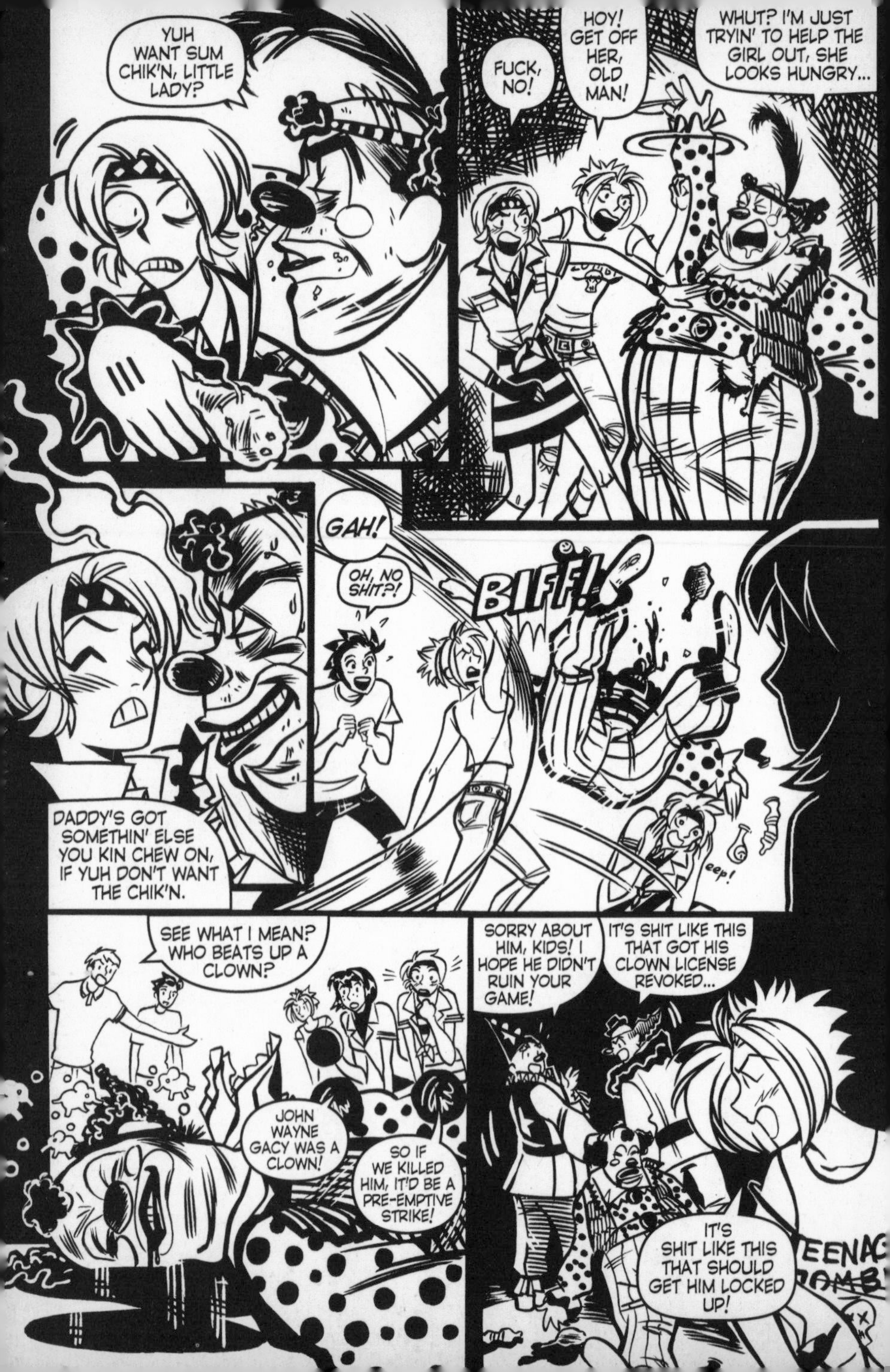
YUH WANT SUM CHIK'N, LITTLE LADY?
FUCK, NO!
HOY! GET OFF HER, OLD MAN!
WHUT? I'M JUST TRYIN' TO HELP THE GIRL OUT, SHE LOOKS HUNGRY...
DADDY'S GOT SOMETHIN' ELSE YOU KIN CHEW ON, IF YUH DON'T WANT THE CHIK'N.
GAH!
OH, NO SHIT?!
BIFF!
eep!
SEE WHAT I MEAN? WHO BEATS UP A CLOWN?
JOHN WAYNE GACY WAS A CLOWN!
SO IF WE KILLED HIM, IT'D BE A PRE-EMPTIVE STRIKE!
SORRY ABOUT HIM, KIDS! I HOPE HE DIDN'T RUIN YOUR GAME!
IT'S SHIT LIKE THIS THAT GOT HIS CLOWN LICENSE REVOKED...
IT'S SHIT LIKE THIS THAT SHOULD GET HIM LOCKED UP!

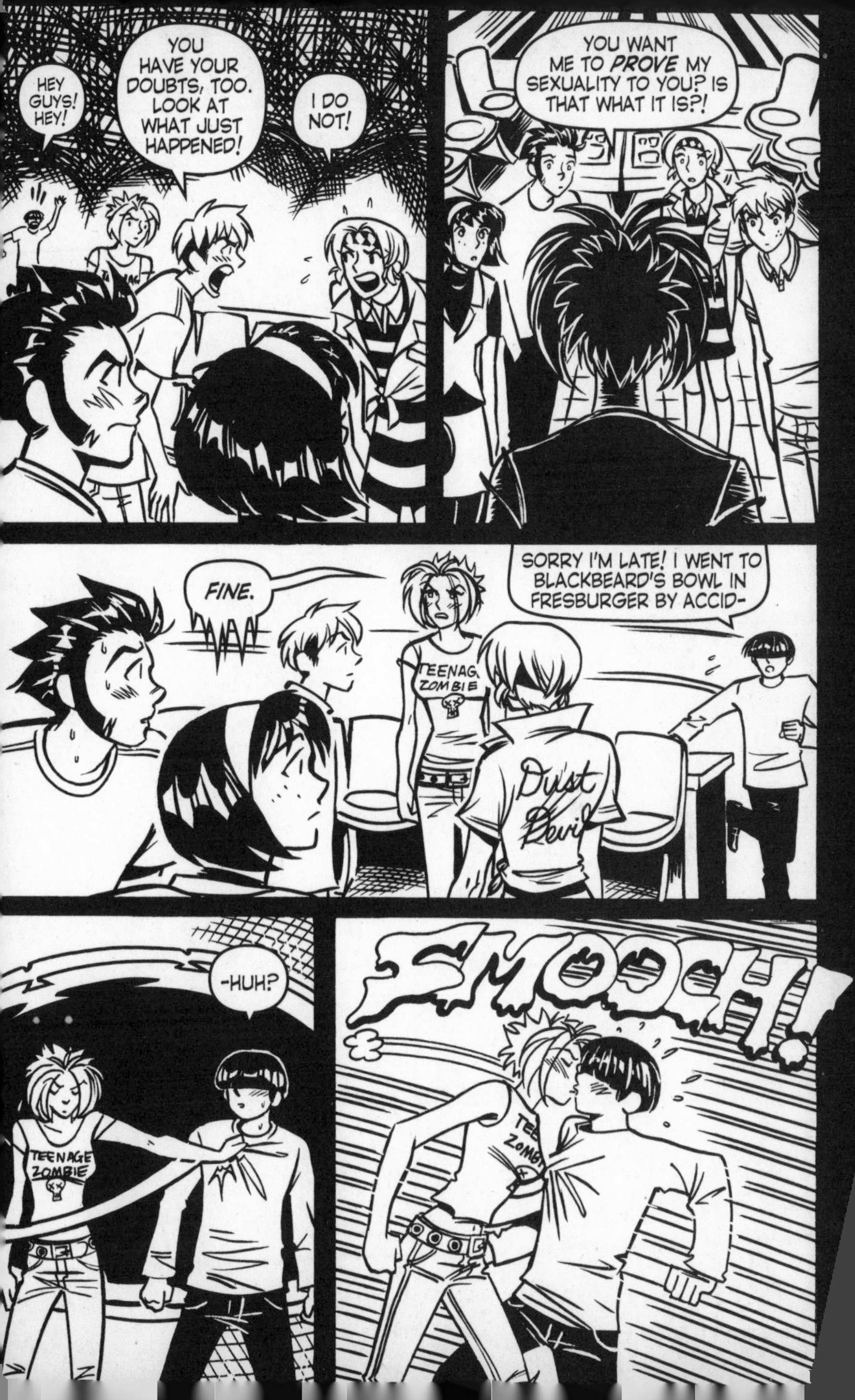
HEY GUYS! HEY!
YOU HAVE YOUR DOUBTS, TOO. LOOK AT WHAT JUST HAPPENED!
I DO NOT!
YOU WANT ME TO PROVE MY SEXUALITY TO YOU? IS THAT WHAT IT IS?!
FINE.
SORRY I'M LATE! I WENT TO BLACKBEARD'S BOWL IN FRESBURGER BY ACCID-
TEENAGE ZOMBIE
Dust Devil
-HUH?
TEENAGE ZOMBIE
SMOOCH!

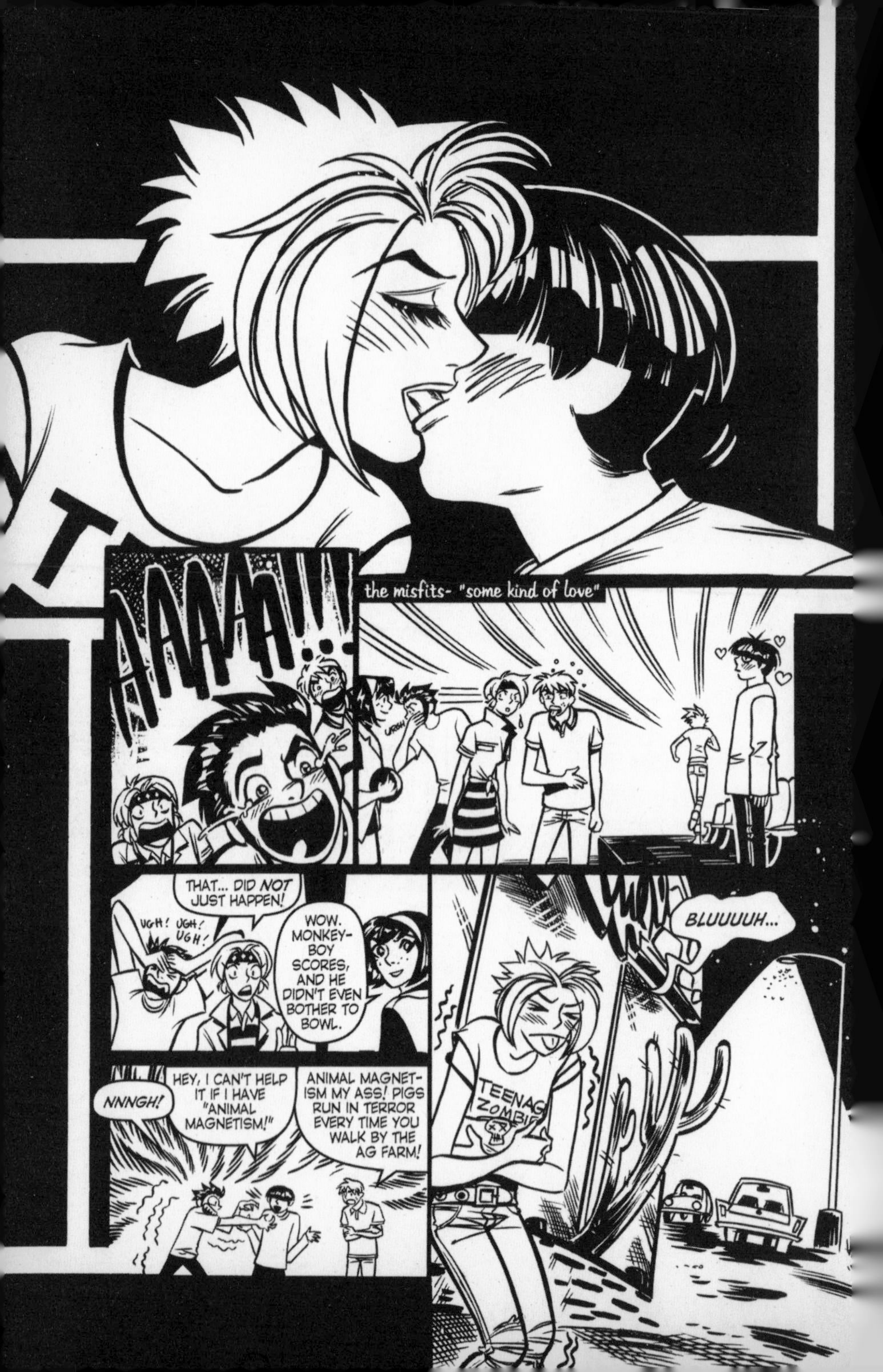

AAAAAA!!!
the misfits- "some kind of love"
URGH
THAT... DID NOT JUST HAPPEN!
UGH! UGH! UGH!
WOW. MONKEY-BOY SCORES, AND HE DIDN'T EVEN BOTHER TO BOWL.
BLUUUUH...
NNNGH!
HEY, I CAN'T HELP IT IF I HAVE "ANIMAL MAGNETISM!"
ANIMAL MAGNET-ISM MY ASS! PIGS RUN IN TERROR EVERY TIME YOU WALK BY THE AG FARM!
TEENAG ZOMBIE

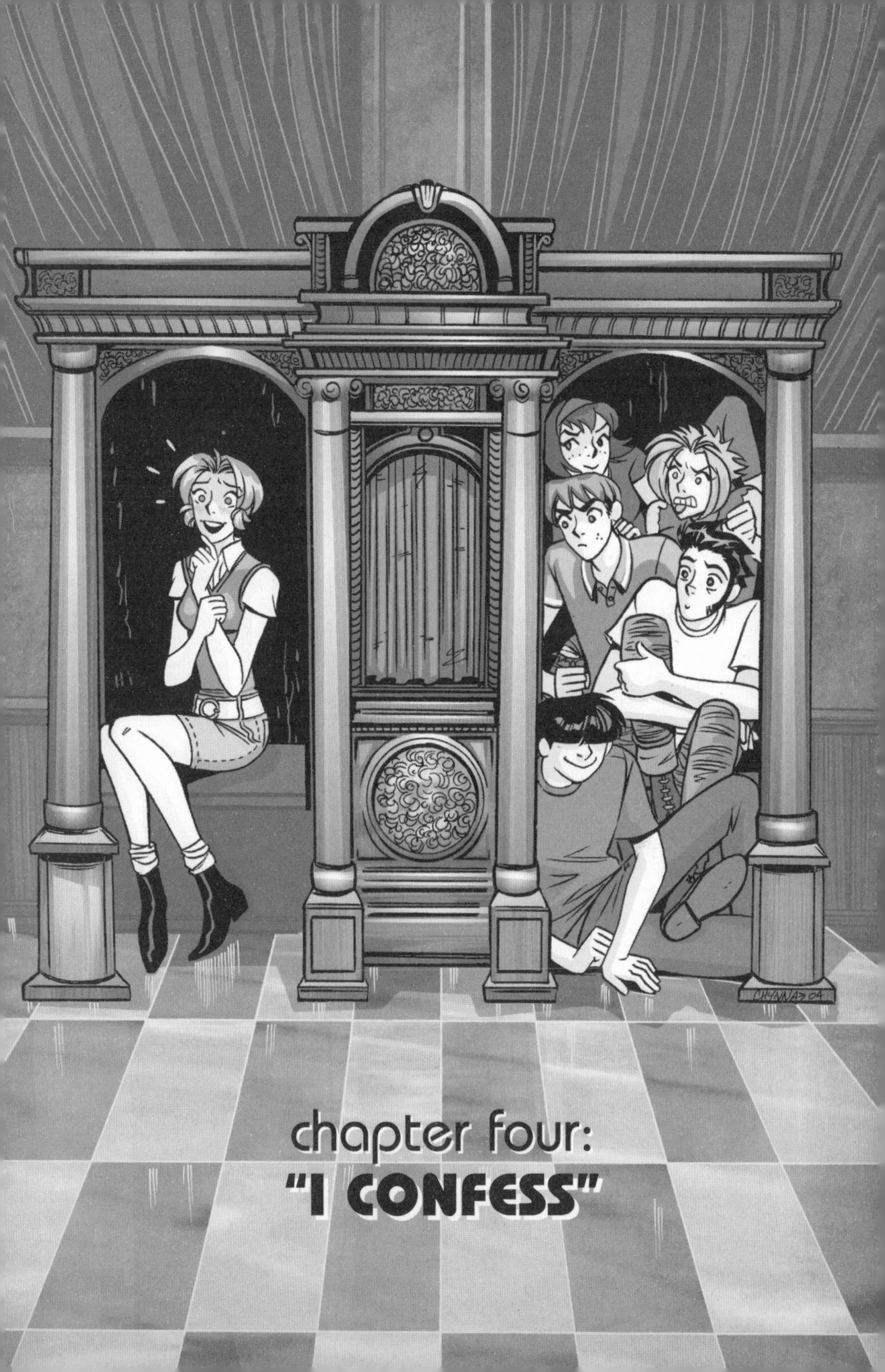

chapter four:
"I CONFESS"

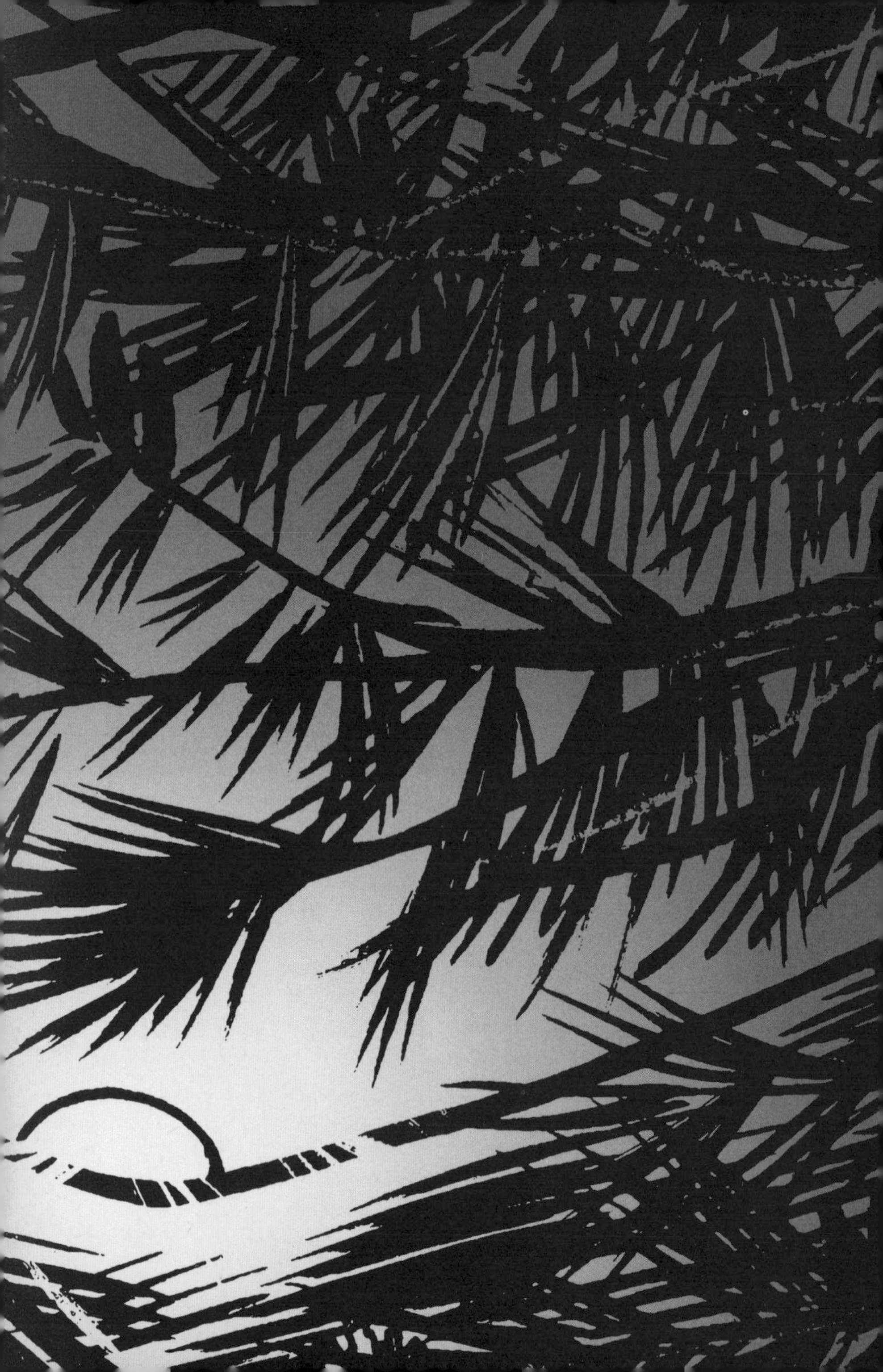

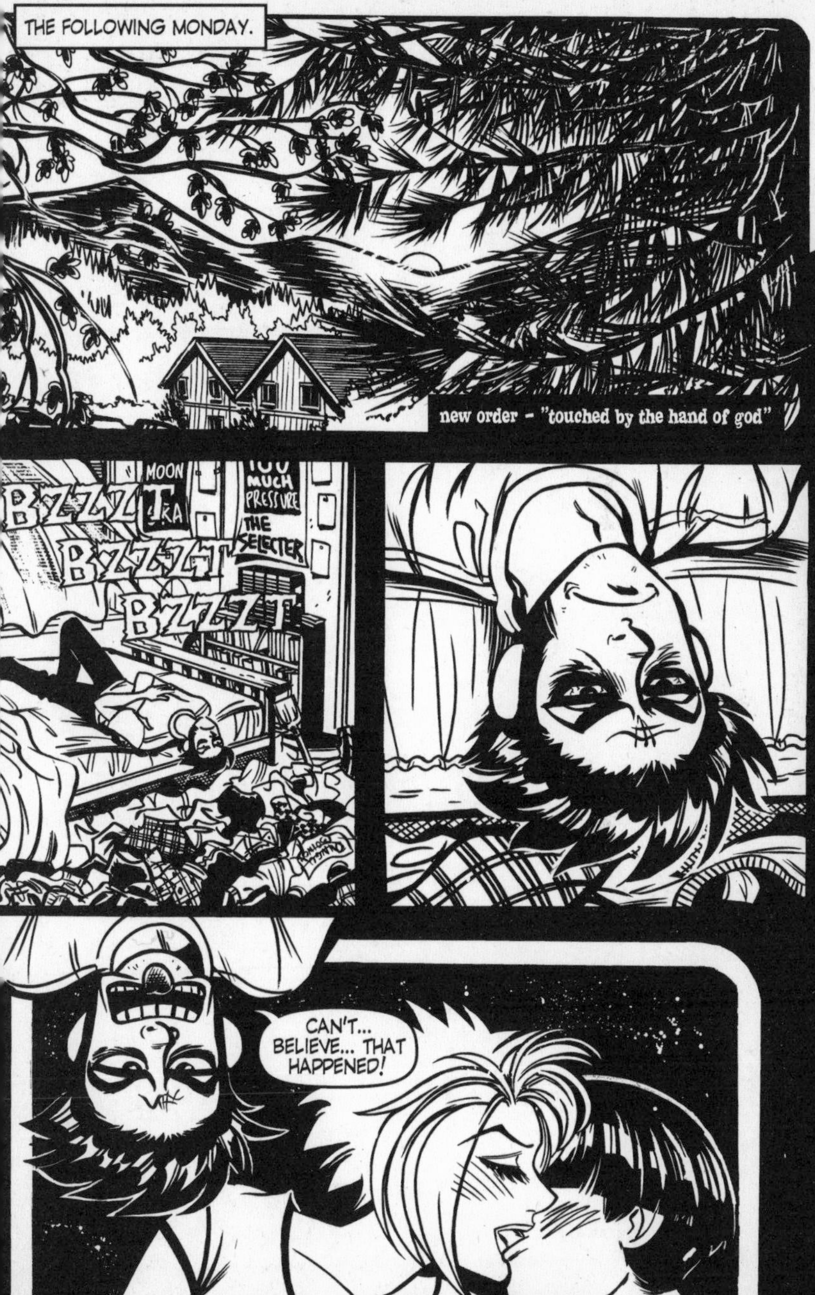
THE FOLLOWING MONDAY.
new order - "touched by the hand of god"
MOON
TRA
TOO MUCH PRESSURE
THE SELECTER
BZZZT
BZZZT
BZZZT
CAN'T... BELIEVE... THAT HAPPENED!

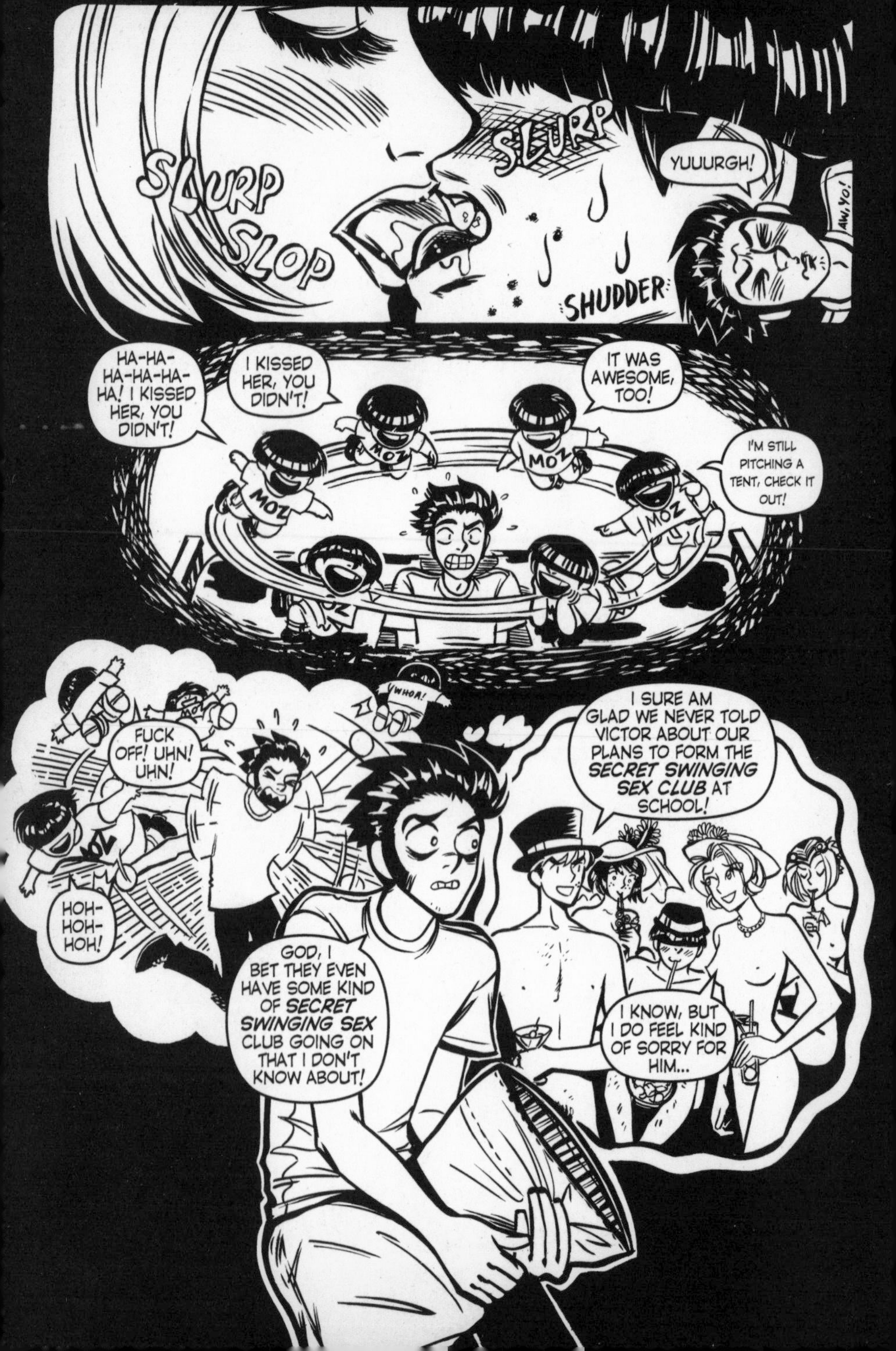
SLURP
SLOP
SLURP
YUUURGH!
AW, YO!
SHUDDER
HA-HA-HA-HA-HA-HA! I KISSED HER, YOU DIDN'T!
I KISSED HER, YOU DIDN'T!
IT WAS AWESOME, TOO!
I'M STILL PITCHING A TENT, CHECK IT OUT!
MOZ
WHOA!
FUCK OFF! UHN! UHN!
HOH-HOH-HOH!
I SURE AM GLAD WE NEVER TOLD VICTOR ABOUT OUR PLANS TO FORM THE SECRET SWINGING SEX CLUB AT SCHOOL!
GOD, I BET THEY EVEN HAVE SOME KIND OF SECRET SWINGING SEX CLUB GOING ON THAT I DON'T KNOW ABOUT!
I KNOW, BUT I DO FEEL KIND OF SORRY FOR HIM...

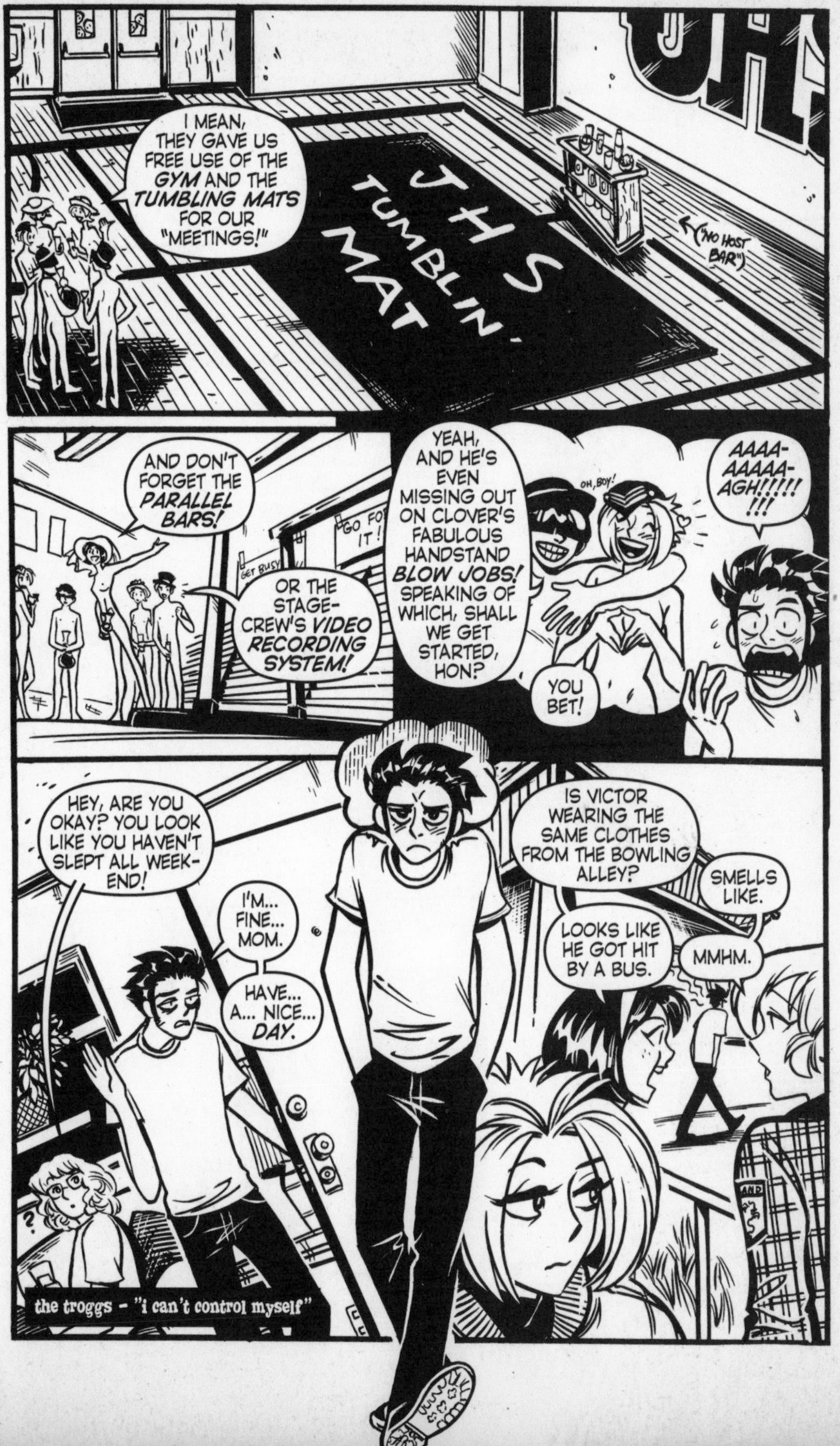
I MEAN, THEY GAVE US FREE USE OF THE GYM AND THE TUMBLING MATS FOR OUR "MEETINGS!"
JHS TUMBLIN' MAT
("NO HOST BAR")
AND DON'T FORGET THE PARALLEL BARS!
GO FOR IT!
GET BUSY
OR THE STAGE-CREW'S VIDEO RECORDING SYSTEM!
YEAH, AND HE'S EVEN MISSING OUT ON CLOVER'S FABULOUS HANDSTAND BLOW JOBS! SPEAKING OF WHICH, SHALL WE GET STARTED, HON?
OH, BOY!
YOU BET!
AAAA-AAAAA-AGH!!!!!!!!!
HEY, ARE YOU OKAY? YOU LOOK LIKE YOU HAVEN'T SLEPT ALL WEEK-END!
I'M... FINE... MOM.
HAVE... A... NICE... DAY.
IS VICTOR WEARING THE SAME CLOTHES FROM THE BOWLING ALLEY?
SMELLS LIKE.
LOOKS LIKE HE GOT HIT BY A BUS.
MMHM.
the troggs - "i can't control myself"

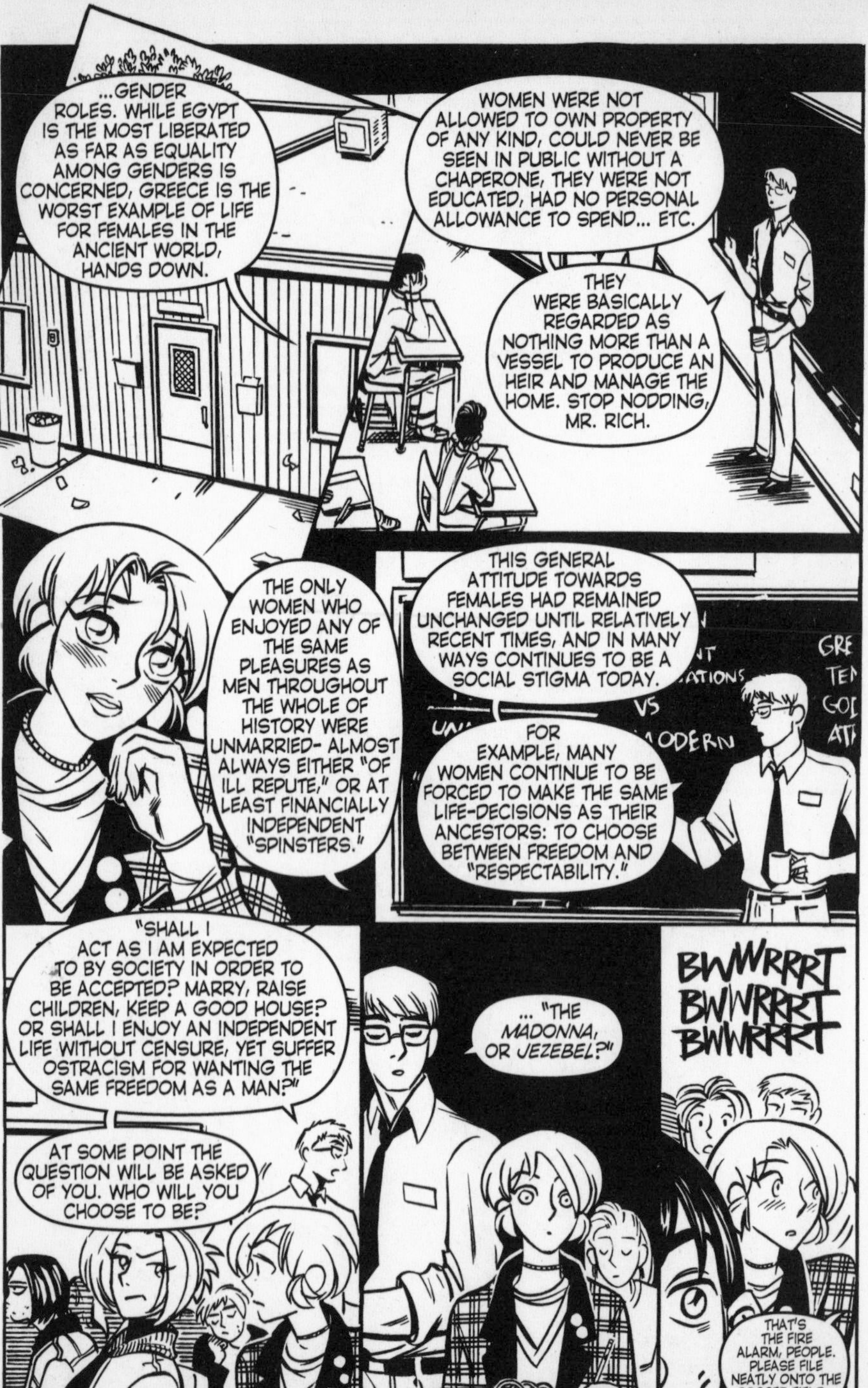
...GENDER ROLES. WHILE EGYPT IS THE MOST LIBERATED AS FAR AS EQUALITY AMONG GENDERS IS CONCERNED, GREECE IS THE WORST EXAMPLE OF LIFE FOR FEMALES IN THE ANCIENT WORLD, HANDS DOWN.
WOMEN WERE NOT ALLOWED TO OWN PROPERTY OF ANY KIND, COULD NEVER BE SEEN IN PUBLIC WITHOUT A CHAPERONE, THEY WERE NOT EDUCATED, HAD NO PERSONAL ALLOWANCE TO SPEND... ETC.
THEY WERE BASICALLY REGARDED AS NOTHING MORE THAN A VESSEL TO PRODUCE AN HEIR AND MANAGE THE HOME. STOP NODDING, MR. RICH.
THE ONLY WOMEN WHO ENJOYED ANY OF THE SAME PLEASURES AS MEN THROUGHOUT THE WHOLE OF HISTORY WERE UNMARRIED- ALMOST ALWAYS EITHER "OF ILL REPUTE," OR AT LEAST FINANCIALLY INDEPENDENT "SPINSTERS."
THIS GENERAL ATTITUDE TOWARDS FEMALES HAD REMAINED UNCHANGED UNTIL RELATIVELY RECENT TIMES, AND IN MANY WAYS CONTINUES TO BE A SOCIAL STIGMA TODAY.
FOR EXAMPLE, MANY WOMEN CONTINUE TO BE FORCED TO MAKE THE SAME LIFE-DECISIONS AS THEIR ANCESTORS: TO CHOOSE BETWEEN FREEDOM AND "RESPECTABILITY."
"SHALL I ACT AS I AM EXPECTED TO BY SOCIETY IN ORDER TO BE ACCEPTED? MARRY, RAISE CHILDREN, KEEP A GOOD HOUSE? OR SHALL I ENJOY AN INDEPENDENT LIFE WITHOUT CENSURE, YET SUFFER OSTRACISM FOR WANTING THE SAME FREEDOM AS A MAN?"
AT SOME POINT THE QUESTION WILL BE ASKED OF YOU. WHO WILL YOU CHOOSE TO BE?
... "THE *MADONNA*, OR *JEZEBEL*?"
BWWRRRT BWWRRRT BWWRRRT
THAT'S THE FIRE ALARM, PEOPLE. PLEASE FILE NEATLY ONTO THE SOCCER FIELD...

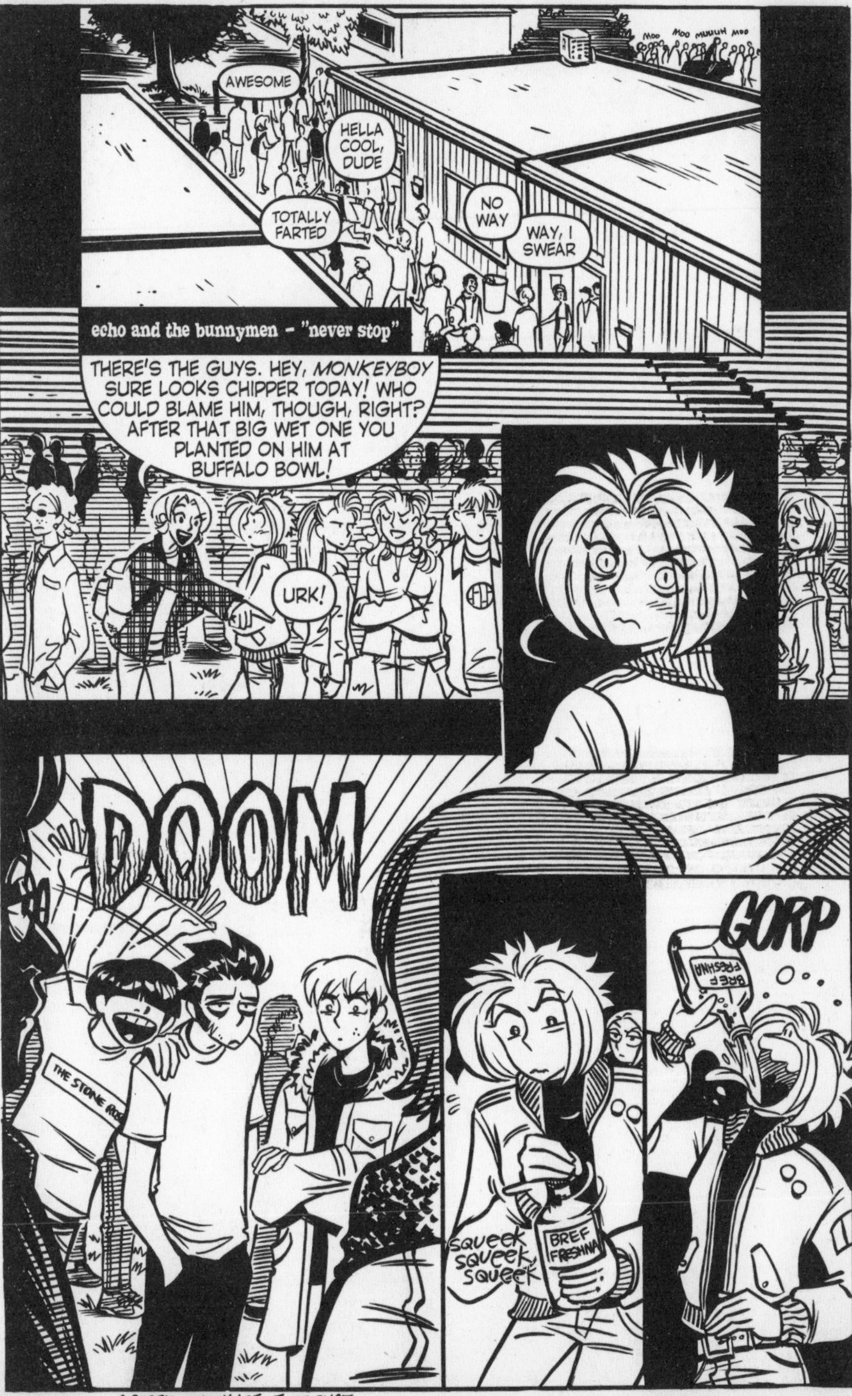
MOO MOO MUUUH MOO
AWESOME
HELLA COOL, DUDE
TOTALLY FARTED
NO WAY
WAY, I SWEAR
echo and the bunnymen - "never stop"
THERE'S THE GUYS. HEY, MONKEYBOY SURE LOOKS CHIPPER TODAY! WHO COULD BLAME HIM, THOUGH, RIGHT? AFTER THAT BIG WET ONE YOU PLANTED ON HIM AT BUFFALO BOWL!
URK!
DOOM
THE STONE RO
squeek squeek squeek
BREF FRESHNA
GORP

A SORRY LOOKIN' LOT, TO BE SURE.

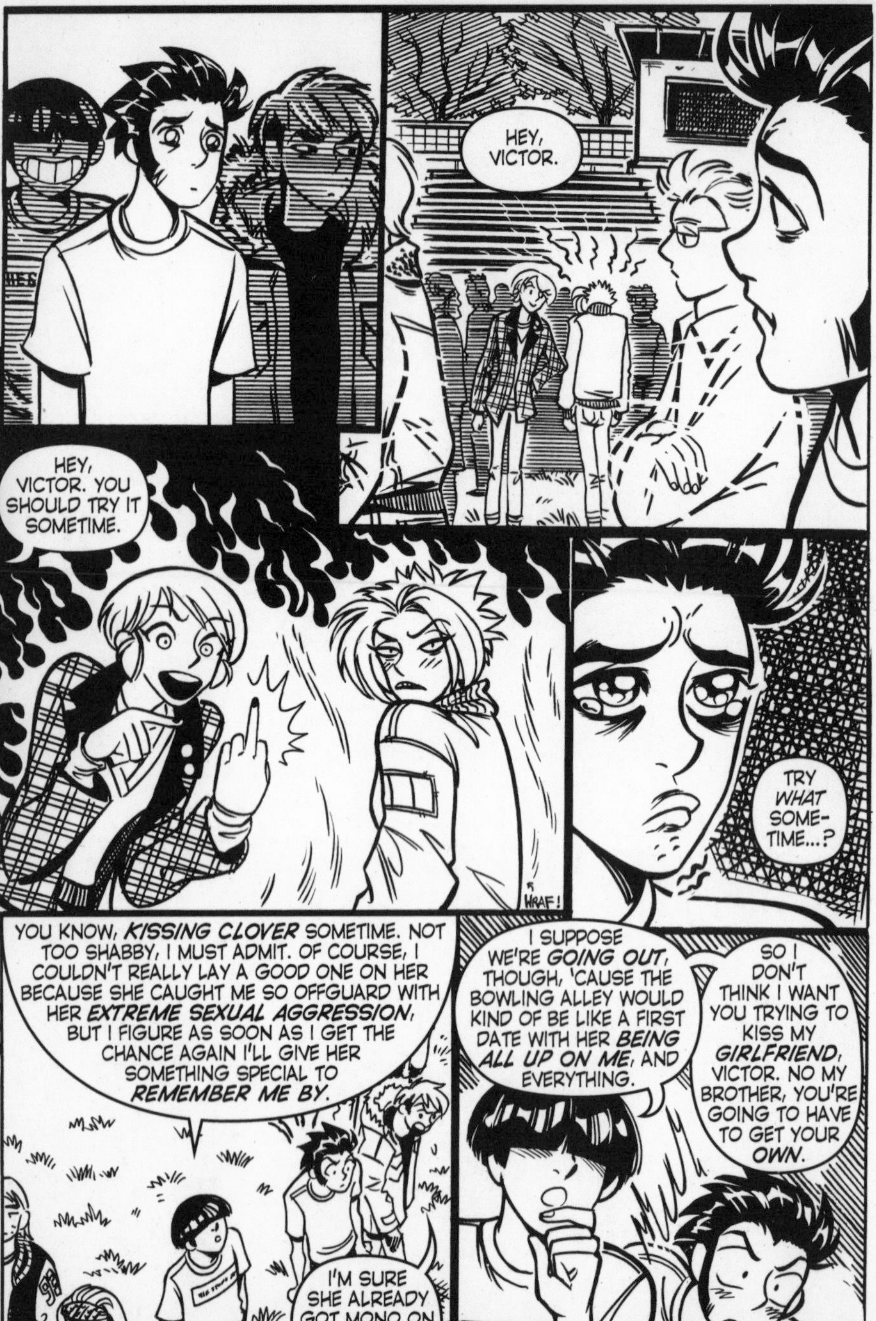
HEY, VICTOR.
HEY, VICTOR. YOU SHOULD TRY IT SOMETIME.
WRAF!
TRY *WHAT* SOME-TIME...?
YOU KNOW, ***KISSING CLOVER*** SOMETIME. NOT TOO SHABBY, I MUST ADMIT. OF COURSE, I COULDN'T REALLY LAY A GOOD ONE ON HER BECAUSE SHE CAUGHT ME SO OFFGUARD WITH HER ***EXTREME SEXUAL AGGRESSION***, BUT I FIGURE AS SOON AS I GET THE CHANCE AGAIN I'LL GIVE HER SOMETHING SPECIAL TO ***REMEMBER ME BY***.
I'M SURE SHE ALREADY GOT MONO ON SATURDAY, ***ASS HEAD***.
I SUPPOSE WE'RE ***GOING OUT***, THOUGH, 'CAUSE THE BOWLING ALLEY WOULD KIND OF BE LIKE A FIRST DATE WITH HER ***BEING ALL UP ON ME***, AND EVERYTHING.
SO I DON'T THINK I WANT YOU TRYING TO KISS MY ***GIRLFRIEND***, VICTOR. NO MY BROTHER, YOU'RE GOING TO HAVE TO GET YOUR ***OWN***.

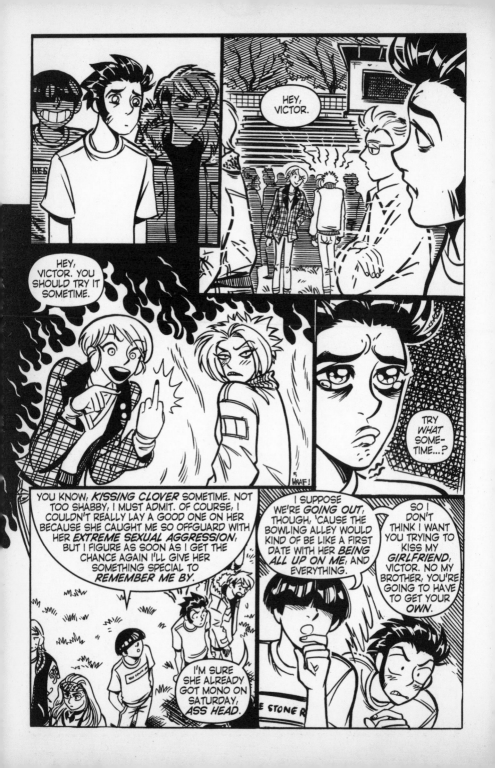

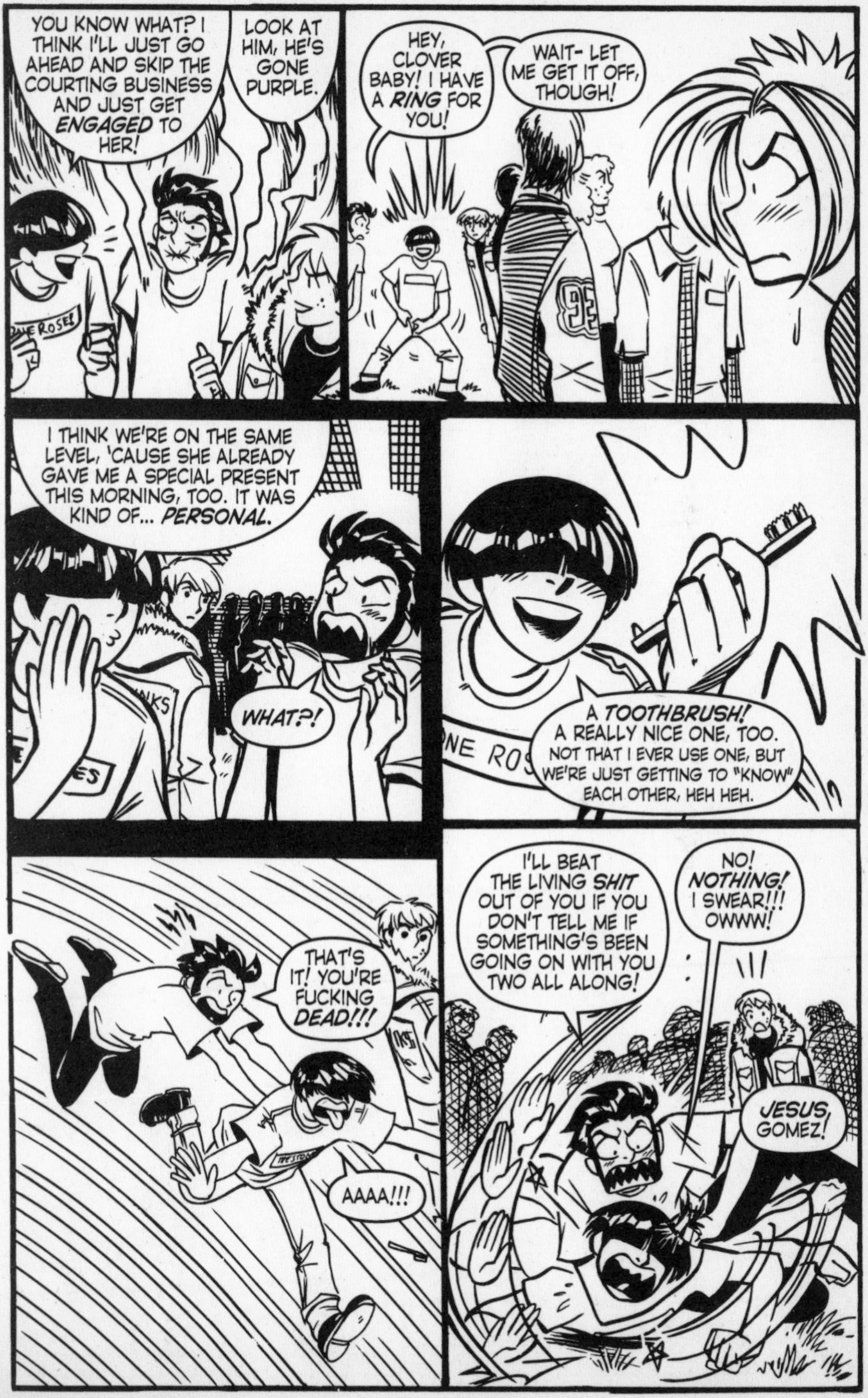
YOU KNOW WHAT? I THINK I'LL JUST GO AHEAD AND SKIP THE COURTING BUSINESS AND JUST GET ENGAGED TO HER!
LOOK AT HIM, HE'S GONE PURPLE.
HEY, CLOVER BABY! I HAVE A RING FOR YOU!
WAIT- LET ME GET IT OFF, THOUGH!
I THINK WE'RE ON THE SAME LEVEL, 'CAUSE SHE ALREADY GAVE ME A SPECIAL PRESENT THIS MORNING, TOO. IT WAS KIND OF... PERSONAL.
WHAT?!
A TOOTHBRUSH! A REALLY NICE ONE, TOO. NOT THAT I EVER USE ONE, BUT WE'RE JUST GETTING TO "KNOW" EACH OTHER, HEH HEH.
THAT'S IT! YOU'RE FUCKING DEAD!!!
AAAA!!!
I'LL BEAT THE LIVING SHIT OUT OF YOU IF YOU DON'T TELL ME IF SOMETHING'S BEEN GOING ON WITH YOU TWO ALL ALONG!
NO! NOTHING! I SWEAR!!! OWWW!
JESUS, GOMEZ!

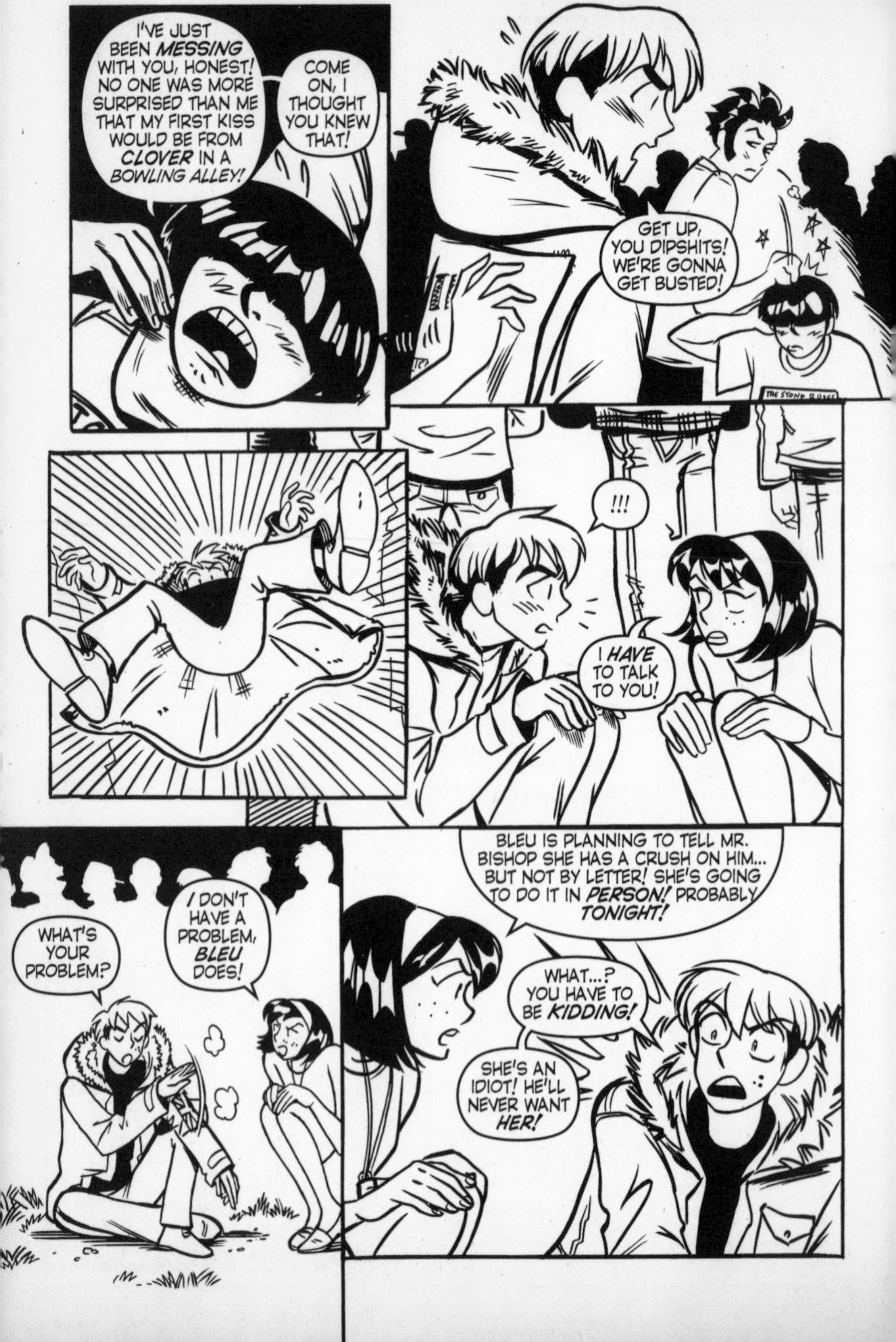

I'VE JUST BEEN MESSING WITH YOU, HONEST! NO ONE WAS MORE SURPRISED THAN ME THAT MY FIRST KISS WOULD BE FROM CLOVER IN A BOWLING ALLEY!
COME ON, I THOUGHT YOU KNEW THAT!
GET UP, YOU DIPSHITS! WE'RE GONNA GET BUSTED!
THE STONE ROSES
!!!
I HAVE TO TALK TO YOU!
WHAT'S YOUR PROBLEM?
I DON'T HAVE A PROBLEM, BLEU DOES!
BLEU IS PLANNING TO TELL MR. BISHOP SHE HAS A CRUSH ON HIM... BUT NOT BY LETTER! SHE'S GOING TO DO IT IN PERSON! PROBABLY TONIGHT!
WHAT...? YOU HAVE TO BE KIDDING!
SHE'S AN IDIOT! HE'LL NEVER WANT HER!

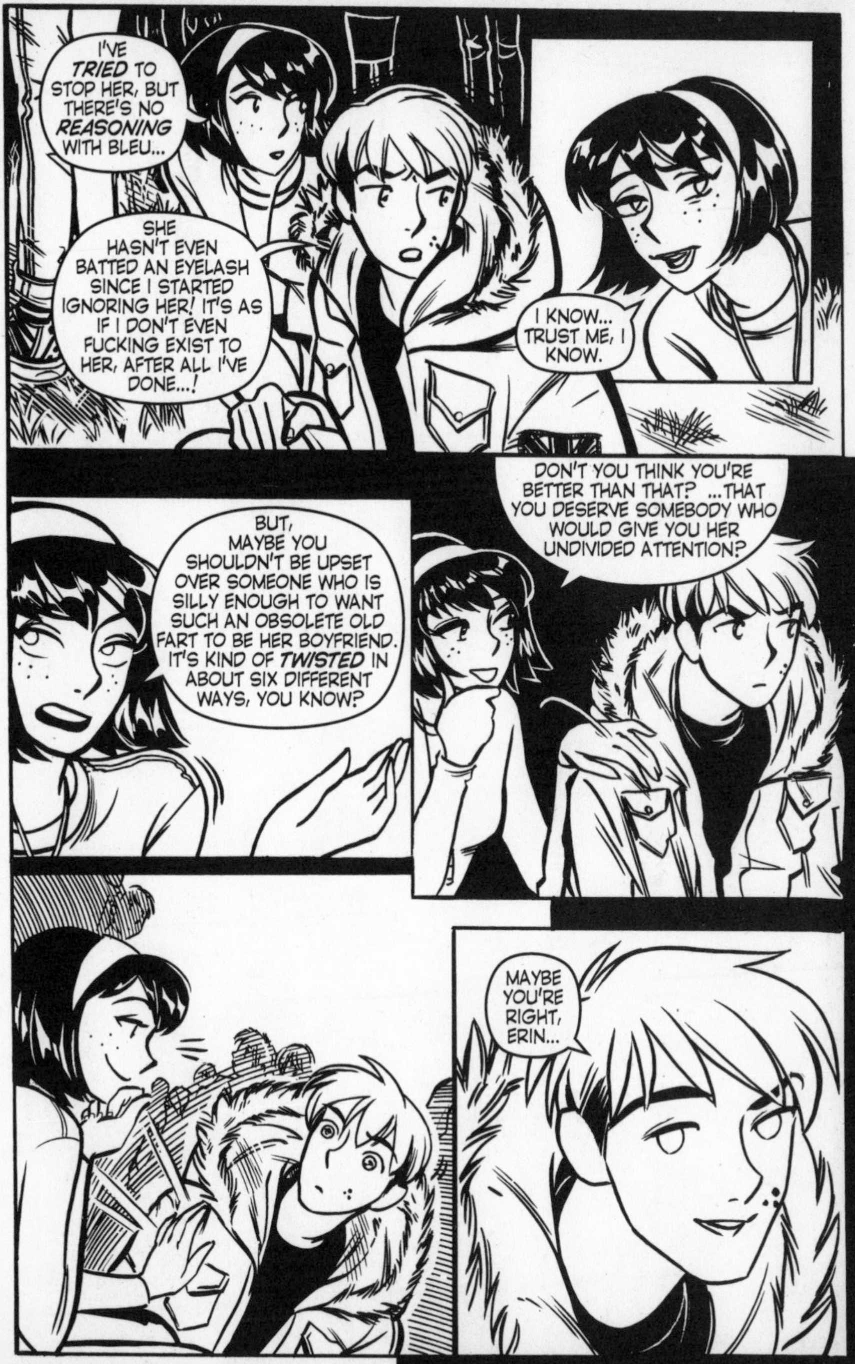
I'VE TRIED TO STOP HER, BUT THERE'S NO REASONING WITH BLEU...
SHE HASN'T EVEN BATTED AN EYELASH SINCE I STARTED IGNORING HER! IT'S AS IF I DON'T EVEN FUCKING EXIST TO HER, AFTER ALL I'VE DONE...!
I KNOW... TRUST ME, I KNOW.
BUT, MAYBE YOU SHOULDN'T BE UPSET OVER SOMEONE WHO IS SILLY ENOUGH TO WANT SUCH AN OBSOLETE OLD FART TO BE HER BOYFRIEND. IT'S KIND OF TWISTED IN ABOUT SIX DIFFERENT WAYS, YOU KNOW?
DON'T YOU THINK YOU'RE BETTER THAN THAT? ...THAT YOU DESERVE SOMEBODY WHO WOULD GIVE YOU HER UNDIVIDED ATTENTION?
MAYBE YOU'RE RIGHT, ERIN...

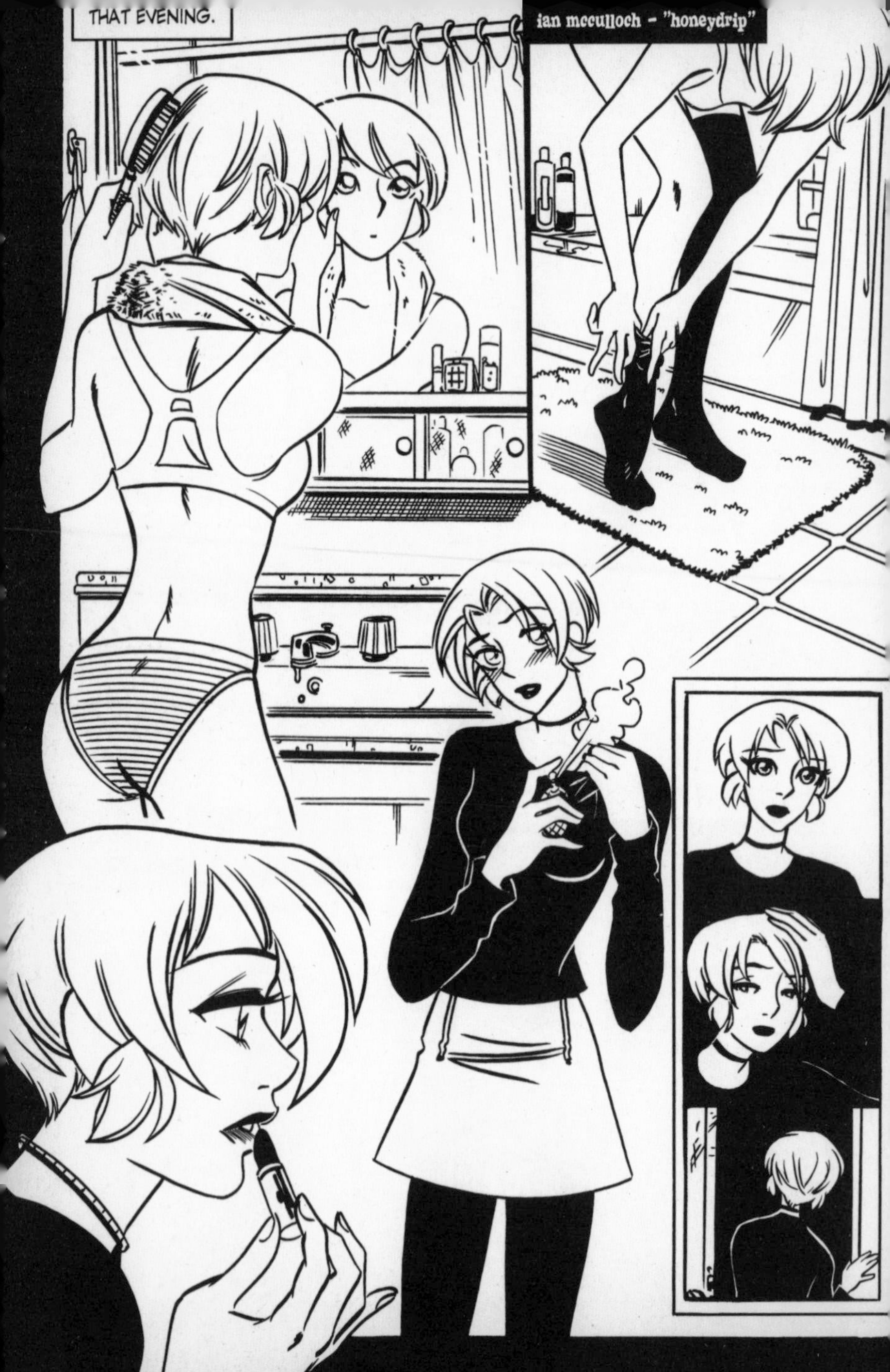

THAT EVENING.
ian mcculloch - "honeydrip"

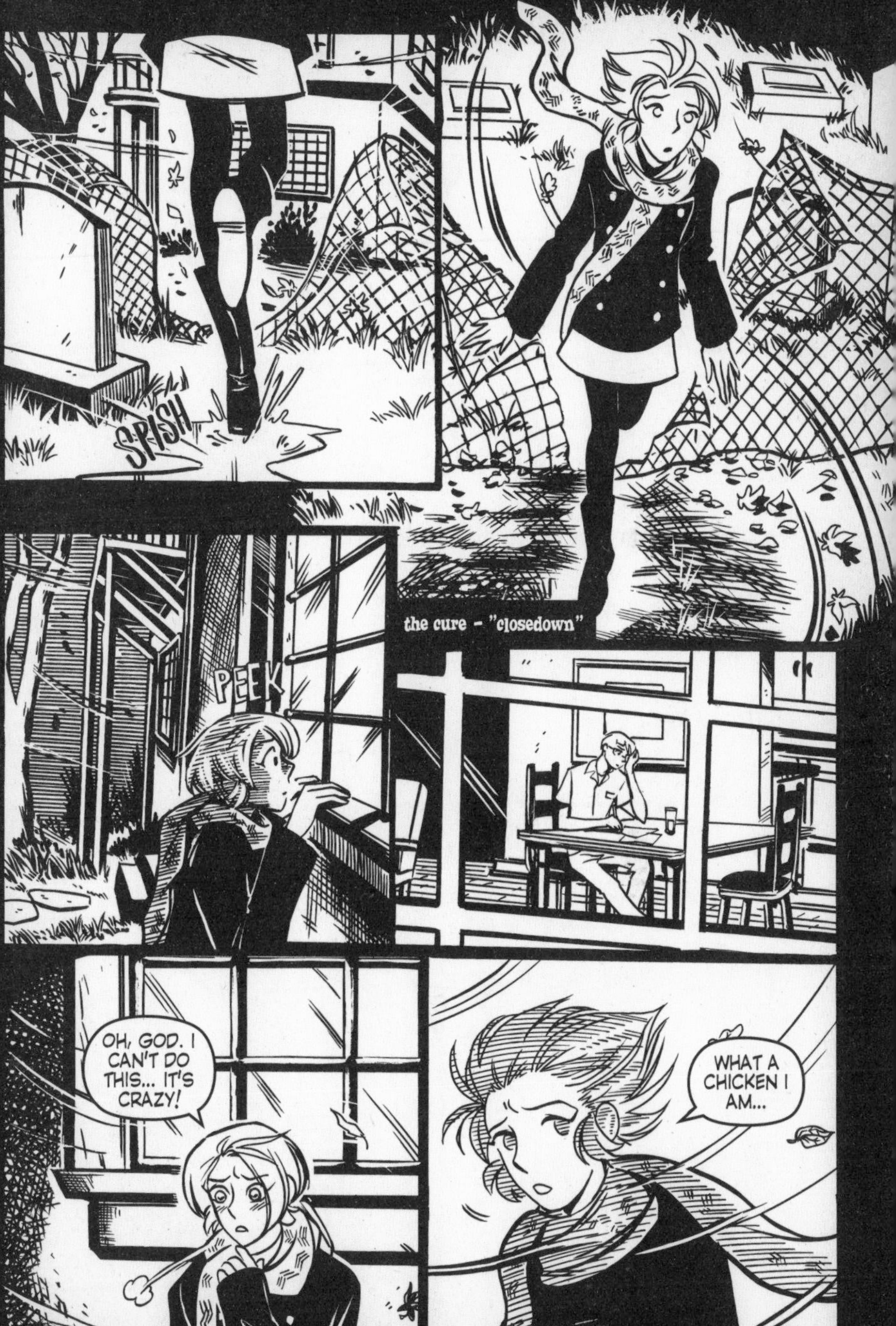
SPISH
the cure - "closedown"
PEEK
OH, GOD. I CAN'T DO THIS... IT'S CRAZY!
WHAT A CHICKEN I AM...

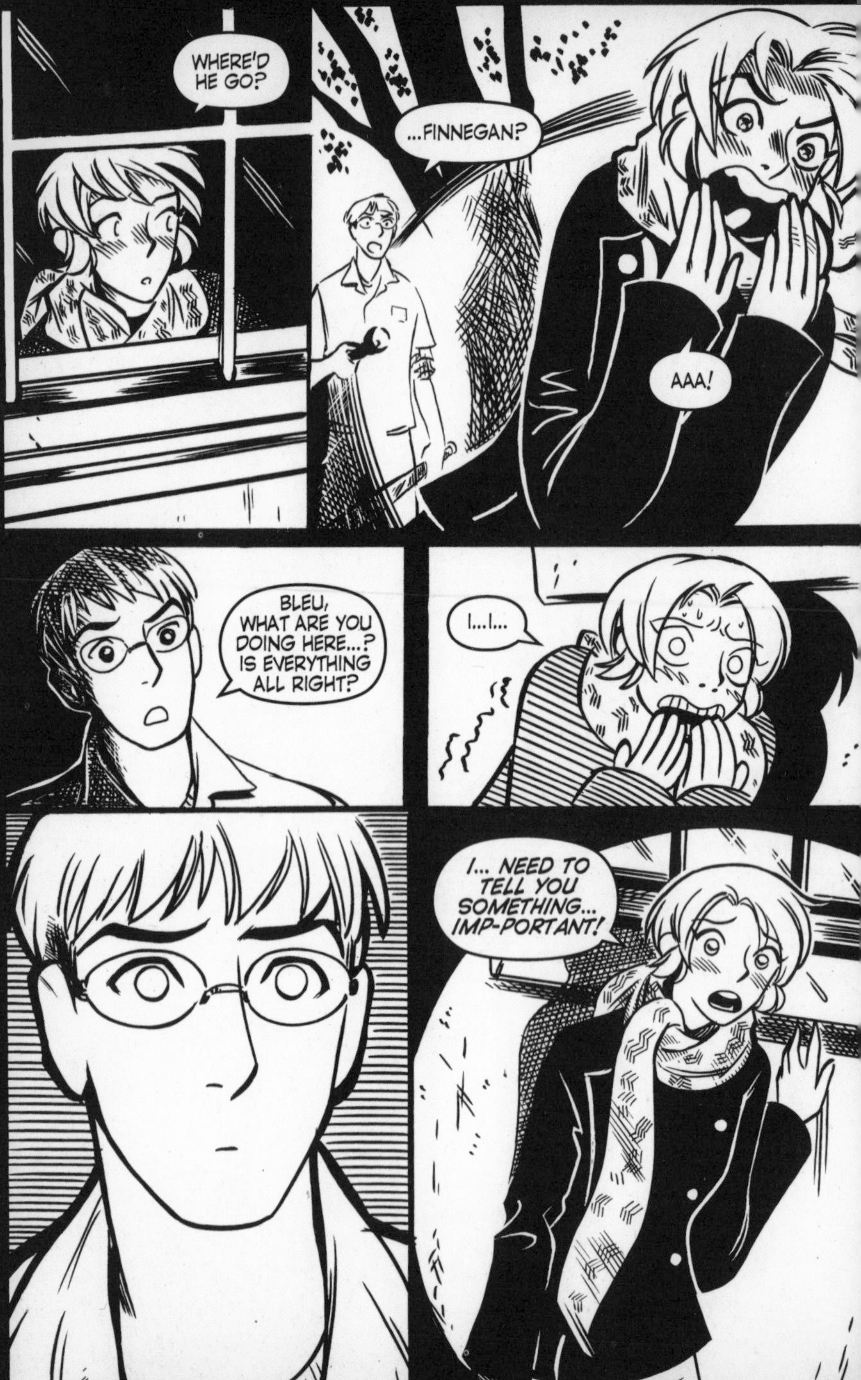
WHERE'D HE GO?
...FINNEGAN?
AAA!
BLEU, WHAT ARE YOU DOING HERE...? IS EVERYTHING ALL RIGHT?
I...I...
I... NEED TO TELL YOU SOMETHING... IMP-PORTANT!

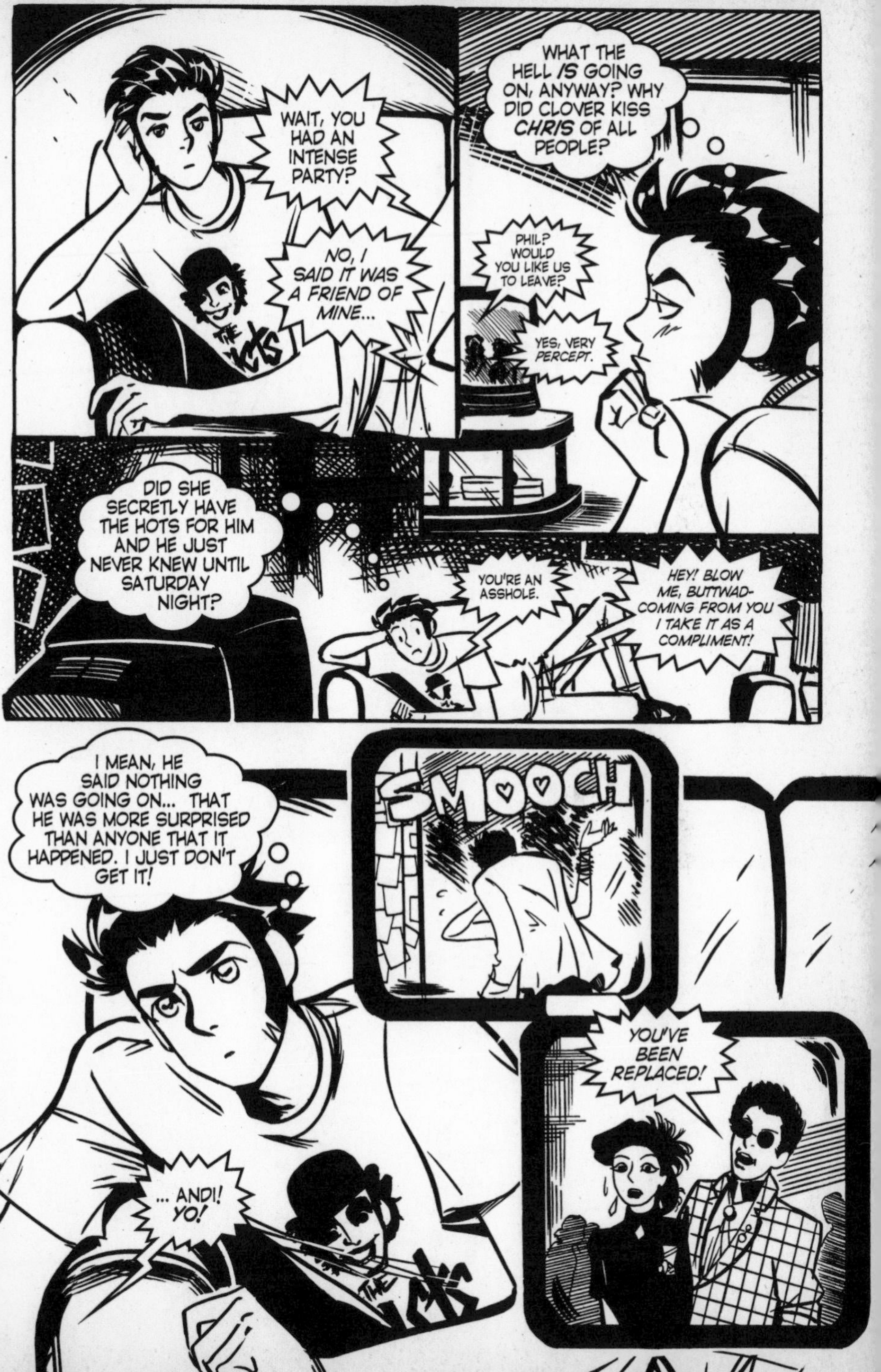
WAIT, YOU HAD AN INTENSE PARTY?
NO, I SAID IT WAS A FRIEND OF MINE...
WHAT THE HELL IS GOING ON, ANYWAY? WHY DID CLOVER KISS CHRIS OF ALL PEOPLE?
PHIL? WOULD YOU LIKE US TO LEAVE?
YES, VERY PERCEPT.
DID SHE SECRETLY HAVE THE HOTS FOR HIM AND HE JUST NEVER KNEW UNTIL SATURDAY NIGHT?
YOU'RE AN ASSHOLE.
HEY! BLOW ME, BUTTWAD-COMING FROM YOU I TAKE IT AS A COMPLIMENT!
I MEAN, HE SAID NOTHING WAS GOING ON... THAT HE WAS MORE SURPRISED THAN ANYONE THAT IT HAPPENED. I JUST DON'T GET IT!
SMOOCH
YOU'VE BEEN REPLACED!
... ANDI! YO!

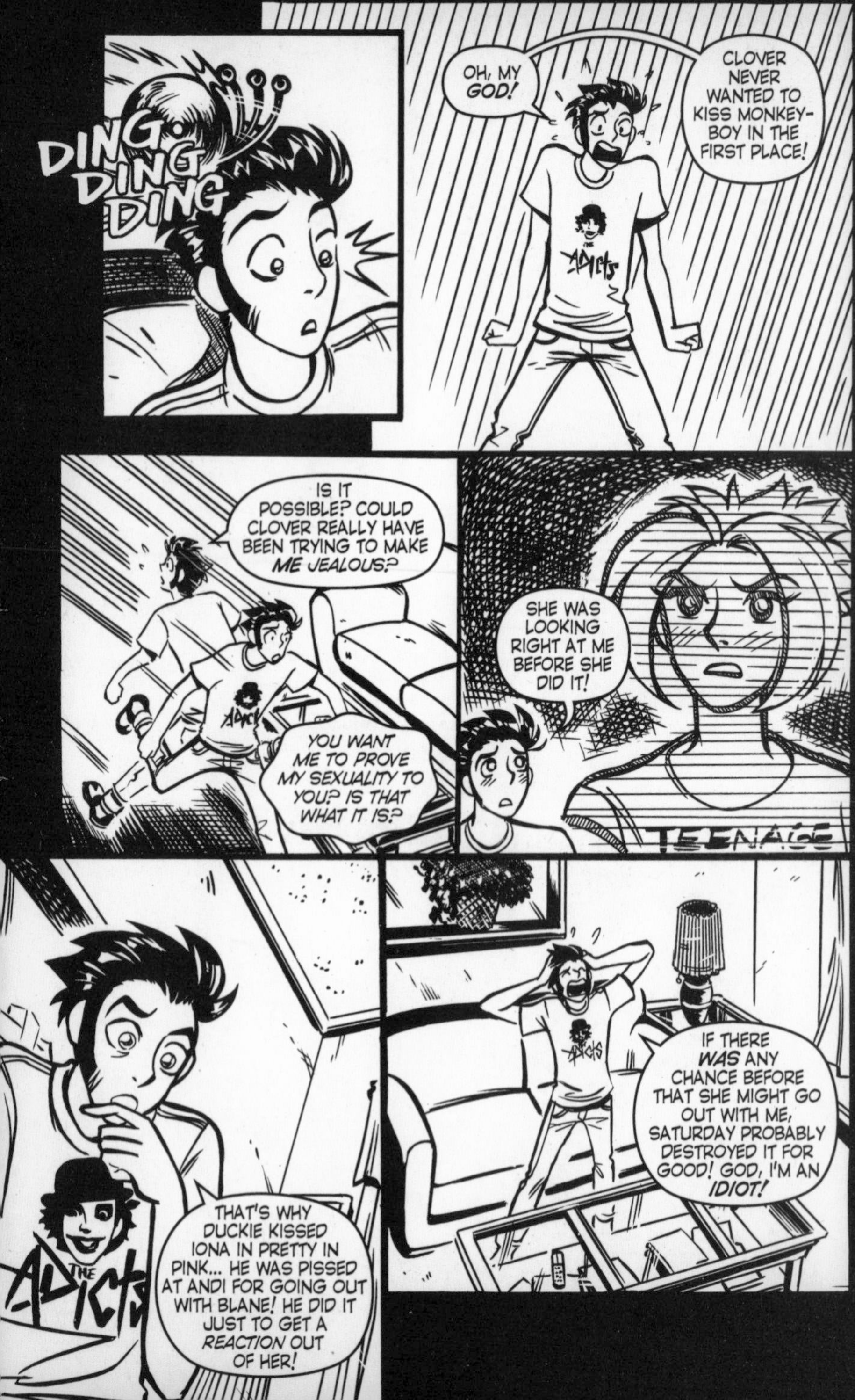
DING DING DING
OH, MY GOD!
CLOVER NEVER WANTED TO KISS MONKEY-BOY IN THE FIRST PLACE!
IS IT POSSIBLE? COULD CLOVER REALLY HAVE BEEN TRYING TO MAKE ME JEALOUS?
YOU WANT ME TO PROVE MY SEXUALITY TO YOU? IS THAT WHAT IT IS?
SHE WAS LOOKING RIGHT AT ME BEFORE SHE DID IT!
TEENAGE
THAT'S WHY DUCKIE KISSED IONA IN PRETTY IN PINK... HE WAS PISSED AT ANDI FOR GOING OUT WITH BLANE! HE DID IT JUST TO GET A REACTION OUT OF HER!
IF THERE WAS ANY CHANCE BEFORE THAT SHE MIGHT GO OUT WITH ME, SATURDAY PROBABLY DESTROYED IT FOR GOOD! GOD, I'M AN IDIOT!

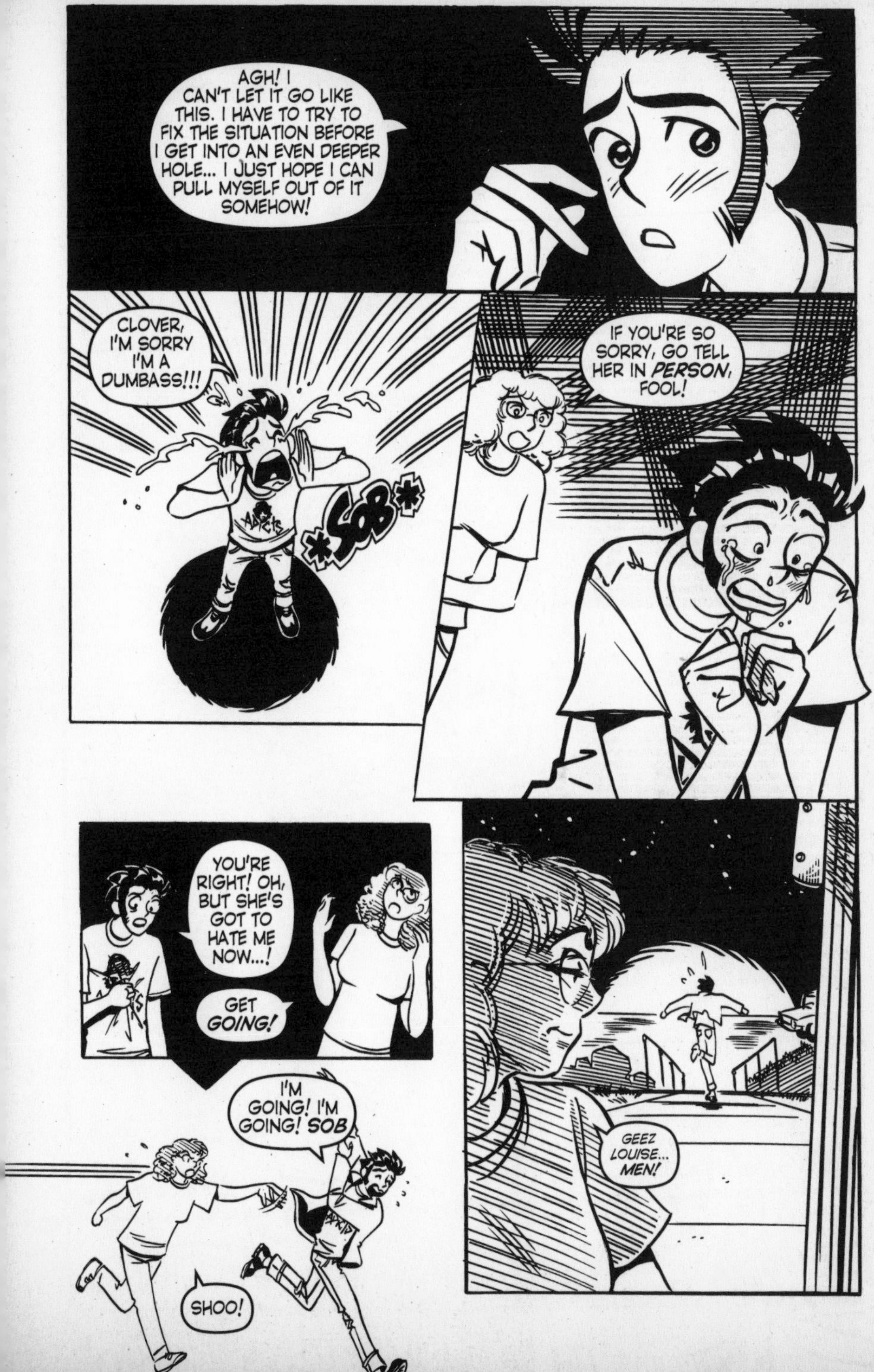
AGH! I CAN'T LET IT GO LIKE THIS. I HAVE TO TRY TO FIX THE SITUATION BEFORE I GET INTO AN EVEN DEEPER HOLE... I JUST HOPE I CAN PULL MYSELF OUT OF IT SOMEHOW!
CLOVER, I'M SORRY I'M A DUMBASS!!!
SOB
IF YOU'RE SO SORRY, GO TELL HER IN *PERSON*, FOOL!
YOU'RE RIGHT! OH, BUT SHE'S GOT TO HATE ME NOW...!
GET *GOING!*
I'M GOING! I'M GOING! *SOB*
SHOO!
GEEZ LOUISE... *MEN!*

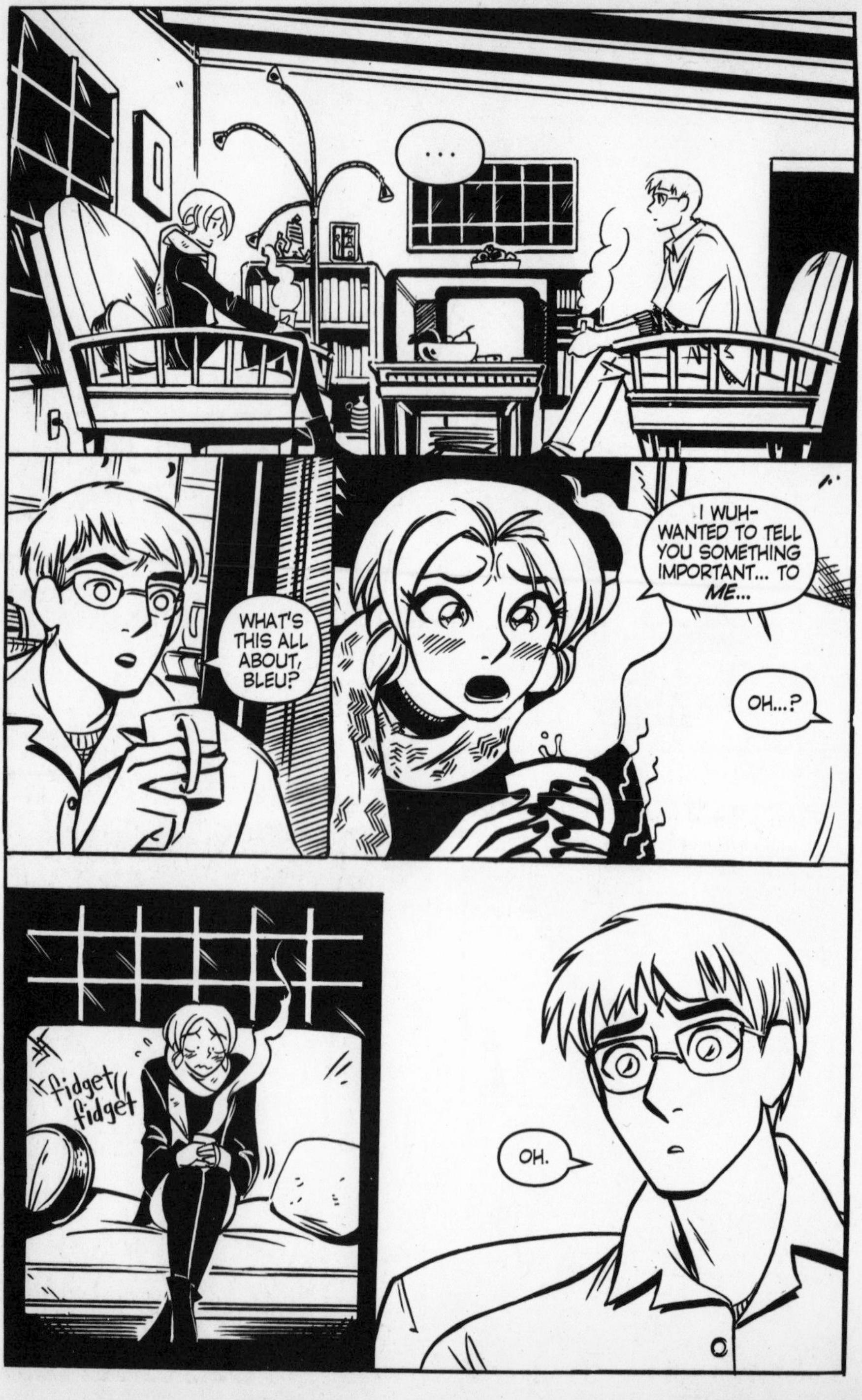
...
WHAT'S THIS ALL ABOUT, BLEU?
I WUH- WANTED TO TELL YOU SOMETHING IMPORTANT... TO ME...
OH...?
fidget fidget
OH.

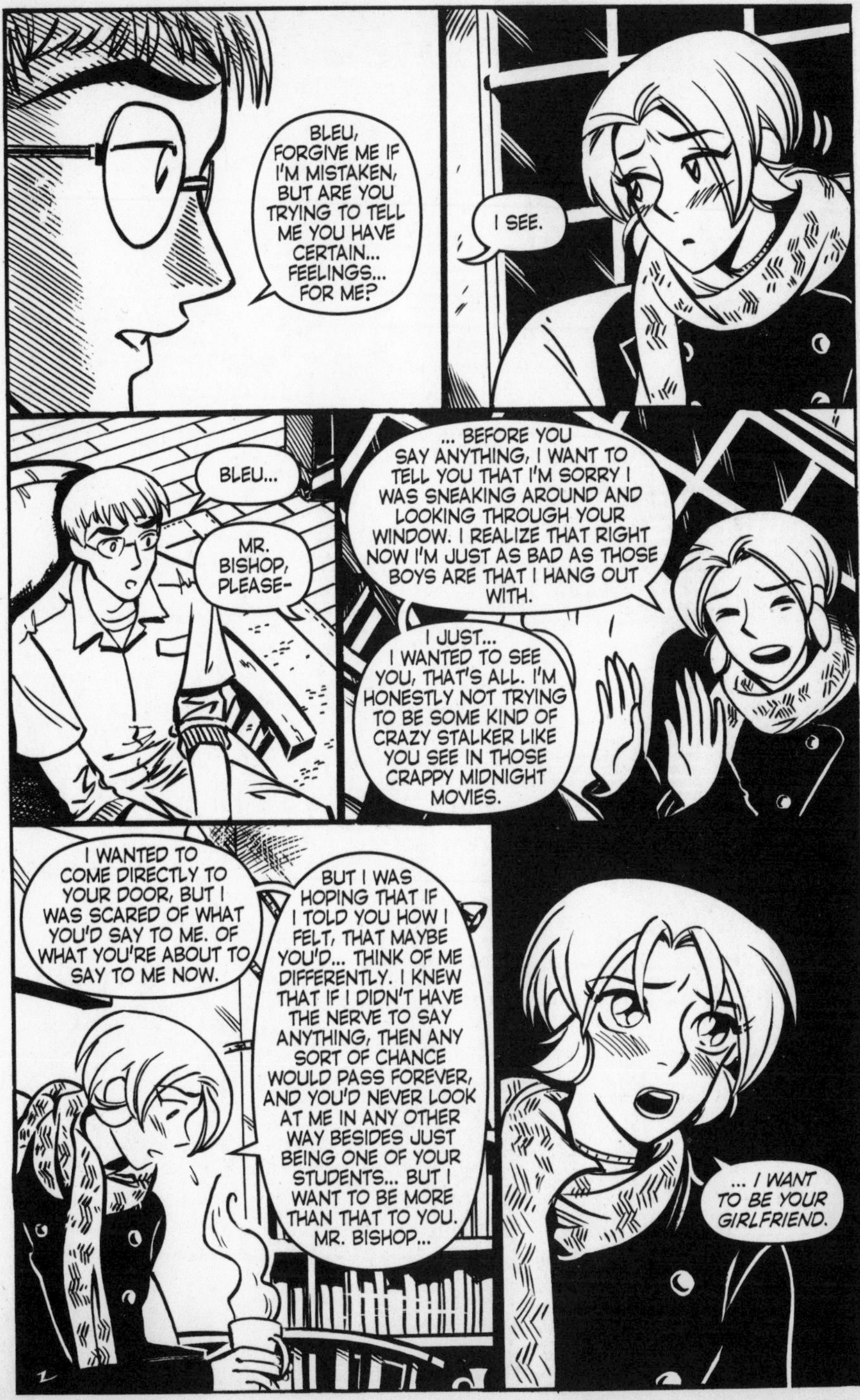
BLEU, FORGIVE ME IF I'M MISTAKEN, BUT ARE YOU TRYING TO TELL ME YOU HAVE CERTAIN... FEELINGS... FOR ME?
I SEE.
BLEU...
MR. BISHOP, PLEASE-
... BEFORE YOU SAY ANYTHING, I WANT TO TELL YOU THAT I'M SORRY I WAS SNEAKING AROUND AND LOOKING THROUGH YOUR WINDOW. I REALIZE THAT RIGHT NOW I'M JUST AS BAD AS THOSE BOYS ARE THAT I HANG OUT WITH.
I JUST... I WANTED TO SEE YOU, THAT'S ALL. I'M HONESTLY NOT TRYING TO BE SOME KIND OF CRAZY STALKER LIKE YOU SEE IN THOSE CRAPPY MIDNIGHT MOVIES.
I WANTED TO COME DIRECTLY TO YOUR DOOR, BUT I WAS SCARED OF WHAT YOU'D SAY TO ME. OF WHAT YOU'RE ABOUT TO SAY TO ME NOW.
BUT I WAS HOPING THAT IF I TOLD YOU HOW I FELT, THAT MAYBE YOU'D... THINK OF ME DIFFERENTLY. I KNEW THAT IF I DIDN'T HAVE THE NERVE TO SAY ANYTHING, THEN ANY SORT OF CHANCE WOULD PASS FOREVER, AND YOU'D NEVER LOOK AT ME IN ANY OTHER WAY BESIDES JUST BEING ONE OF YOUR STUDENTS... BUT I WANT TO BE MORE THAN THAT TO YOU. MR. BISHOP...
... I WANT TO BE YOUR GIRLFRIEND.

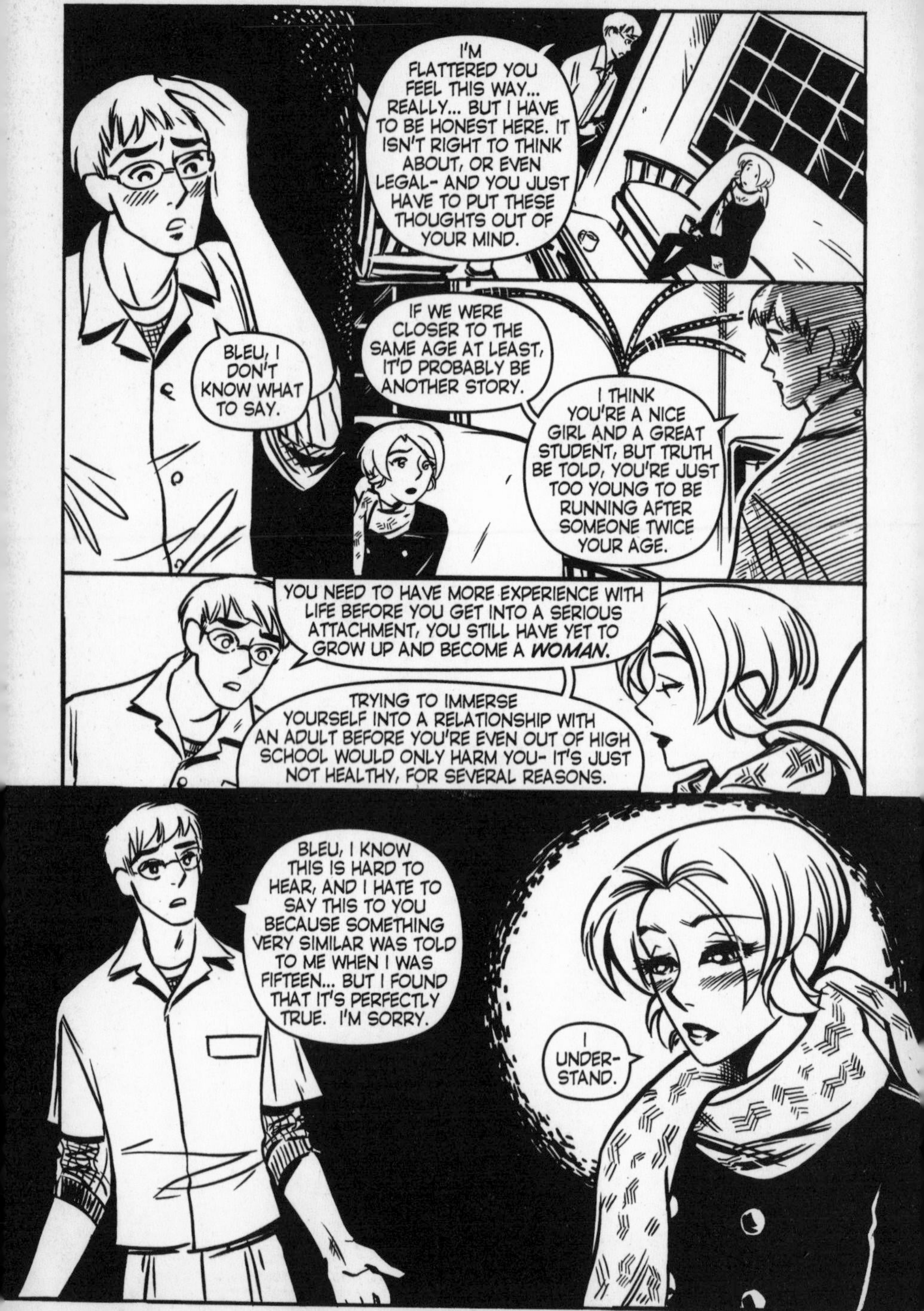
I'M FLATTERED YOU FEEL THIS WAY... REALLY... BUT I HAVE TO BE HONEST HERE. IT ISN'T RIGHT TO THINK ABOUT, OR EVEN LEGAL- AND YOU JUST HAVE TO PUT THESE THOUGHTS OUT OF YOUR MIND.
BLEU, I DON'T KNOW WHAT TO SAY.
IF WE WERE CLOSER TO THE SAME AGE AT LEAST, IT'D PROBABLY BE ANOTHER STORY.
I THINK YOU'RE A NICE GIRL AND A GREAT STUDENT, BUT TRUTH BE TOLD, YOU'RE JUST TOO YOUNG TO BE RUNNING AFTER SOMEONE TWICE YOUR AGE.
YOU NEED TO HAVE MORE EXPERIENCE WITH LIFE BEFORE YOU GET INTO A SERIOUS ATTACHMENT, YOU STILL HAVE YET TO GROW UP AND BECOME A *WOMAN*.
TRYING TO IMMERSE YOURSELF INTO A RELATIONSHIP WITH AN ADULT BEFORE YOU'RE EVEN OUT OF HIGH SCHOOL WOULD ONLY HARM YOU- IT'S JUST NOT HEALTHY, FOR SEVERAL REASONS.
BLEU, I KNOW THIS IS HARD TO HEAR, AND I HATE TO SAY THIS TO YOU BECAUSE SOMETHING VERY SIMILAR WAS TOLD TO ME WHEN I WAS FIFTEEN... BUT I FOUND THAT IT'S PERFECTLY TRUE. I'M SORRY.
I UNDER-STAND.

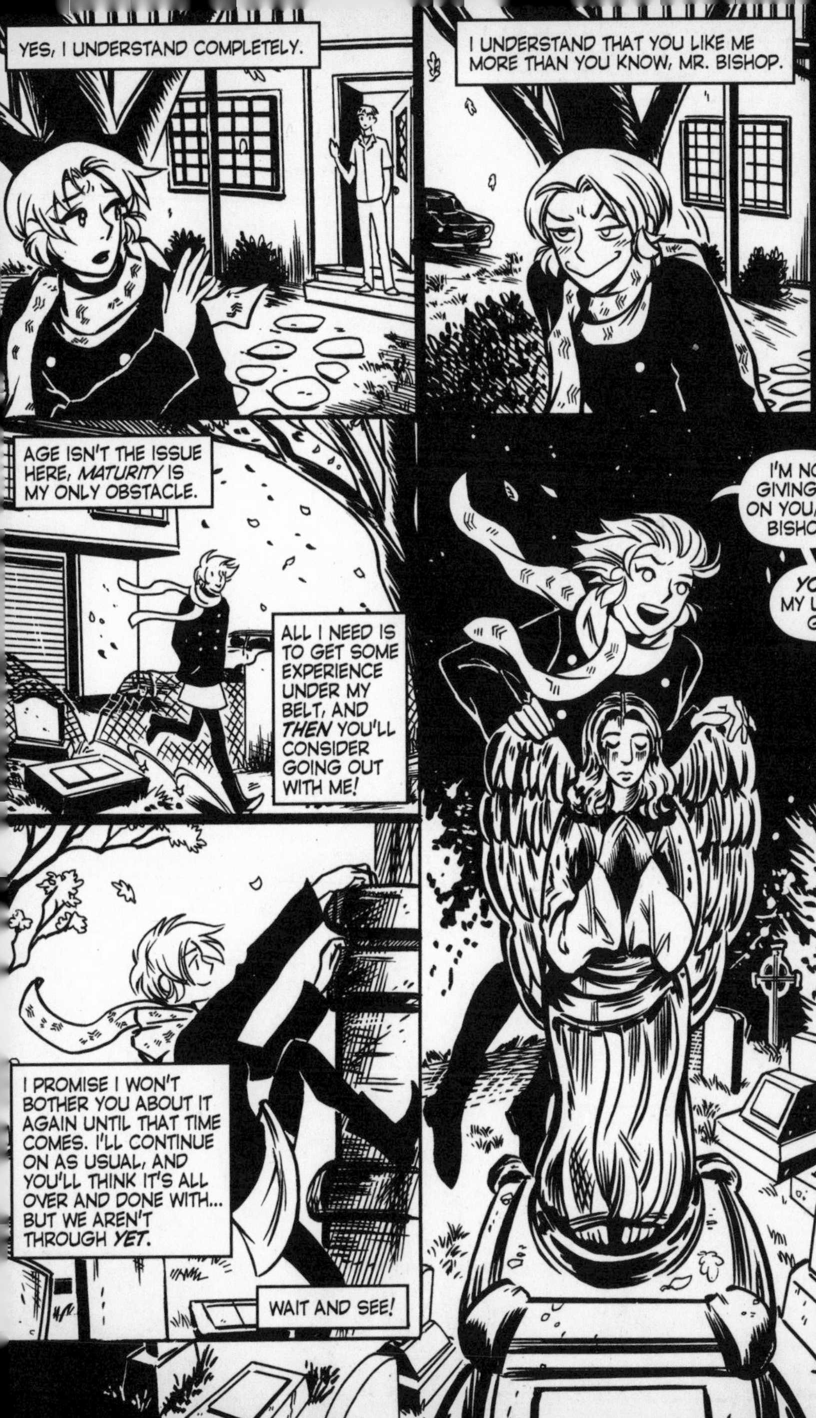
YES, I UNDERSTAND COMPLETELY.
I UNDERSTAND THAT YOU LIKE ME MORE THAN YOU KNOW, MR. BISHOP.
AGE ISN'T THE ISSUE HERE, *MATURITY* IS MY ONLY OBSTACLE.
ALL I NEED IS TO GET SOME EXPERIENCE UNDER MY BELT, AND *THEN* YOU'LL CONSIDER GOING OUT WITH ME!
I PROMISE I WON'T BOTHER YOU ABOUT IT AGAIN UNTIL THAT TIME COMES. I'LL CONTINUE ON AS USUAL, AND YOU'LL THINK IT'S ALL OVER AND DONE WITH... BUT WE AREN'T THROUGH *YET*.
WAIT AND SEE!
I'M NOT GIVING UP ON YOU, MR. BISHOP!
YOU ARE MY ULTIMATE GOAL!

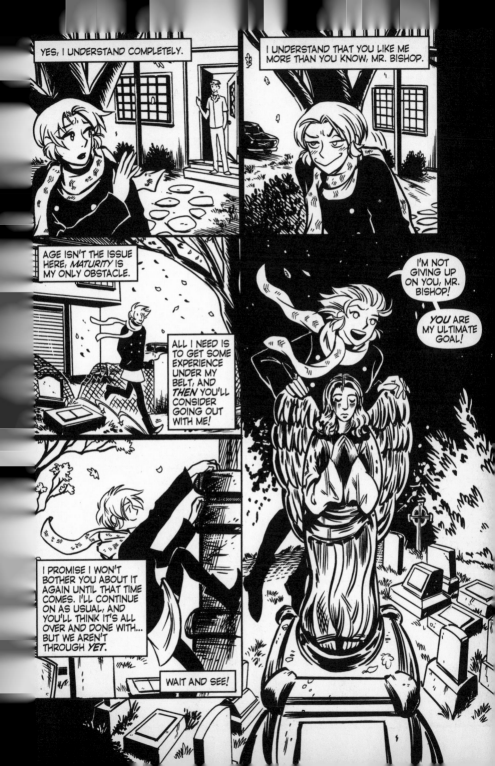

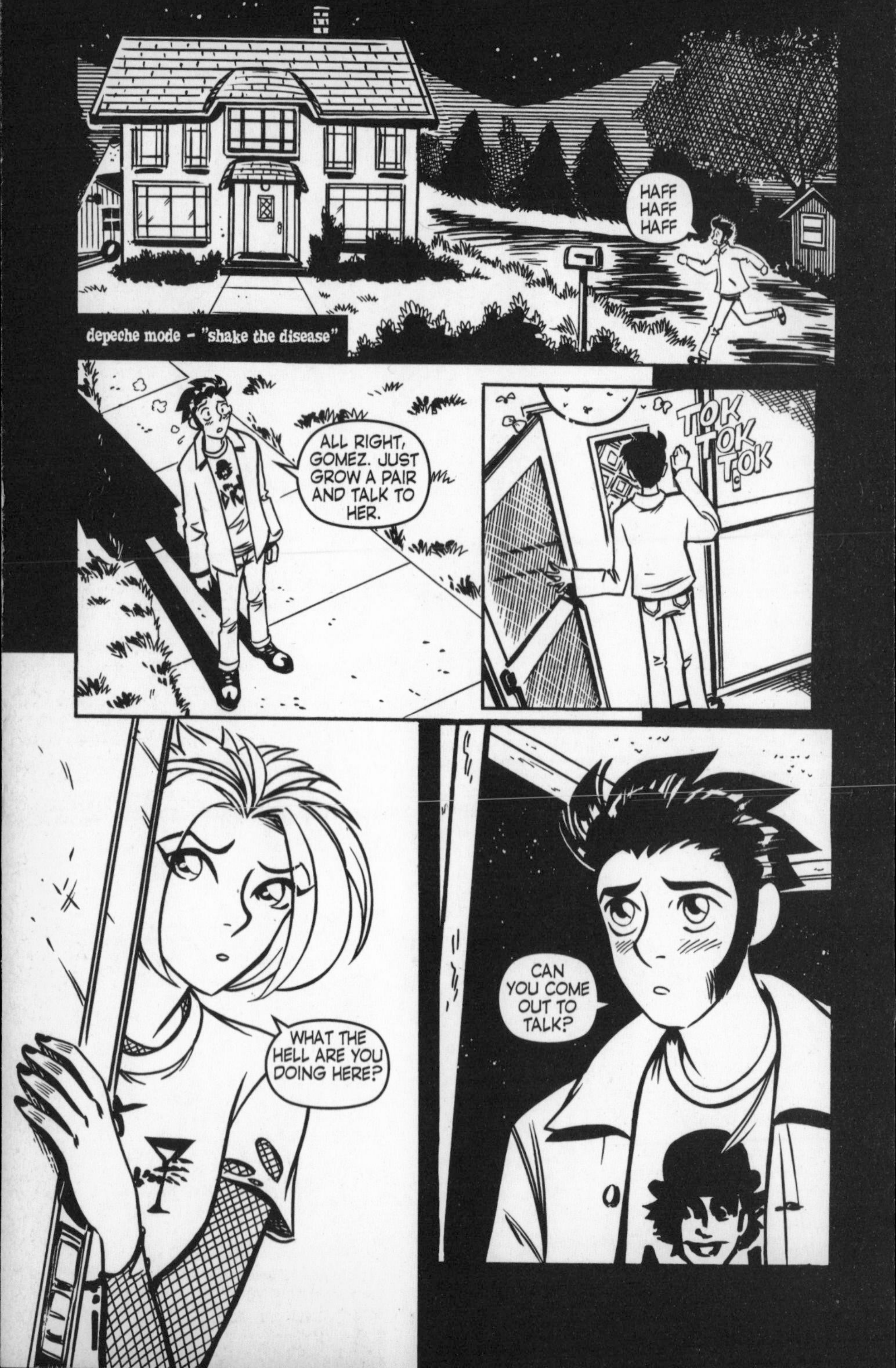
HAFF HAFF HAFF
depeche mode – "shake the disease"
ALL RIGHT, GOMEZ. JUST GROW A PAIR AND TALK TO HER.
TOK TOK TOK
WHAT THE HELL ARE YOU DOING HERE?
CAN YOU COME OUT TO TALK?

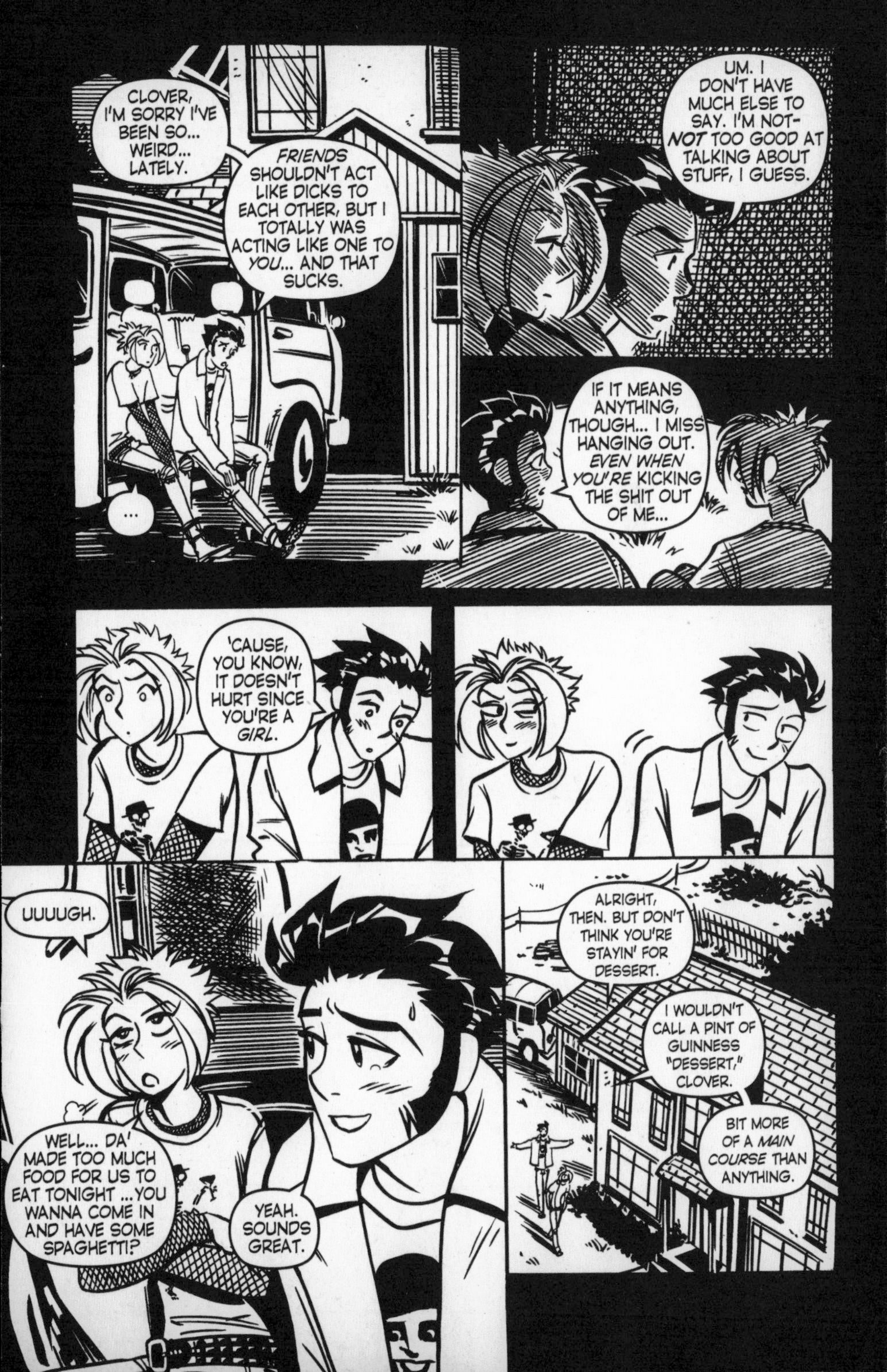
CLOVER, I'M SORRY I'VE BEEN SO... WEIRD... LATELY.
FRIENDS SHOULDN'T ACT LIKE DICKS TO EACH OTHER, BUT I TOTALLY WAS ACTING LIKE ONE TO YOU... AND THAT SUCKS.
...
UM. I DON'T HAVE MUCH ELSE TO SAY. I'M NOT- NOT TOO GOOD AT TALKING ABOUT STUFF, I GUESS.
IF IT MEANS ANYTHING, THOUGH... I MISS HANGING OUT. EVEN WHEN YOU'RE KICKING THE SHIT OUT OF ME...
'CAUSE, YOU KNOW, IT DOESN'T HURT SINCE YOU'RE A GIRL.
UUUUGH.
WELL... DA' MADE TOO MUCH FOOD FOR US TO EAT TONIGHT ...YOU WANNA COME IN AND HAVE SOME SPAGHETTI!?
YEAH. SOUNDS GREAT.
ALRIGHT, THEN. BUT DON'T THINK YOU'RE STAYIN' FOR DESSERT.
I WOULDN'T CALL A PINT OF GUINNESS "DESSERT," CLOVER.
BIT MORE OF A MAIN COURSE THAN ANYTHING.

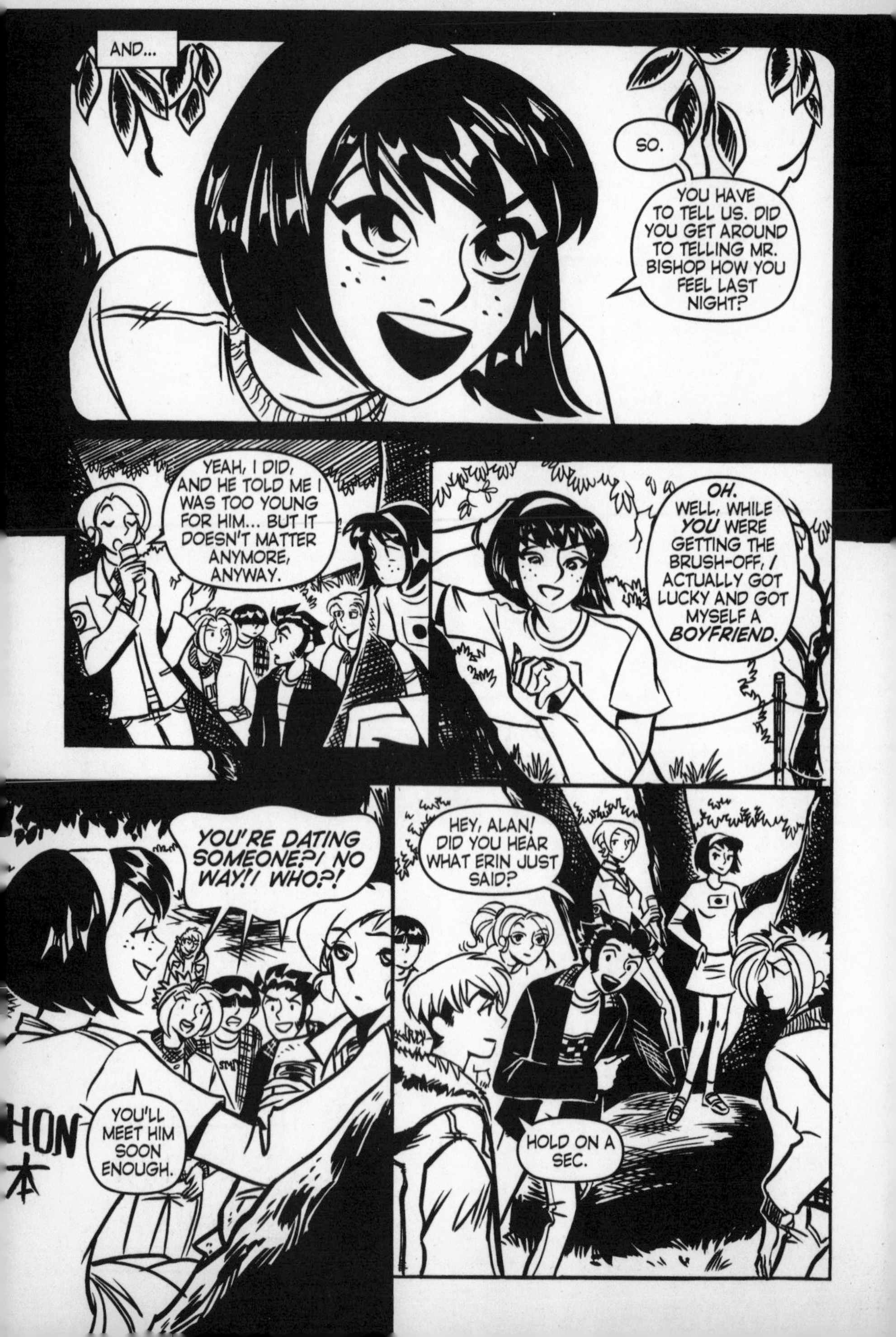
AND...
SO.
YOU HAVE TO TELL US. DID YOU GET AROUND TO TELLING MR. BISHOP HOW YOU FEEL LAST NIGHT?
YEAH, I DID, AND HE TOLD ME I WAS TOO YOUNG FOR HIM... BUT IT DOESN'T MATTER ANYMORE, ANYWAY.
OH. WELL, WHILE YOU WERE GETTING THE BRUSH-OFF, I ACTUALLY GOT LUCKY AND GOT MYSELF A BOYFRIEND.
YOU'RE DATING SOMEONE?! NO WAY!! WHO?!
YOU'LL MEET HIM SOON ENOUGH.
HEY, ALAN! DID YOU HEAR WHAT ERIN JUST SAID?
HOLD ON A SEC.

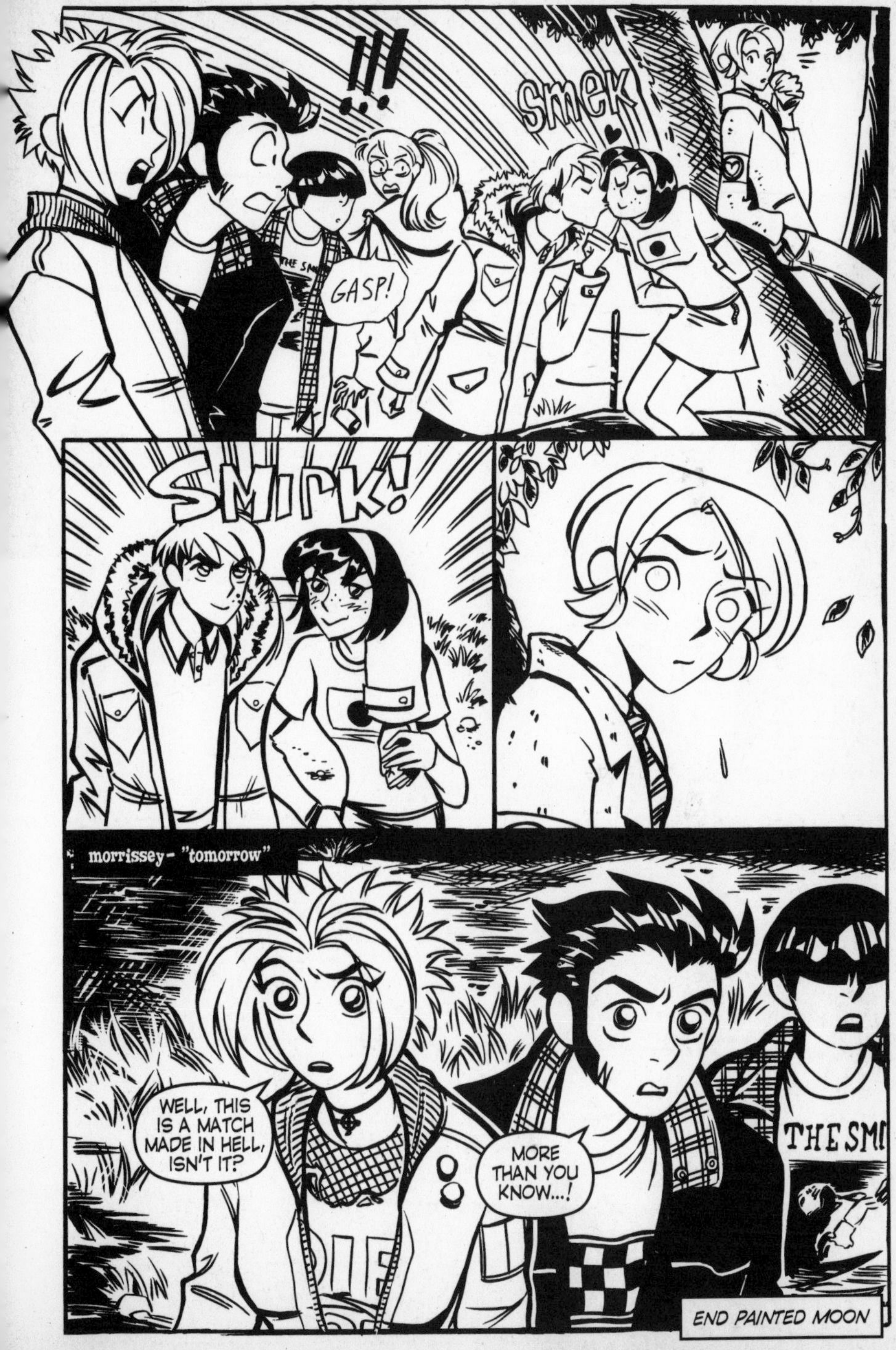
!!!
SMEK
GASP!
SMIRK!
morrissey- "tomorrow"
WELL, THIS IS A MATCH MADE IN HELL, ISN'T IT?
MORE THAN YOU KNOW...!
THE SM
END PAINTED MOON

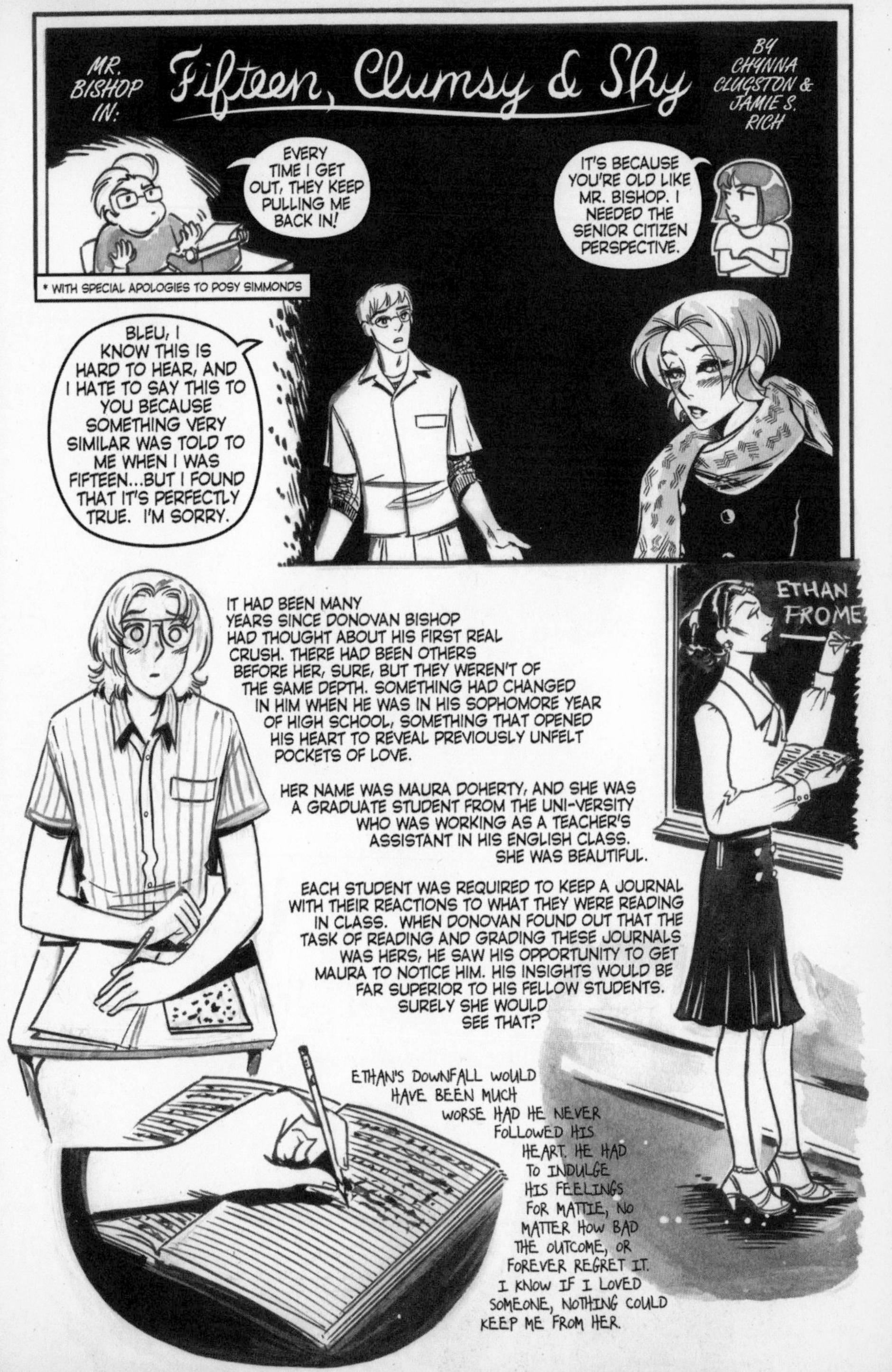
MR. BISHOP IN:
Fifteen, Clumsy & Shy
BY CHYNNA CLUGSTON & JAMIE S. RICH
EVERY TIME I GET OUT, THEY KEEP PULLING ME BACK IN!
IT'S BECAUSE YOU'RE OLD LIKE MR. BISHOP. I NEEDED THE SENIOR CITIZEN PERSPECTIVE.
* WITH SPECIAL APOLOGIES TO POSY SIMMONDS
BLEU, I KNOW THIS IS HARD TO HEAR, AND I HATE TO SAY THIS TO YOU BECAUSE SOMETHING VERY SIMILAR WAS TOLD TO ME WHEN I WAS FIFTEEN...BUT I FOUND THAT IT'S PERFECTLY TRUE. I'M SORRY.
ETHAN FROME
IT HAD BEEN MANY YEARS SINCE DONOVAN BISHOP HAD THOUGHT ABOUT HIS FIRST REAL CRUSH. THERE HAD BEEN OTHERS BEFORE HER, SURE, BUT THEY WEREN'T OF THE SAME DEPTH. SOMETHING HAD CHANGED IN HIM WHEN HE WAS IN HIS SOPHOMORE YEAR OF HIGH SCHOOL, SOMETHING THAT OPENED HIS HEART TO REVEAL PREVIOUSLY UNFELT POCKETS OF LOVE.
HER NAME WAS MAURA DOHERTY, AND SHE WAS A GRADUATE STUDENT FROM THE UNI-VERSITY WHO WAS WORKING AS A TEACHER'S ASSISTANT IN HIS ENGLISH CLASS. SHE WAS BEAUTIFUL.
EACH STUDENT WAS REQUIRED TO KEEP A JOURNAL WITH THEIR REACTIONS TO WHAT THEY WERE READING IN CLASS. WHEN DONOVAN FOUND OUT THAT THE TASK OF READING AND GRADING THESE JOURNALS WAS HERS, HE SAW HIS OPPORTUNITY TO GET MAURA TO NOTICE HIM. HIS INSIGHTS WOULD BE FAR SUPERIOR TO HIS FELLOW STUDENTS. SURELY SHE WOULD SEE THAT?
ETHAN'S DOWNFALL WOULD HAVE BEEN MUCH WORSE HAD HE NEVER FOLLOWED HIS HEART. HE HAD TO INDULGE HIS FEELINGS FOR MATTIE, NO MATTER HOW BAD THE OUTCOME, OR FOREVER REGRET IT. I KNOW IF I LOVED SOMEONE, NOTHING COULD KEEP ME FROM HER.

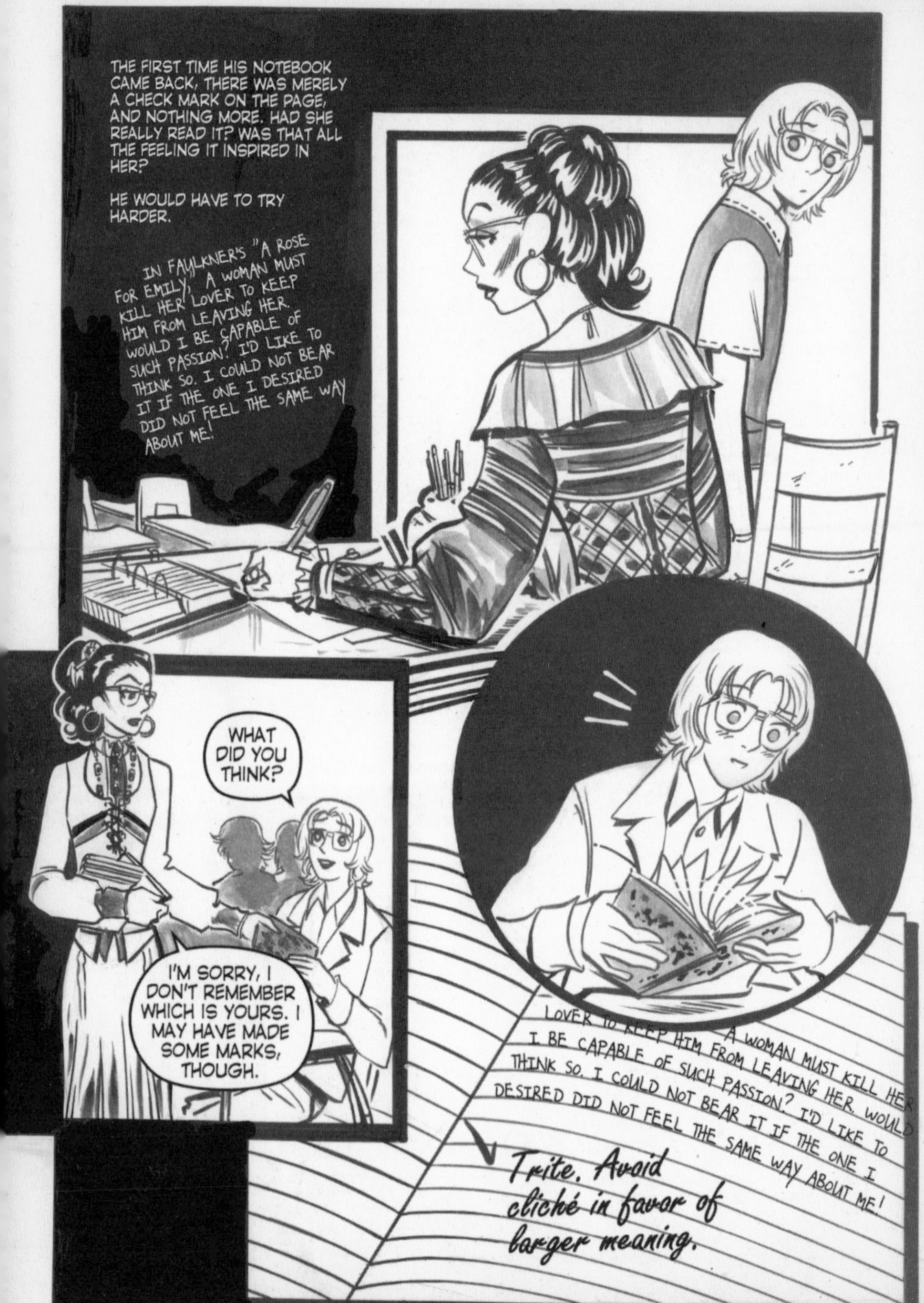
THE FIRST TIME HIS NOTEBOOK CAME BACK, THERE WAS MERELY A CHECK MARK ON THE PAGE, AND NOTHING MORE. HAD SHE REALLY READ IT? WAS THAT ALL THE FEELING IT INSPIRED IN HER?
HE WOULD HAVE TO TRY HARDER.
IN FAULKNER'S "A ROSE FOR EMILY," A WOMAN MUST KILL HER LOVER TO KEEP HIM FROM LEAVING HER. WOULD I BE CAPABLE OF SUCH PASSION? I'D LIKE TO THINK SO. I COULD NOT BEAR IT IF THE ONE I DESIRED DID NOT FEEL THE SAME WAY ABOUT ME!
WHAT DID YOU THINK?
I'M SORRY, I DON'T REMEMBER WHICH IS YOURS. I MAY HAVE MADE SOME MARKS, THOUGH.
A WOMAN MUST KILL HER LOVER TO KEEP HIM FROM LEAVING HER. WOULD I BE CAPABLE OF SUCH PASSION? I'D LIKE TO THINK SO. I COULD NOT BEAR IT IF THE ONE I DESIRED DID NOT FEEL THE SAME WAY ABOUT ME!
Trite. Avoid cliché in favor of larger meaning.

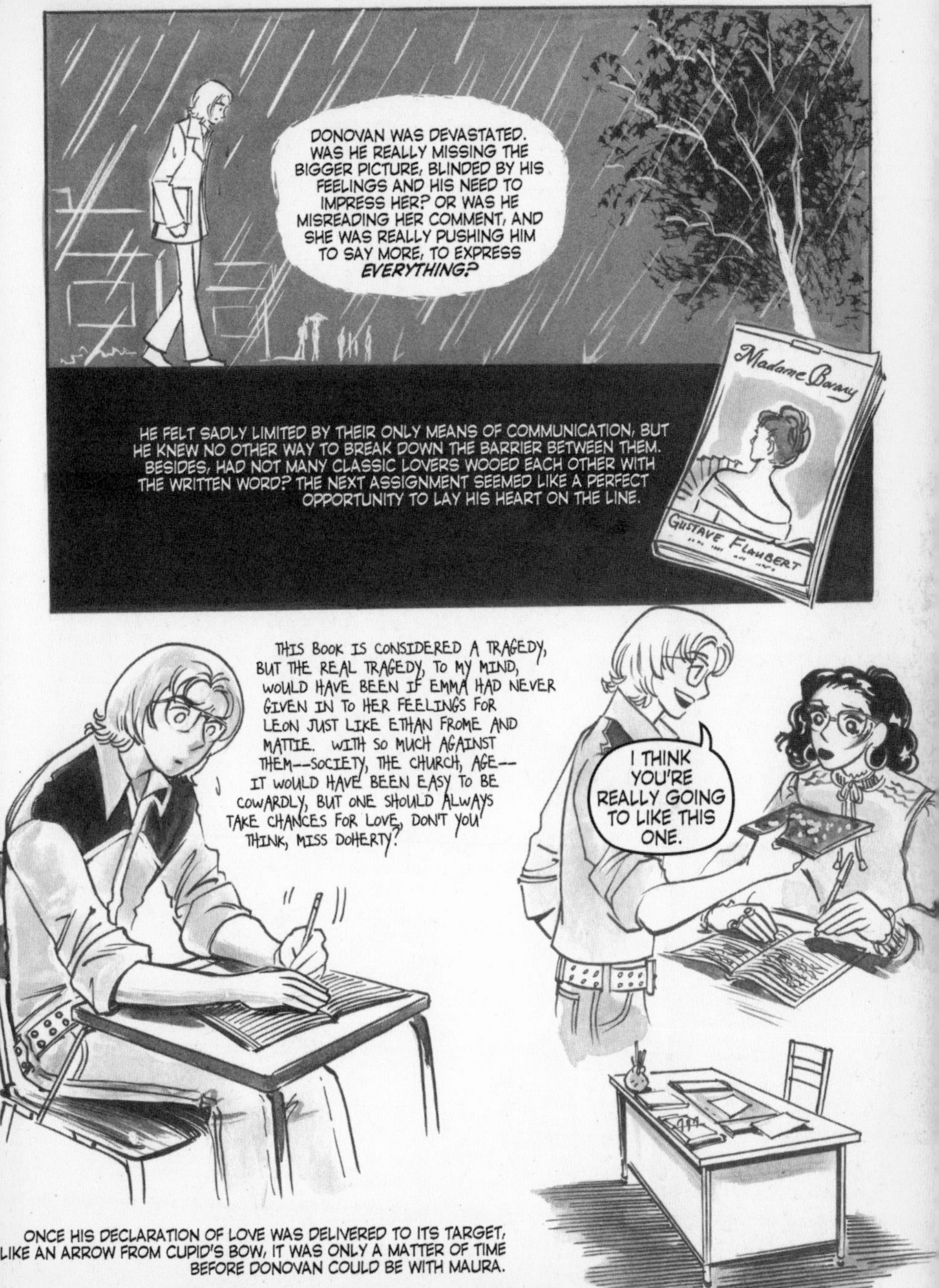
DONOVAN WAS DEVASTATED. WAS HE REALLY MISSING THE BIGGER PICTURE, BLINDED BY HIS FEELINGS AND HIS NEED TO IMPRESS HER? OR WAS HE MISREADING HER COMMENT, AND SHE WAS REALLY PUSHING HIM TO SAY MORE, TO EXPRESS *EVERYTHING?*
Madame Bovary
GUSTAVE FLAUBERT
HE FELT SADLY LIMITED BY THEIR ONLY MEANS OF COMMUNICATION, BUT HE KNEW NO OTHER WAY TO BREAK DOWN THE BARRIER BETWEEN THEM. BESIDES, HAD NOT MANY CLASSIC LOVERS WOOED EACH OTHER WITH THE WRITTEN WORD? THE NEXT ASSIGNMENT SEEMED LIKE A PERFECT OPPORTUNITY TO LAY HIS HEART ON THE LINE.
THIS BOOK IS CONSIDERED A TRAGEDY, BUT THE REAL TRAGEDY, TO MY MIND, WOULD HAVE BEEN IF EMMA HAD NEVER GIVEN IN TO HER FEELINGS FOR LEON JUST LIKE ETHAN FROME AND MATTIE. WITH SO MUCH AGAINST THEM--SOCIETY, THE CHURCH, AGE--IT WOULD HAVE BEEN EASY TO BE COWARDLY, BUT ONE SHOULD ALWAYS TAKE CHANCES FOR LOVE, DON'T YOU THINK, MISS DOHERTY?
I THINK YOU'RE REALLY GOING TO LIKE THIS ONE.
ONCE HIS DECLARATION OF LOVE WAS DELIVERED TO ITS TARGET, LIKE AN ARROW FROM CUPID'S BOW, IT WAS ONLY A MATTER OF TIME BEFORE DONOVAN COULD BE WITH MAURA.
ONLY DONOVAN HADN'T REALIZED THAT THE LESSON OF FLAUBERT WAS THAT GOING AGAINST THE GRAIN HAD CONSEQUENCES, EVEN IN THE NAME OF LOVE.

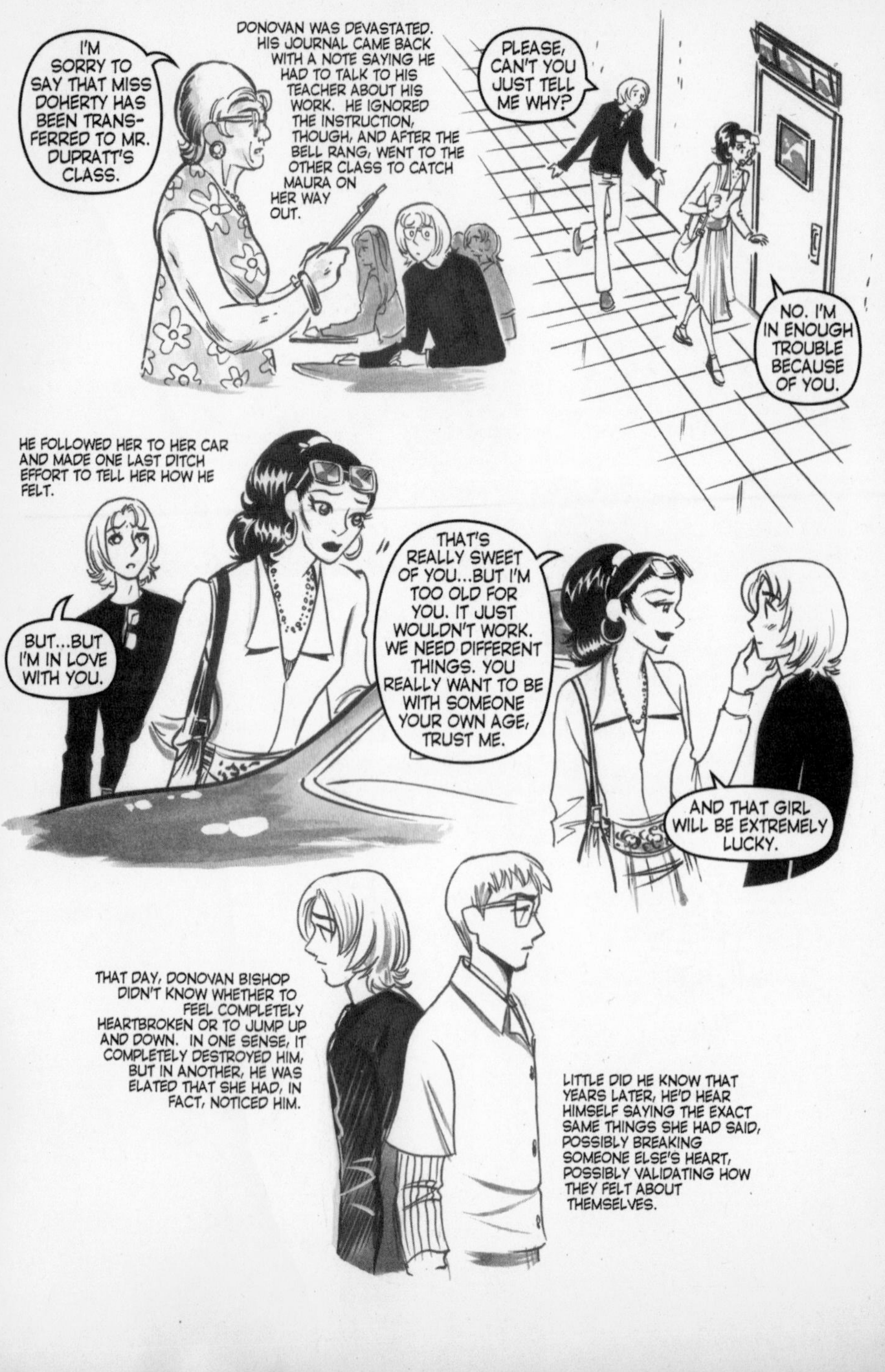

I'M SORRY TO SAY THAT MISS DOHERTY HAS BEEN TRANS-FERRED TO MR. DUPRATT'S CLASS.
DONOVAN WAS DEVASTATED. HIS JOURNAL CAME BACK WITH A NOTE SAYING HE HAD TO TALK TO HIS TEACHER ABOUT HIS WORK. HE IGNORED THE INSTRUCTION, THOUGH, AND AFTER THE BELL RANG, WENT TO THE OTHER CLASS TO CATCH MAURA ON HER WAY OUT.
PLEASE, CAN'T YOU JUST TELL ME WHY?
NO. I'M IN ENOUGH TROUBLE BECAUSE OF YOU.
HE FOLLOWED HER TO HER CAR AND MADE ONE LAST DITCH EFFORT TO TELL HER HOW HE FELT.
BUT...BUT I'M IN LOVE WITH YOU.
THAT'S REALLY SWEET OF YOU...BUT I'M TOO OLD FOR YOU. IT JUST WOULDN'T WORK. WE NEED DIFFERENT THINGS. YOU REALLY WANT TO BE WITH SOMEONE YOUR OWN AGE, TRUST ME.
AND THAT GIRL WILL BE EXTREMELY LUCKY.
THAT DAY, DONOVAN BISHOP DIDN'T KNOW WHETHER TO FEEL COMPLETELY HEARTBROKEN OR TO JUMP UP AND DOWN. IN ONE SENSE, IT COMPLETELY DESTROYED HIM, BUT IN ANOTHER, HE WAS ELATED THAT SHE HAD, IN FACT, NOTICED HIM.
LITTLE DID HE KNOW THAT YEARS LATER, HE'D HEAR HIMSELF SAYING THE EXACT SAME THINGS SHE HAD SAID, POSSIBLY BREAKING SOMEONE ELSE'S HEART, POSSIBLY VALIDATING HOW THEY FELT ABOUT THEMSELVES.

SKETCH GALLERY

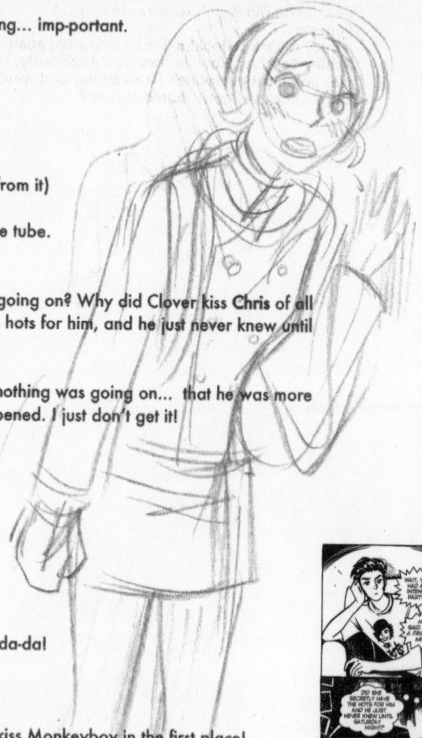

Panel 6
She can't make eye contact.
Bleu: I... need to tell you something... imp-portant.

__**Page Thirteen**__

Panel 1
We cut to Victor at home.
TV SFX: (see below- insert quote from it)
Panel 2
He's watching **Pretty In Pink** on the tube.
TV SFX: (another quote.)
Panel 3
Victor (thought): What the hell is going on? Why did Clover kiss **Chris** of all people? Did she secretly have the hots for him, and he just never knew until Saturday night?
Panel 4
Victor (thought): I mean, he said nothing was going on... that he was more surprised than anyone that it happened. I just don't get it!
TV SFX: ... Andi!
Panel 5
Scene where duckie kisses Iona.
Panel 6
Duckie: *You've been replaced!*

__**Page Fourteen**__

Panel 1
Fire alarms go off in his head. Da-da-da!
Panel 2
Victor leaps up.
Victor: Oh, my ***god!***
Victor/2: Clover never wanted to kiss Monkeyboy in the first place!
Panel 3
V starts pacing.
Victor: Is it possible? Could Clover really have been trying to make **ME** *jealous?*
Floating balloon: *You want me to PROVE my sexuality to you? Is that what it is?*

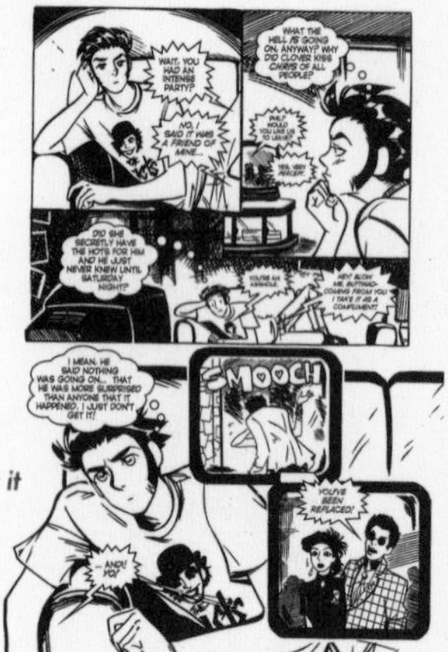
WAIT, YOU HAD AN INTENSE PARTY?
NO, I SAID IT WAS A FRIEND OF MINE...
WHAT THE HELL IS GOING ON, ANYWAY? WHY DID CLOVER KISS CHRIS OF ALL PEOPLE?
DID SHE SECRETLY HAVE THE HOTS FOR HIM AND HE JUST NEVER KNEW UNTIL SATURDAY NIGHT?
I MEAN, HE SAID NOTHING WAS GOING ON... THAT HE WAS MORE SURPRISED THAN ANYONE THAT IT HAPPENED. I JUST DON'T GET IT!
SMOOCH
YOU'VE BEEN REPLACED!
... ANDI! YO!

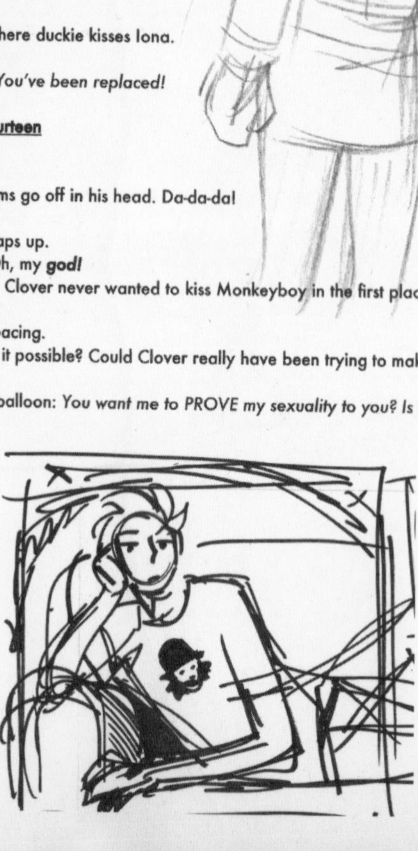

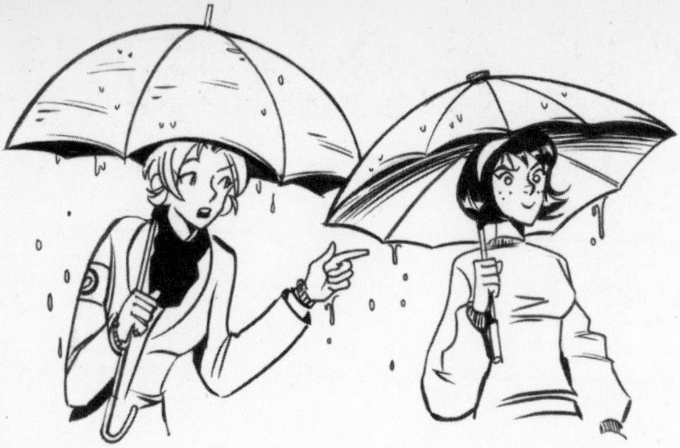

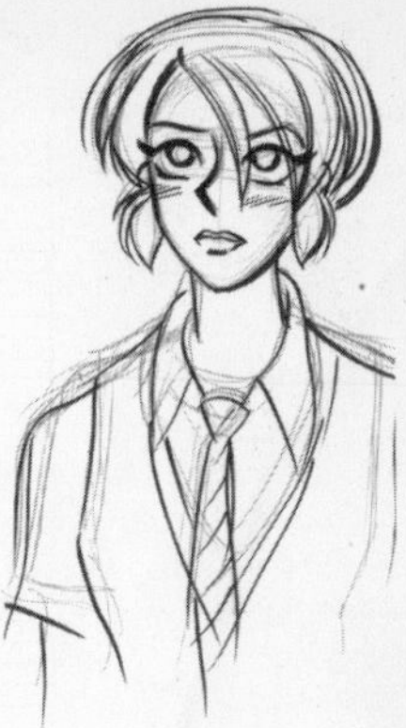

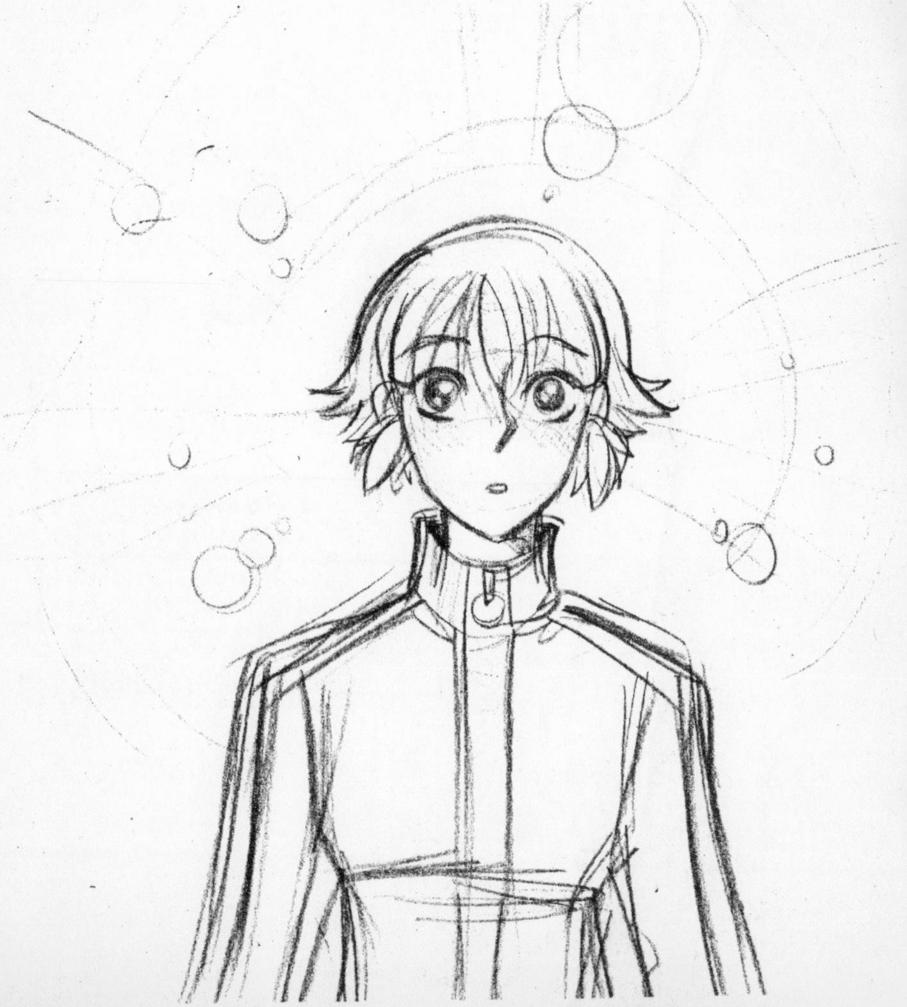

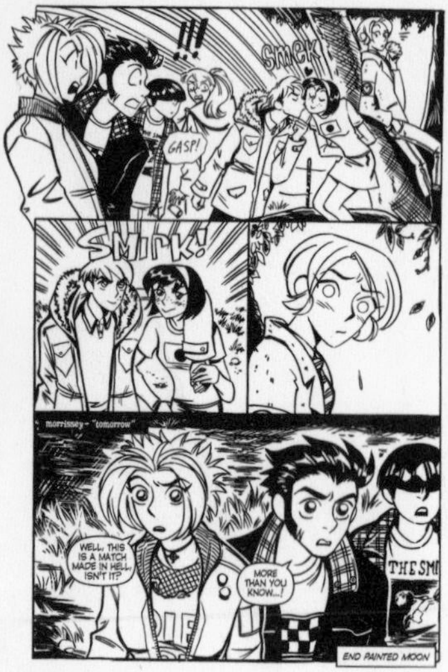
!!!
SMCK
GASP!
SMIRK!
morrissey– "tomorrow"
WELL, THIS IS A MATCH MADE IN HELL, ISN'T IT?
MORE THAN YOU KNOW...!
THE SM
END PAINTED MOON

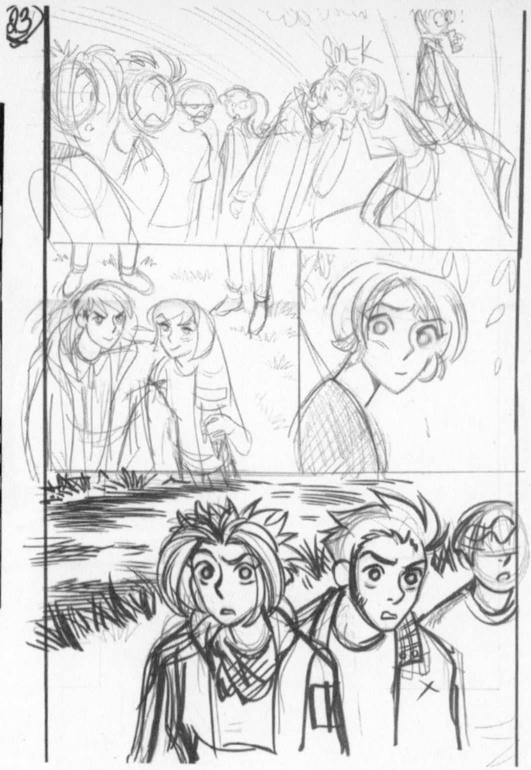
23
Smck

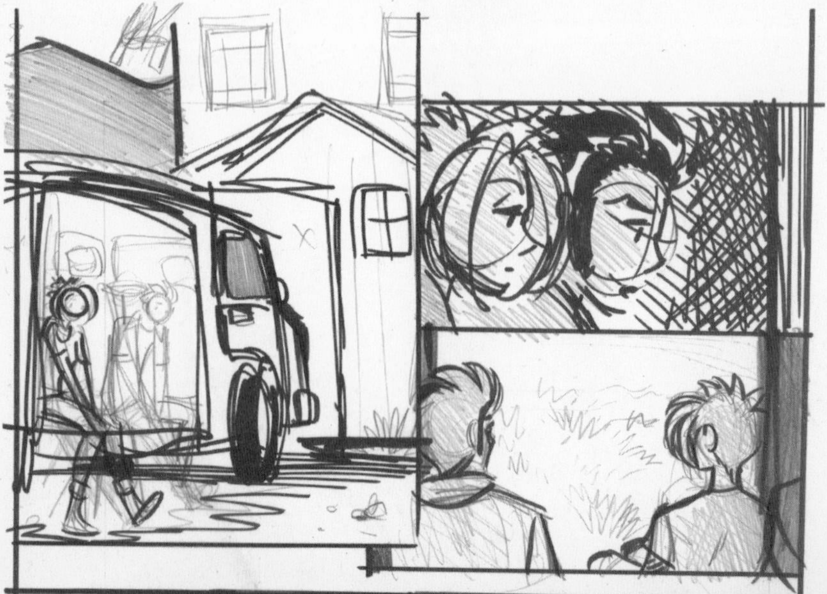

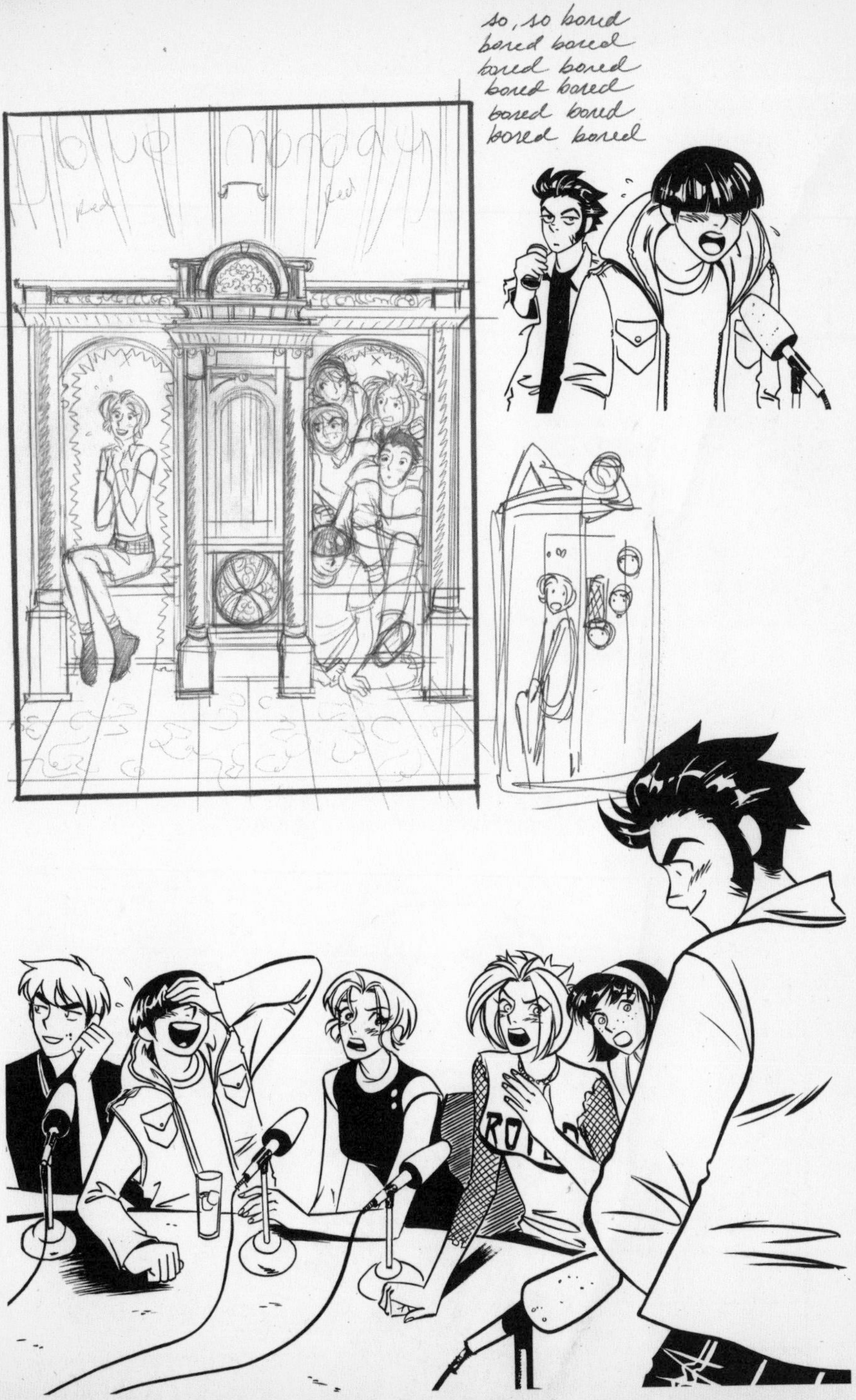
so, so bored
bored bored
bored bored
bored bored
bored bored
bored bored

Special thanks to:

Chris Brosnahan, who has been Clover's slang guide for much of this series. "The Kit Kat Shuffle" would have never happened without his enlightenment.

The Sugar Skulls Bicycle Gang, for being the raddest bike gang ever! Bowser!

The Lips, RIP, Mongo get your lame ass back to California. No culture, my eye.

Sir Tuffy, also a slang guide, even though he's just a dumb Limey and probably has no idea what he's talking about.

Thanks too Guy Major, Keef Wood, Butter Bear, Ginger Job and Froggy, for working on my stupid book with me.

Rest of the thanks go to the usual gang of idiots, especially Jon Flores, a constant inspiration and seriously hot babe, (especially when he walks like a baboon in Target...) and Buster, my favorite bully, who is sulking away as usual.

Congrats to Guy & Jackie, Tim & Theresa, Go-Go & Mary-Mo, Andrew & Renee and whoever else has decided to take the big plunge this year. What is this, a plague?

Also, special congrats to my old buddy Syd & her husband Makoto Takigawa for the upcoming sapling!

Good luck to all!